S0-EGK-437

GOLDEN GATE SEMINARY LIBRARY

# CHRISTIAN WHOLISM

## Theological and Ethical Implications in the Postmodern World

## John B. Wong

University Press of America,® Inc.
Lanham · New York · Oxford

GOLDEN GATE SEMINARY LIBRARY

BT
766,
W 66
2002
c. 2

Copyright © 2002 by
University Press of America,® Inc.
4720 Boston Way
Lanham, Maryland 20706

PO Box 317
Oxford
OX2 9RU, UK

All rights reserved
Printed in the United States of America
British Library Cataloging in Publication Information Available

**Library of Congress Cataloging-in-Publication Data**

Wong, John B.
Christian wholism : theological and ethical implications in the
   postmodern world / John B. Wong.
      p.   cm.
1. Perfection—Religious aspects—Christianity. I. Title.

BT766 .W76 2002
233'.5—dc21          2002028738 CIP

ISBN 0-7618-2391-3 (clothbound : alk. ppr.)
ISBN 0-7618-2392-1 (paperback : alk. ppr.)

♾™ The paper used in this publication meets the minimum
requirements of American National Standard for Information
Sciences—Permanence of Paper for Printed Library Materials,
ANSI Z39.48—1984

*To every man and woman buffeted by life's stresses and strains, pains and sorrows, who with sincerity of heart yet rises up in faith to respond "yes" to the Christ who asks, "Wilt thou be made whole?" John 5:6*

# CONTENTS

Preface

1. Introduction                                                          1
   Purpose and direction of this book  1
   Definition of Christian Wholism  1
   Chapters' overview  5

2. Theological And Philosophical Implications  11
   Metaphor, analogy, accommodational statement  12
   Meaning of peace, wholeness, joy  13
   Spiritual wholeness and *shalom*  14
   Biblical concept of spiritual wholeness  15
   Possible theological, philosophical, and intellectual
      barriers to Christian grounding of wholism  19
   Authority and reliability of the Bible  19
   The Divinity of Christ  22
   The Resurrection and the resurrected body  26
   Christian Wholism and religious pluralism  27
      Confucianism, Taoism, Buddhism, Islam, Judaism,
      Marxism, Secular Humanism, New Ageism,
      Radical Postmodernism

3. Faith And Intellect In Christian Wholism     39
   *Sum, ergo Deus est*  39
   Definition of intellect and faith defined  44
   Conflicts between faith and intellect—4 patterns  45
      Creationism and evolution, theology and science 46
      The problem of evil and human freedom.  56
      God's love, omniscience, omnipotence  65
      Where was God on 9-11-01?  67

## 4.  Christian Wholism And The Body            69

The human person  69
Unique multilayered personal identity  78
Christian anthropology supportive of
    Christian Wholism  82
    Spirit, soul, body, person, human nature,
    Tripartite, bipartite, monistic
Wholistic concept of the Image of God   94
    Summary statement  of the Biblical concept
    of the human  97
    Physical health and Christian Wholism  98
    Emphasis on whole person care  100
    Two worldviews for health professionals  103
    Education of Christian physicians  105
    Proposing a physical wholeness model
        Including spirituality  110
        10 characteristics of ideal spirituality

## 5.  Christian Wholism And Psychology        113

Six psychological personality maturity criteria
    Congruent with Christian Wholism  113
Destructive emotions a barrier to
    Christian wholeness  117
Psychology and the Christian faith  121
    God concept  122
    Psychological perspectives of religion  123
Psychology of religion and Christian Wholism  127
Psychoneuroendocrinoimmunology  132
Christian Wholism and human sexuality  138

**6. Christian Wholism And Christian Ethics,
   And Culture, Finance, And Ecology        141**
   Ethics review  142
   Normative ethics  143
   Christian ethics  145
   Definition of ethics in the context of wholeness  149
   Ethical decision-making  149
      Ethicist, norms, person in need, situational concerns
   Sexual ethics—abortion, homosexuality  151
   Music, arts, literature, mission outreach and sharing
      Christian Wholism  156
   Christian Wholism in the area of finance  165
      Nine guidelines to heed
   Christian Wholism and ecology  170

**7. Christian Wholism vs. Human Brokenness  175**
   Mind-brain discussion  176
      Epiphenomenalism, emergence, supervenience,
      Consciousness, reductive materialism, nonreductive
      Physicalism
   Proposing nonreductionistic transphysicalism  182
   Grace of wholeness—a human story  188
   Christian Wholism and faith and hope and the
      believer's resurrected body  189

**Notes**                                   **191**

**Index**                                   **226**

**About the Author**                        **229**

# *PREFACE*

In several careers and different seasons of my life, I have personally witnessed, coped with, and vicariously experienced brokenness and lostness in the many dimensions of a person. So this idea of wholeness has been growing in my heart and mind for a long time.

The urge to formally write on this subject did not come until I was studying theology and ethics in a Seminary a few years ago. This book in a sense could be considered a sequel to my book *The Resurrected Body*, which is eternity and future oriented. In faith and patience we wait for that morning splendor; in hope we rejoice in the ultimate consummation of our highest aspirations. But in the interim what do we do?

This book is my attempt to address this question. I argue that while we strain forward to reach for that "not yet," we have a task here on earth. It is to be made whole in ourselves by God's grace and power and to teach others and help them to be whole. Research and reflections on this topic have helped me posit Christian Wholism as a Christian theology for the postmodern man and woman. The contents of Christian Wholism, in concept and practice, can address the need for healing in the different spheres of a person's life. The first portion of this book discusses specific concerns in the spiritual, theological, intellectual, and physical realms in the context of Christian Wholism. And the ensuing chapters deal with the issues in the psychological, ethical, cultural, relational, sexual, and ecological domains.

With fear and uncertainty gripping the hearts of many in our post 9-11-2001 world, the need for wholeness, which I argue is the path to peace and joy, is never more urgent. Admittedly, our quest to be made whole in spirit, soul, mind, and body is an ongoing challenge. But in faith and with courage, our search cannot but lead us to that promised land. For there waiting on the other side is Christ the Lord who has already trodden the path. He was broken in all dimensions, and yet has conquered and become whole again. He is risen from the dead! He is now in the task of making us whole not only here on earth but also in the eternal life to come by gifting us with the resurrected body—the ultimate wholeness.

Now a brief word of acknowledgment. The summary of this book was the subject of discussion during a recent faculty presentation at the Loma Linda University Faculty of Religion. Among those present were Gerald Winslow, PhD; Wil Alexander, PhD; David Larson, D.Min, PhD; Ivan Blazen, PhD; Ron Carter, PhD; Louis Venden, PhD; James Walters, PhD; Soroj Sorajjakool, PhD; David Taylor, D.Min; Johnny Ramirez, EdD; Mark Carr, PhD; James Greek, D.Min; Leigh Aveling, D.Min; and others. I appreciated the interest generated and the questions raised. Formal answers to some of the questions are included in the last chapter of this book. I also want to thank Ray Anderson, PhD; Russell Rohde, MD, FACP; Scott Clark, D.Phil.; Wilma McClarty, EdD; Robert Brown, PhD; Lisa Beardsley, PhD; Amos Yong, PhD for reading and/or discussing certain parts of my book. To the editors of the University Press of America I give my thanks and appreciation. I take responsibility, however, for any oversights that might have escaped my detection.

Special thanks go to my wife, psychologist Alice Wong, PhD, who through all these years has helped make my life more whole and tolerable for both of us and others. And finally to God be the glory for instilling in my mind the seminal idea which has grown into Christian Wholism that you find in this book.

Rolling Hills, Fallbrook
California, USA
May 26, 2002

# CHAPTER 1

---

# INTRODUCTION

People universally yearn for peace and joy. In a post 9-11-01 world, security and certainty seem illusory and elusive. For Christians and all those with religious faith, however, life's tragedies and crucible of suffering are not the final word. But peace and joy must be the ultimate answer.

In this book I want to invite you to consider Christian Wholism as a path to peace and joy. But is wholism merely a nice-sounding term, empty rhetoric, or largely a vacuous concept for armchair discussion by detached spectators? Or is there concreteness to the idea and application? If so, what is its content and the factors that shape the outcome of ethical, theological and philosophical arguments?

In the following chapters I shall attempt to address these issues regarding wholism's concept and praxis. First, a working definition will give you some ideas about the discussions and the direction in which we are headed.

**Christian Wholism** is a belief and practice that is grounded in God's creation of the human as a unitary whole person with integrated, interrelated, interdependent attributes. This multidimensional person expresses himself/herself in physical, mental-intellectual, emotional, relational, socio-cultural, and spiritual modes in a dynamic interaction with the environment, the ecosystem. Christian Wholism extends beyond the mere absence of disease. It is more than physical health or mental and emotional well-being. It is greater than relational calm and social adjustments.

The biblical locus of **Christian Wholism**, I argue, is in the New Testament's record of Jesus' affirming the overarching, most important, first commandment, "Love the Lord your God with all your heart (*kardias*) and with all your soul (*psyches*) and with all your mind (*dianoias*) and with all your strength (*ischus*)." The second is this: "Love your neighbor as yourself. There is no commandment greater than these." Mk.12:30-31; Mt.22:37-40; Lk.10:27. The polyspheric, overlapping compositions of a person are represented here by the **heart**—the seat of physical, spiritual and mental life, encompassing the whole inner life of thinking, understanding, spiritual enlightenment, volition, will, moral decisions, emotions, love, desires, wishes, feelings; and by the **soul**—the center of life in its many and varied aspects, in all the expressions of what makes a human human;[1] and by the **mind**— the reasoning, thinking, intellectual, cognitive, creative, purposive, imaginative, conceptual and psychological domains; and by the **strength**—the physical, corporeal, tangible, sexual, biological, bodily dimension of a person.

Loving our neighbor presupposes a relational, social, cultural element. In addition, humans are designed to interact with the environment and ecosystem as recorded in Genesis' creation account, "God created man in His own image…male and female He created them. Let them rule…over all the earth, and over all the creatures…. Now the Lord God planted a garden…And the Lord God took the man and put him in the garden of Eden to work it and take care of it." Gen. 1: 27, 26: 2:8, 15.

**Christian Wholism** is, from another perspective, the progressive integration of the spiritual attributes of love, faith, hope, freedom, creativity, humility, and forgiveness with the other dimensions of personhood in an ongoing process of peace and joy toward a perfectly harmonious development intended by God. This ideal of Christian Wholism may not be realizable in our lifetime in that its praxis is an ongoing, lifelong process.

Theologically and philosophically, **Christian Wholism** can be viewed as a foundational Christian concept based on the doctrine of Creation, Christian anthropology, the image of God, Christian ethical reflection, the mission of Christ, the *telos* of God's redemptive activities, and God's sovereign will for fallen humanity. Its full expression will be culminated in our resurrected bodies at the eschaton. While wholism's ultimate actualization is still "not yet," its praxis finds ample applications in our daily Christian life.

For example, the Saturday or Sunday Sabbath [2] can become a recurrent, periodic, insulated time for the practice of Christian Wholism. Study and research stretches the boundary of intellectual wholeness. Family and community fellowship enacts a micro-version of that quintessential relational wholeness in Heaven. Eating, exercise, conjugal sex, other biological activities and artistic pursuits all foreshadow the physical and mental wholeness to be experienced in the earth made new. And worship here on earth adumbrates the divine-human wholistic encounter yet to come.

The Christian theme of the Second Advent, I submit, is God's appointed time for the ultimate fulfillment of Christian Wholism in believers' resurrected bodies. The biblical imagery and concept of salvation (Greek *sozo, soter, soteria, hugies, hugiaino, iaomai*)—to save, make whole, to heal, to be well; savior, salvation, healing, wholeness—all are intimately tied to the concept of Christian Wholism under discussion here. To paraphrase Acts 4:12 using the shared meaning between wholeness and salvation and possibly holiness, the text might read, "Wholeness is found in no one else, for there is no other name under Heaven given to men and women by which we must be made whole." [3]

When Jesus says in Matt. 5:48, "Be perfect, therefore, as your heavenly Father is perfect," is He quoting or referring to Leviticus 19:2 "Be holy, because I, the Lord your God, am holy," which was also quoted by Peter in 1Pet.1:16? The NIV Study Bible seems to point that way. Or is Jesus calling us to be merciful as God is merciful, to love our enemies and to have our righteousness surpass that of the Pharisees and the teachers of the law? Lk. 6:36; Mt. 5:20. Matthew Henry takes the saying to mean that Christians are to press towards a perfection in grace and holiness. The 2001 Oxford Bible Commentary states, "Jesus' call to perfection is a call to completeness." [4] One could certainly equate completeness with wholeness. Paul in 2 Corinthians 7:1 exhorts, "Let us purify ourselves from everything that contaminates body and spirit,

4          *Christian Wholism*

perfecting holiness out of reverence for God." In 1 Thessalonians 3:13; 4:7, he continues, "May He strengthen your hearts so that you will be blameless and holy in the presence of our God and Father when our Lord Jesus Christ comes with all His Holy Ones." "For God did not call us to be impure, but to live a holy life." In Ephesians 5:27, Paul speaks of Christ's intention for the Christian Church, "And to present her to Himself as a radiant church, without stain...blemish...but holy and blameless." Eph. 5:27.

The word "holy" (Heb. *Qadowsh, qadhosh, qodesh, chacyid, hasid*; Gk *hagios, hagnos*) [5] has two basic meanings: (1) what is intrinsically sacred, distinct, separate, unique, apart from what is common; (2) moral, pure, good, kind, godly, merciful, saintly, sanctified, consecrated, dedicated, hallowed. The word "whole" (Heb. *Tamem, tam*; Gr. *holos*) means complete, integral, without defect, flawless, blameless, upright, faithful, morally perfect. Could the first meaning of "holy" in the context of wholeness possibly refer to <u>separation</u> from the brokenness of sin, <u>apartness</u> from the chaos of emotional turmoil, the <u>antithesis</u> of physical dysfunction, and its <u>uniqueness</u> among the banalities and frenzies of the world?

Avoiding the etymological fallacy of using linguistic linkage as the only guide to words' meanings, one is free to explore concepts and significance that have been accorded to a word whether by usage, tradition or context and semantic range. Important also are the perceived meaning of the text and literary genre, intent of the author, readers' expectation, their self-understanding and response, and other factors. Historically, the English word "wholeness" is related to the English word "holiness" (German *heil*=whole/ intact/healed; *heilig*= holy/sacred). Again, holy is from *holi, halig, haleg,* var. *hal*=whole). Wholism and holism have the root word from Greek *holos*=whole. Then, is it not permissible to somehow conjoin the significance of the symbolism suggested by both the words "holy" and "whole," even in their original Hebrew they may not mean quite the same thing? [6]

And if "holy" embodies the notion of wholeness, "Remember the Sabbath day to keep it holy," could include the suggestion to keep it wholistic. To keep it wholistic is to keep it according to the perceived needs and composition of the multiple dimensions of our personhood.

I shall argue that Christian Wholism is the path to peace and joy here and now as well as there and then for eternity. The Hebrew word *shalom (shalam)* which occurs rather frequently in the Old Testament, embodies the ideas of peace, completeness, making whole, soundness, welfare, contentment, peace with God, making good, restoring what was lost or stolen (see fuller discussion of *shalom* in chapter 3). It is a gift of God by His grace. It is the ultimate demonstration of Jesus' love for the undeserving—the making good of God's promise to restore fellowship with humankind through the ministration of the Holy Spirit in the context of the grand Biblical theme of redemption.

Here on earth, the fruition of a Spirit-filled life parallels the praxis of Christian Wholism. The fruit of the Spirit is love, joy, peace, patience, kindness, goodness, faithfulness, gentleness and self-control (Gal. 5:22, 23). What is peace? Is it not joy in its rest mode? And what is joy? Can we not think of it as peace in its excitation mode? Peace and joy are thus intricately linked. They are the gifts from God who is love. They are the hallmark of those who love while practicing Christian Wholism.

In Chapter 2, I shall describe how to achieve wholeness in the spiritual and theological domains by proposing an existential wholistic Divine-human encounter. My discussion will explain our vertical interaction with the Divine and the obstacles that hamper wholism. We shall examine how certain intellectual barriers to faith can create an impasse to joy and peace and undermine wholism. Some solutions are suggested. The authority of the Bible, the Divinity of Christ, Mary's surrogacy, the human fallen condition and redemption, Resurrection, Heaven and hell, will be dealt with in brief. In a multicultural, postmodern era, a discussion on what is truth and who is the real God among all the gods of religious pluralism cannot be avoided. Christian Wholism presupposes a certitude, albeit only in the context of probability stemming from our finitude and imperfect knowledge in a fallen world, that hinges its hope on a transcendent yet immanent, all powerful, all-knowing God who can make Christian Wholism whole and realizable.

For those serious-thinking people with a penchant for theology and philosophy, wholeness must embrace other inquiries. As a concept of Christian theology and ethics, it must be juxtaposed and argued against other philosophies and worldviews that proffer the "same" peace, harmony, and human solution. I shall argue that Confucianism, Taoism, Buddhism, Islam, Judaism, Marxism, secular humanism, New Ageism, radical postmodernism among others, all pale in comparison to Christian Wholism.

Chapter 3 probes faith and intellect in the context of Christian Wholism. Interactions between science and theology, conflict between creationism and evolutionary theory, the conundrum of a good God in the face of evil and suffering, and God's foreknowledge and reflection on open theism will occupy our attention.

Chapter 4 deals with Christian wholeness in the physical realm. Here Christian anthropology, the image of God, human nature whether it is unitary, bipartite, tripartite, or nondescript will be the focus of discussion. How the understanding of human nature influences our ethical and moral deliberation will also be examined. The psychosomatic implication in health and illness, faith and healing, whole-person care and spirituality, and the body's role in the achievement of Christian wholeness will be investigated. A practical, physical wholeness model in acrostic is proposed, and the essence of genuine Christian spirituality defined.

Chapter 5 discusses wholeness in the psychological sphere. Inquiry is directed to those areas that encompass emotions, attitudes, human motivations and behavior, "God concept," psychological perspectives of religion, psychology-theology dialogues, "psychology as religion," psychology's role in promoting spiritual wholeness, and psychology collaborating with religion and theology in providing resources for removing roadblocks to Christian wholeness. In arguing for the validity of Christian Wholism, I shall briefly examine William James, Carl Jung, Sigmund Freud and others. Under examination will be some of the psychological theories that are antithetical to Christian philosophy as well as psychological insights that can illumine religious faith and practice in the journey toward peace and joy. Finally, I want to introduce to the readers the scientific research in psychoneuroimmunology, which adds to the biological foundation of Christian wholism. Psychoneuroendocrinoimmunology is an interdisciplinary study of the interactions among psychological, behavioral, neural, endocrine functions, and immune system processes. Central to human interactions with the external environment including its hostile components is a single, integrated network of defenses. Each component of this defensive system serves specialized functions and, at the same time, monitors and responds to information derived from the others in the network. Psychonueroimmunology studies the relationship among these systems. Two pathways bridge the brain and the immune system: autonomic nervous system activity through the sympathetic and parasympathetic nerves and neuroendocrine outflow from the pituitary. Primary and secondary lymphoid organs are sympathetically innervated, and these nerve fibers form neuroeffector junctions with lymphocytes, monocytes, macrophages, and granulocytes that possess receptors for these neurotransmitters.

There is a prevalent mindset among neuroscientists that all manifestations of the mind, all psychological states, emotions, will, judgment, behaviors, human free choice are ultimately reducible to and explainable by neural activities, i.e. biochemicoelectrical events. I shall argue against the fallacy of such assumptions and projects. A brief discussion of human nature, body, soul and spirit is included anticipating a fuller discussion in chapter 7 on scientific reductionism and the brain-mind relationship.

The big picture that I want to construct in this chapter which discusses psychoneuroendocrinoimmunology is: Beginning from the spiritual composition of our being with its cognitive and emotional aspects of religious life most likely arising in the limbic-hypothalamic-pituitary axis of the brain, through the mental-intellectual dimension and psychological components, to the physical dynamics of health and immunity defense which can be influenced by psychosocial factors and one's environment, the loop of wholistic relatedness finally closes. That closure is located in the unified complex of a person that is secure in God's making, enhancement and preservation. To put it in practical terms, the spiritual experience which begins in the highest faculty of the mind at zenith, as it were, signals an emotional response which then is translated into actions and behavior. The latter through the neuropathways and neurotransmitters in turn signals the body's cellular and immune response that science now is able to locate and map out. But this is only part of the story. There is a bidirectional pathway by which the immunal, hormonal, neural events at the nadiral pole of the loop also effect what transpires at the spiritual/mental zenith, as borne out by research studies.

Incorporated in this chapter, additionally, is a discussion on Christian Wholism in light of human sexuality.

Chapter 6 introduces us to the ethical, socio-cultural realm in the context of Christian Wholism. I shall address sexuality and some of the contentious issues of sexual ethics, such as abortion and homosexuality. I argue that Christian ethics fundamentally is a lifelong discipline learning how to be the Christian moral person in wholeness by the grace of God. In a practical way, this discipline involves one's seeking to analyze and internalize the criteria of good and bad, right and wrong. It calls for the systematic study of reflective choices and attainable goals in its horizontal encounter with humanity. Most importantly, in the midst of such pursuit, Christian ethics is learning to be and to do that which glorifies God by one's passion in restoring wholeness to self and others.

Since humanity has been created in the Image of God with the capacity for social interaction and the need for relations, the significance of society and culture in their contribution to wholeness comes to the foreground. I shall discuss how music, literature, arts, architecture, involvement with humanity in projects of outreach and service can all add to the joy of wholistic Christian life experience. Financial wholeness is also discussed as a related topic.

I shall also make forays into environmental wholeness and its ecological implications from the theological and ethical perspectives. God's natural world is intimately bound with God's creatures. Christian Wholism as defined at the beginning of this chapter seeks a harmonious development by balancing the creaturely needs with preservation of God's ecosystem based on the concept of stewardship and entrustment. The original Edenic abode for humans bespeaks the idyllic relationship that is part of the trajectory toward ultimate wholeness in "being" and in "relations" with self, the universe, and God.

Chapter 7 summarizes the all-encompassing concept of Christian Wholism as we survey all the separate, albeit at times overlapping, domains and dimensions which are constitutive of humanity made in the image of God after His likeness. In this chapter, I examine mind-brain relationship in the context of Christian wholism. We attempt to deal with questions of whether the mind is material, non-material, or supramaterial. If the mind is not material nor non-material, what then is it and how does it relate to the brain? As a tentative approach to this conundrum, I submit my model of nonreductionistic transphysicalism. In the discussion to follow, I include the unlikelihood of success of scientific reductionistic projects in reducing theology, ethics, philosophy, psychology, anthropology, sociology to molecular biology, chemistry, then to physics, then to quarks and antiparticles with their intrinsic angular momentum measured in Planck's constant divided by 2п. Their success notwithstanding, though most unlikely, I shall argue that my construct of nonreductionistic transphysicalism is capable to withstand such onslaught.

I would be perfectly satisfied and immensely grateful to God if scientists are able to isolate a biochemical endorphin-like substance produced in my brain that accounts for the feeling of joy and peace and a sense of wholeness. What is that substance that circulates in my system when I am overwhelmed by beauty and transcendence in music, art, poetry, the human form, nature, inspiration, thought, human relation, and encounter with God?

If atoms and molecules are the substrate of this biochemical entity, should I not rejoice in the work of the Creator who created these subatomic particles? Should I not give Him praise for the stimulus, the signaling for the production of these endorphin-like substance? Reductionistic explanation would not detract one whit from crediting my joy and peace to His infinite provisions. For those who believe in a self-existent, self-conscious soul, reductionism does pose a daunting threat to one's theology. But this is not a problem in my theological construct as elsewhere I have already defined what the "soul" is in Chapter 4. Questions as how to present the concept of wholeness to those with missing organic parts, such as the amputees and those with post-mastectomy scars or terminal illnesses are also examined in this last chapter.

I shall argue that Christian wholism is an answer to human lostness. Our sin nature and the evil confronting our world evidence that we have lost the clarity of God's image in us, lost our rightful position before God, and our ability to directly communicate with Him. We have lost our inheritance and abode in His Kingdom, our fellowship with Him and almost the possibility for eternal life. Physically we have lost our perpetual renewal and healing gene; psychologically our capacity for intimacy with God and other people because of our estrangement. Mentally, we are deprived of the ability to comprehend the universe and God, and spiritually our *shalom*.

Our journey and aspiration in quest for wholism must be an ongoing and progressive experience. Realism mandates our admission of failure, faulty steps, and perhaps many trials and disappointments. Nonetheless, Christian Wholism is sustained by Christian faith and hope that are anchored to a Creator who knows no impossibility. Even more so, He is truth and love personified, the grantor of our promised resurrected body—the ultimate fulfillment of Christian Wholism in style and substance.[7]

In conclusion, it is my hope and prayer that this book may provoke further discussion on the meaning of existence and about the content of an authentic and abundant life with wholeness as its goal. And on a practical level, may the readers find useful suggestions to defuse tension in every aspect of their life. Postmodern men and women need to heed the Apostle Paul's admonition: "Rejoice in the Lord always. I will say it again: Rejoice!" Phil.4:4. "Don't fret or worry. Instead of worrying, pray. Let petitions and praises shape your worries into prayers, letting God know your concerns. Before you know it, [*the peace of God*], a sense of God's wholeness, everything coming together for good, will come and settle you down. It's wonderful what happens when Christ displaces worry at the center of your life." Phil. 4: 6-7. [8]

Empowered by God's Spirit and made whole by His grace, we can all become God's instruments of wholeness and healing for our fragmented world and in our own Christian walk live wholesomely in peace and joy.

# CHAPTER 2

## THEOLOGICAL AND PHILOSOPHICAL IMPLICATIONS

The concept of Christian Wholism is grounded in the doctrine of Creation and redemption as expounded in the Bible. God is the Creator of all there is, animate, inanimate, life, non-life, time, space, matter, energy and every dimension of reality. "In the beginning God created the heavens and the earth." (Gen. 1:1). "God created man in His own image, in the image of God He created him; male and female He created them." (Gen. 1:27). "God saw all that He had made, and it was very good...." (Gen. 1:31). We humans are His creatures and crowning work. As our Maker fashioning us in His own image and likeness, He knows what constitutes wholeness and perfection for His created beings. He has the blueprint, the implementing skill, the resources, and creativity to complete the master project of redemption, transformation, glorification, and making us whole for eternity. "...He who began a good work in you will carry it on to completion until the day of Christ Jesus." (Phil. 1:6).

This process of restoring us to perfect wholeness is related to the basic Christian theme of God's redemptive work in saving sinners by grace through the life, death, resurrection of the God-Man Jesus Christ. "For it is by grace you have been saved, through faith—and this not from yourself, it [either faith as such or faith and salvation together] is the gift of God" (Eph. 2:8).[9]

I shall argue that actualization of wholeness in the spiritual, theological and philosophical domains requires us to examine, at the minimum, our existential relationship with God at the very fundamental level. This in turn calls forth our inquiry about the authority of the Bible, the Divinity of Christ, the human fallen condition, the sin nature that fractures wholeness, the solution provided by God through the redemptive activities of Christ whose resurrection paves the way for our inheritance in the heavenly kingdom with our resurrected bodies.

What are the barriers to such beliefs? One could not be spiritually whole when one constantly vacillates between overwhelming doubts and tenuous beliefs. Like the tempest-tossed boat, such a mind could not be the homing ground of peace and joy, the inner and outer manifestation of Christian wholeness.

Before we examine the list of obstacles to our Christian faith and roadblock to wholeness, we do well to clarify our methodology and terms we apply in our discussion.

In theology, so-called God-talk, and in philosophy and ethics we often use analogical and metaphorical language. Professor Alister McGrath of Oxford provides us with a useful handle by quoting Aquinas and Ian Ramsey. Analogy emphasizes likeness and correspondence of two things, which appear appropriately so even though there are genuine points of dissimilarity. For example, in saying that God is our Father, we want to convey the meaning that God is like a human Father, instrumental in bringing us into existence, having authority over us, caring and providing for us. However, like all figures of speech, analogies have their limits and break down when pressed further. God is like our human father, but He is totally different from our earthly father. God can create *ex nihilo*, does not need a wife/woman to generate us, is not a physical person with measurements, will not grow old and die.

Metaphor, on the other hand, is a way of speaking about one thing in terms which are suggestive of another.[10] Metaphors stress both similarity and dissimilarity between the two things being compared (analogies stress more the similarity). "A mighty fortress is our God," "The Lord is my shepherd," "God is light," are metaphors, which have an open-ended character inviting readers to discover further levels of meaning. They often carry strong emotional overtones calling forth response and commitment during worship and private devotion.

In theology and in the Bible, one should also be alert to the language of accommodation in God's self revelation. He adjusts and adapts His activities and words to the level of His creatures of finitude, with their imperfect development of mind and heart. God stoops down, as it were, to our human level to make known His truth and love.

To say some of the biblical terms and statements are analogical, metaphoric, or accommodational is not to say that they are not important. Even metaphors point to the truth behind the shifted contexts. Similarly, in our discussion of Christian Wholism, I argue that God has the blueprint for restoring us to wholeness. Metaphorical language, yes! The levels and depths of meaning are nonetheless inviting and awaiting us to explore.

**The Meaning of Peace, Wholeness, and Joy**

Christian wholeness leads to peace and joy. Or one can say that peace and joy affirm the reality of wholeness in a Christian life. As I suggest earlier that <u>peace is joy in its rest mode and joy is peace in its excitation mode</u>; wholeness therefore can assume dual expressions. Let us now analyze the biblical conception and also the etymology of peace.

Peace from the Latin derivation of *pax, pacem* is equivalent to the Hebew word *shalom*, which in the Septuagint, the oldest Greek version of the Old Testament, is almost invariably translated into the Greek word *eirene.*

*Shalom*, which occurs some 250 times in the OT, has a basic meaning of completeness, soundness, welfare, peace, contentment, peace with God, <u>making whole,</u> making good, restoring what was lost or stolen (Joel 2:25, Exo. 21:37).[11]  The word embodies the meaning of material prosperity in Psalms 73:3, and physical safety and emotional calm in Psalm 4:8. It also carries the comprehensive meaning of rest, freedom from care, safety, trustfulness, and ease; communal well-being in contrast to war; and a state of law and order leading to prosperity. It denotes bodily health; contentedness on living and at death. It also has the sense of salvation (Isa. 43:7, Jer. 29:11; 14:13). It has a social and political reference beyond the personal dimension. It is associated with righteousness, concrete ideas of law and judgment. [12]

The essence of *shalom* climaxes in the familiar form of OT blessing from Yahweh, "The Lord bless you and keep you; the Lord make His face shine upon you and be gracious unto you; The Lord turn His face toward you and give you peace" (Num.6:24-26). According to Professor J. I. Durham, *shalom* is the gift of God, and can be received only in His presence. It is intended as a description of the man (woman) who is blessed and treated graciously by God; the one who is doubly in God's presence, the one who is "fulfilled," and so "complete." Indeed, asked Prof. Durham, "Has such a person answered the NT commandment, 'You, therefore, must be perfect, as your heavenly Father is perfect.'"

Durham, quoted by Prof. H. Beck and Prof. Brown, further contends that *shalom* in the OT indicates a comprehensive kind of fulfillment or completion, indeed of a perfection in life and spirit which quite transcends any success which the human alone, even under the best of circumstances, is able to attain. Thus it is ultimately a gift from God. [13]

Thus the concept of *shalom* (peace) in the OT is congruent with the concept of Christian Wholism. In the above quoted blessing motif, when the Lord blesses His people with peace, He is in essence blessing them with "wholeness."

In the New Testament, the word peace (classical Greek *eirene* meaning a state of law and order resulting from the cessation of war) occurs 91 times. It has an extensive meaning linking it with love (2 Cor. 13:11), grace (Rom. 1:7; 1 Cor. 1:3), life (Rom 8:6), righteousness (Rom 14:7), and nearly always carries a spiritual connotation.[14] It points to harmony, the essence of *summum bonum* the ultimate good, messianic salvation, peace brought by Christ, peace on earth (Lk 2:14).[15]

In the NT, peace has a specific reference to the peace which is the gift of Christ (Jn. 14:27, 16:33, Rom. 5:1, Phil. 4:7), and to His mission and His purpose of coming into the world (Mk. 5:34, Lk 1:79).

In announcing His mission on earth in Luke 4:18,19, Jesus proclaimed that He was to bring good news to the poor (I interpret this to mean, among other things, restoring dignity and self-worth, and offering salvation to those poor in worldly goods and/or in spiritual awareness). He was to proclaim freedom for the prisoners—making whole and restoring freedom to those in physical, emotional and spiritual slavery. His mission was to recover physical and spiritual sight, restoring wholeness to one's worldview and life's perspective; and releasing those oppressed by disease, psychological pain, relational dysfunction, and spiritual conflicts.

In sum, Jesus' mission was to restore wholeness, restore *shalom*, peace, and joy to everyone alienated from God's perfect plan for humanity.

The term peace also captures the essence of the gospel--"the good news of peace through Jesus Christ." (Acts 10:36, Eph. 6:15). Here peace refers to the reconciliation and fellowship restored and made whole between God and the human, through Christ's life, death, and resurrection. Thus peace with God and in God is the privilege with which every sinner is conditionally accorded. J. H. Thayer describes peace as a conception distinctly peculiar to Christianity, the tranquil state of a soul assured of its salvation through Christ, and so fearing nothing from God and content with its earthly lot, of whatever sort that is.[16]

### The Biblical Concept of Spiritual Wholeness

In the Book of Romans, after discussing God's wrath against mankind, righteous judgment, God's faithfulness, righteousness through faith, and Abraham's justification, the Apostle Paul pauses and unveils the main thrust of his message. He declares, "Therefore (in view of what I have stated), since we have been justified through faith, we have peace (*eirenen*) with God through our Lord Jesus Christ, through whom we have gained access by faith into the grace in which we now stand. And we rejoice in the hope of the glory of God...Since we have now been justified by His blood, how much more shall we be saved from God's wrath through Him! For if when we were God's enemies, we were reconciled to Him through the death of His Son, how much more, having been reconciled, shall we be saved through His life! Not only is this so, but we also rejoice in God through our Lord Jesus Christ, through whom we have now received reconciliation (Rom. 5:1,2, 9-11).

Though St. Paul did not use the word wholeness, his theology is consonant with Christian wholism. We cannot have peace which flows out of wholistic living without first being justified and reconciled—restored to relational wholeness between parties in conflict. Here God's holiness and human's sin (as a result of misuse of freedom) are in opposition. I shall not deal at length the theological interpretation of the term "God's wrath," whether it is a subjective, personal, angry frame of God's mind, or some impersonal, automatic, causal effects of an abstract law, or a peculiar holy pathos expressing an act of His will, or His judgmental condemnation of sin and sinners. It is the case for our inquiry that God's wrath, manifested as a consequence of the violations of God's law and as perceived by the recipients of His wrath, is an obstacle to wholeness both in the context of the divine-human relationship and one's existential life.

Paul states that we can have peace (wholeness under discussion) after being justified through faith in Jesus Christ. What then is justification? Tomes of Christian literature have been written on this subject. Since it is not the main focus of our discussion, a brief word will serve the purpose.

Justification (to justify—Heb. *Sadeq,* Gk. *Dikaioo*) is a legal term, which means to pronounce a verdict of acquittal (thus penally not liable) on the person who has been charged with crimes. The person is then declared just and accepted back into society with all the privileges accorded to those who keep the law. Justification, by the act itself, restores the full legal status of the person, removing from him or her any possibility of condemnation by the law.

In Christian theology, justification is achieved by God's sovereign will, mediated by His love and grace through the believer's faith in Christ's atoning death and resurrection (Eph. 2:8, Gal.3:6-9; Phil. 3:7-11, Rom. 10: 9-13). In justification, God is declaring "through a judicial act" that the sinner is righteous through the imputed righteousness of Christ. Righteousness (Heb. *tsadaq*) is living up to the standards set for a relationship.[17] In the divine-human interaction, God, the Creator of the universe and humanity, is the ultimate standard of righteousness since He is the final authority of all ethics and morality. God is the judge as well as the administrator for justice. The created beings including the angels are the jury or spectators witnessing the cosmic drama of creation, sin, fall, redemption, God's initiative of love and grace, human response—positive or negative. The God-given faith that we exercise, appropriates the grace that He offers. This faith, however, is authenticated by our good works, in the life and from a heart overflowing with gratitude. While the Apostle Paul warns of salvation through dead works (Romans 3, 4, 5 and Ephesians 2), James the apostle cautions us about salvation by dead faith (Jas. 2:14-26).

Questions can be raised as to the propriety and ethics of imputing Jesus' righteousness to sinners and transferring sinners' sin and guilt to the Innocent One. Is not the acquitting of the guilty unrighteous itself an unrighteous act on the part of God? Is God making sinners something they are not? Does God play games and not seeing through sinners' real characters when they are cloaked with "the robe of Christ's righteousness?" And is not the condemning of the innocent Jesus with the requirement of death on the cross the epitome of injustice? In human justice system, one person cannot die for the one condemned to die. The guilty one alone must pay the death penalty.

How can we have spiritual and theological wholeness (peace) while encountering such intellectual challenge to our minds? Theologians and ministers have debated long and hard the theories of justification, sanctification, atonement, election, regeneration, salvation, and other related subjects. My own tentative response is that we have to begin with the presupposition that God is love and justice personified, and that He is the ultimate paragon of all goodness, truth, and virtue. There is nothing He does that would violate the highest norm of morality and ethics.[18]

I argue that since God is the final authority of the moral and physical laws of the universe, He can devise any system of justice to His liking. He makes the laws. The laws do not control Him. If He designs a legal system in which a willing sinless one can die for the sinners to whom all the benefits accrue, and the sinless one being Himself, who can say there is no justice? The only one who could complain about injustice would be Christ Himself. But He is the One who willingly suffered the injustice. So the argument becomes an abstraction, if not moot. In the willing acceptance of such injustice, God's love is revealed to the created order.

Again I argue that in justification when Christ's righteousness is imputed to us as if it were our own, God is accepting our faith, thus our potential to truly conform to Christ's righteousness in an ongoing process. God is acting on faith Himself, humanly speaking, to believe in the final actualization of our intended goal to become like Christ. In reality, by virtue of God's omniscience and omnipotence, He knows who through His enabling would actualize the initial faith manifested when a sinner is justified. There is no disappointment with God. Justification, then, is not a make-believe; it is true belief in the making.

Existentially we know we have sin and guilt to contend with, ever since God has gifted us with limited genuine freedom which Adam and Eve abused. This is the biblical portrayal and reality of humanity's fall. Historically and culturally, there is no dispute as to the sinfulness and wickedness of human nature and its heinous manifestation. Individually and for the human family, there is a need for forgiveness and justification by God—vertically from above and horizontally among us. Because He is love, the method He uses must be for our ultimate good. Being just, He employs the means of justification with equal concern for both the sinner and the sinless. So there cannot be an unjust treatment for Christ, who volunteered to be the instrumentality of God's salvation for humanity. As truth personified, He does not engage in self-deception or deceptively manipulating His created beings and pretending to transfer our sins to Christ and impute Christ's righteousness to us. Because He is all-knowing and wise, His method of justifying the sinners is the best chosen, and being all-powerful, there is nothing He could not have done to find the best solution for the sin problem and our being made whole for His fellowship.

Forgiven by God, we are free to progress in the path of peace and joy. Justified and declared righteous before the Creator God, we partake of God's gifts of faith, hope, and love, and eternal life which begins even now. Spiritual wholeness is letting our spiritual life co-mingle with our other life's dimensions of personhood in a progressive, harmonious development of our God-given attributes.

Wholeness in the spiritual sphere seeks to modulate the deficiency of other domains. It leads where the others lack behind. It nurtures the other dimensions of the person, because it itself is nurtured by God.

## Possible Theological, Philosophical, and Intellectual Barriers to Christian Grounding of Wholism

Since I argue that Christian wholism is built on the Christian doctrines of Creation and redemption and other Biblical wisdom, it is only reasonable that we address the issues of the authority of the Bible, the Divinity of Christ, His Resurrection, and distinctiveness of Christian beliefs in our religious pluralistic world.

### Authority and Reliability of the Bible

God, our Creator, is transcendent and immanent (dwells in us through His Spirit). His transcendence precludes our ever finding and knowing Him unless He first reveals to us through self-disclosure. The Bible is such specific self-revelation by God. His other means of making Himself known to us is His general revelation through Nature. The structure of traditional Christianity rests on this fundamental assertion.

I argue that the Bible, the Word of God—both the Old and New Testaments, is totally trustworthy in the autographs and most translations, and is an infallible expression of God's will for the salvation of humankind. "...the Scriptures (Scriptures means writings) are the faithful testimony of the godly to the God whom they loved and served...from another standpoint, through a unique exercise of divine overruling in their composition, they are God's own testimony and teaching in human form." [19]

In His task of communicating to us whom He created, He has, by His sovereign will, employed sinful and fallible humanity as is, with all its imperfections, biases, and educational and cultural preconditioning. The product is a document, or better named a library of 66 books by some 40 writers of varied stations in life and living in 10 different countries.

This Bible, God's message to humankind, was written in three languages (Hebrew, Aramaic, Greek), with more than 3,000 human characters depicted in over 1,000 locations and spanning some

1,500 years. It deals with human history, nature, and God's interaction with His creatures. It describes Creation, sin and grace, Satan and the Fall. It portrays the redemptive mission of the Redeemer, His ministry, earthly life, death, and resurrection. It promises hope for human restoration, bodily resurrection, Heaven, and finally the end of the cosmic drama.

An exhaustive critique of modern Biblical scholarship and criticisms of the Bible will necessarily include textual, source, form, redaction, historical and literary criticism. Such an endeavor would be outside the ambit of our discussion. Nonetheless, it is necessary to emphasize that in all His dealings with us, God delights in the joint participation of both divinity-the-transcendent and humanity-with-all-its-vagaries. Analogous to the unfathomable mystery of the Incarnation, the Bible is fully divine and fully human.

In a Divine-human encounter, God seldom if ever bypasses the human mind, which houses all our memory, learning, experience, our cognitive as well as emotional components. In general, He makes no exception to the rule, not even in the work of redeeming the human race or revealing His sovereign plan in Scripture.

Is there any wonder then that some textual inconsistencies (real or apparent), some errors in copying and translating the Bible (accidental or willful), some misdating of chronology (careless or ignorant), should surface to our attention? Even so, one encounters only relatively small number of discrepancies. None of these would significantly affect our knowledge of salvation and God's will for us. The surprise should rather be that there are not any more. That there is a deep unity underlying this remarkable document we call the Bible makes it even more credible and creditable.[20]

The canonical boundaries of the Old and New Testaments automatically exclude certain interpretations of the Christian faith. Conversely, the same canonical walls also encompass a variety of hermeneutical enterprises to foster diversity of faith and meaning. The Scriptural Canon is a safeguard against capricious, unlimited theological speculations and philosophical sophistry.

Aside from the academic and public interpretations of the Bible, there is yet the all-important personal response to whatever meaning one places on Scripture. One must diligently guard against a manipulative reading of the word of God so as to promote one's self-interest, whether conscious or unknowing. The Bible student must desist from salving his/her conscience with Biblical confirmation, even by a sense of need while blinded by self-deception.

A critical evaluation as to the Bible's claim to be the Word of God yields the following. Christ's own testimony in Matthew 4, 5, 12, 15, 19, 22, 24 and John 3, 10, 17 lends authority to the Old Testament. A circularity-criticism argument may not prevail as long as we broaden the circle with warrants supporting the ultimate criterion of our assertion using archaeological data, historical writings, fulfilled prophecies to accord divine authority to Jesus of history as the Christ of our faith.

For the New Testament, there are thousands of earlier manuscripts available to document its authenticity (fragments dating back to the late 1st century). The numerical number of good manuscripts exceeds that of any book of antiquity.[21]

Miracles, prophetic utterances, accurate fulfillment of biblical prophecies, archaeological confirmations, all testify to the inspiration and reliability of the Bible. The Bible has been the source of wisdom, the motive power behind selfless service. It has inspired scientists and philosophers, and became the engine for democratic ideas and social reform. It has been the germinating field for scientific inventions and the flourishing of arts, music, and literature. Religious atrocities in the name of Christianity and systematic dehumanization based on twisted biblical hermeneutics notwithstanding, only the Western civilization nurtured mainly by biblical wisdom and morality is noted for the founding of innumerable hospitals, orphanages, social support agencies, research, and higher learning institutions.

From a personal and existential perspective, the transforming power of the gospel through the God-Man Jesus, the main focus and unitary theme of the Bible, speaks again and again of the authenticity of its moral and divine Source. The biblical message can be understood by people of little learning, yet it poses challenge to the most brilliant minds. In life and near death, the Scripture with its wisdom, counsel, guidance, and consoling voice is without peers. Countless people down through the centuries have testified to the life-enriching, life-supporting function of the Christian Bible.

For our purpose, the Bible with all the accumulated reflections and traditions thereof can more than provide a total, coherent theology of Christian Wholism under discussion. No other religious book could take its place.

## The Divinity of Christ

The deity of Christ has been a contentious issue ever since the founding of Christianity. Whether Christ is believed to have one nature, two natures, how they are related, and how they are expressed has been the basis of heretical trials in many Church Councils. Since a thorough examination of this topic is beyond the scope of our discussion, a brief description may suffice. Arianism claims that only God has deity; and Christ is the first and highest of created beings, who created the world; "there was a time when he was not," thus Christ is not self-existent. Docetism maintains that Christ, though appeared human, was really divine. Ebionitism—Jesus was an ordinary human being possessing unusual wisdom and righteousness; not preexistent. Nestorianism—Jesus' human nature was under the complete control of His divine nature; Nestorians are against unity of person and believe that the human Jesus who died on the cross was not the same as the Divine Son for whom death is impossible. Appollinarianism—Christ did not have a human mind, He had the divine Logos, which is reason in humanity. Eutychianism (monophysitism)—Jesus' human nature was absorbed into the divine resulting in a new third nature *(tertium quid)*; Christ's humanity thus deemphasized. Monarchianism: dynamic and adoptionistic variety—Jesus was a mere man endowed with the Holy Spirit; the divine Logos not personal but simply God's inherent rationality; modalistic—Sabellianism, a divine Monad, revealed as Father the Creator and Lawgiver, as Son the Redeemer, as Spirit the Giver of grace; three different modes revealing the same divine Person.

Since the patristic period and through the middle ages, the Christian churches have accepted the Divinity of Christ as enunciated in the Nicene, Athanasian, Chalcedonian creeds, which state, "We believe in one God...and in one Lord Jesus Christ, the only begotten Son of God, begotten of the Father before all worlds; God of God, Light of Light, Very God of Very God, begotten, not made, being of one substance with the Father; by whom all things were made...incarnate by the Holy Ghost of the Virgin Mary, and was made man ...crucified ...suffered ...buried ...and the third day He rose again...and ascended into Heaven...He shall come again, with glory, to judge the quick and the dead; whose kingdom shall have no end...we look for the resurrection of the dead, and the life of the world to come." [22]

Martin Luther subscribed generally to the credo orthodoxy with emphasis of mutual interpenetration of Jesus' divine and human qualities or properties. John Calvin was careful to insist that Christ's two natures are distinct though never separate, in the unity of Christ's person. Calvin stressed the assumption of the human nature into the divine person of the Son, in whom there is a direct union between the two natures.

Theologian of the 20th century Karl Barth argued Christology from top down, starting with God, Trinity, then Incarnation downward, looking at Jesus' humanity against the transcendent context. Wolfhart Panneberg went the opposite way, viewing Christology from below, "moving upward from Jesus' life and death toward His transformation in His resurrection and exaltation through the grace of God." Roman Catholic Karl Rahner posited Jesus' divine and human natures beginning from His humanity in the context of anthropology. [23]

Oscar Cullmann emphasized Jesus' function and work rather than His ontological nature. Using "salvation history" and a functional approach, Cullmann concentrated on what Jesus had done in history.[24]

Approaching this subject of the divinity of Christ from a different angle, Professor McGrath, theologian and Research Lecturer from Oxford with a PhD in microbiology, comments that there have been people in history who have made great sacrifices for those they loved, so that if He was not God, "Jesus cannot be singled out for special discussion unless he *is* something or someone qualitatively different from us." Only when God suffered in Christ, is the love of God truly manifest.

McGrath continues, "...A nonincarnational Christianity is unable to convincingly anchor the person of Jesus Christ as the center of the Christian faith...The divinity of Christ, given expression in the doctrine of the Incarnation, is an essential and integral part of the authentically Christian understanding of reality. Faith in the resurrection and Incarnation is what kept and keeps Christianity growing and spreading...Only a form of Christianity that is convinced that it has something distinctive, true, exciting, and relevant to communicate to the world in order to transform it will survive." [25]

Evangelical Christians have generally argued for the divinity of Christ along the following lines: (1) Jesus claimed to be God (Jn. 17:5, Rev. 1:17, to be equal with God (Mk. 2:5-11), to be honored with God (Jn.5:23), to accept worship due God (Mt. 8:2, 9:18, Jn.20-28), to have equal authority with God (Mt. 5-21-22; 28:18-19); (2) He fulfilled scores of prophecies regarding a Messiah—the probability of having all these prophecies fulfilled in one man boggles the mind—one chance out of trillions and trillions and trillions, the number goes on; (3) He alone lived a sinless life and performed many miracles, (4) He predicted His resurrection and fulfilled it—He rose from the dead.[26]

At this point, one might ask why in the discussion of Christian Wholism such a review of the Divinity of Christ is necessary. My response is: There are important implications of the Divinity of Christ as well as its nexus to a theology of Christian Wholism.

1) Christian wholism is tied to the saving mission of Christ. After sin's rupture of God's original plan for the human family, God's redemptive activity for lost humanity mediated through Christ has been set in motion. The scope of redemption extends to the total restoration of God's image in humans, which includes all dimensions of personhood, beginning here and now, culminating in our resurrected bodies in the eternal Kingdom.

2) It was not a mere good human being, a moral teacher, a prophet, an ambassador of God who came to live, die, and save us. It was Christ, the very God of very God, who came to live among us and promised to take us to where He is—God's eternal Kingdom. It was Christ Jesus, God Himself who said, "I am the resurrection and the life. He who believes in me will live, even

though he dies, and whoever lives and believes in me will never die." Because Christ is God, we can trust His promise, including the restorative work of making us whole in every dimension of life.

3) The Creator God is transcendent, is beyond our time-space domain. He appears so far, far away in the seeming infinity of space and time. Our human quest would only end in futility had Christ, the Godhead, not come. The incarnational Christ in its profound mystery crosses over the humanly unbridgeable gulf between Creator and creatures. His purpose is to make human whole with no spheres untouched. Being God, He comes to dwell among us. God is no longer an unfeeling Great Principle, an Ideal, a Platonic Form, The Other, the Unmoved Mover. He is immanent, personal, Immanuel—God with us. Jesus' deity puts a human face on God, analogically speaking. Answering Philip's question about wanting to see God the Father, Jesus answered, "Anyone who has seen me has seen the Father. Don't you believe that I am in the Father and the Father is in me?" Jn.14:9.

4) God in the Person of Christ did not shun the human body for inhabitance. It is the human body in which the Spirit delights to dwell. Surely, such a body is worth God's restoring or made whole! It is looking to the end and *telos* and into God's divine intention for humanity, culminated in the resurrection body of the believers, that Christian Wholism draws courage and hope.

5) While on earth, the God who lives among us practices Christian Wholism. Repeatedly, He made people whole physically, emotionally, spiritually. Not an angel, not an Ideal, not a mortal man, but God, love-incarnate, stoops down to our level in His capacity of full divinity. That makes a difference! This is love genuine and transparent. If a God of love and miracles is in charge, the Christian hope of wholism leading to everlasting peace and joy can find its sure moorings.

6) As an ancillary issue, we may inquire whether Jesus inherited Adam's and Eve' prelapsarian (before the Fall) nature or their postlapsarian sin nature in the context of His incarnation? With the knowledge of modern-day reproductive technology and in-vitro fertilization, let me posit that Mary could very well have been a surrogate mother consenting to be the recipient of a perfect, sinless, God-embryo, via the Holy Spirit, that grew up to be Jesus.

Jesus then had neither an earthly father nor an earthly mother. The human genome has been contaminated by the cumulative effects of fallen nature. The latter, however, did not taint God's Son. The God-embryo during gestation was nourished by Mary's blood. Mary's fallen nature manifested through the placental circulation suppressed the expression of certain perfect genes, resulting in Jesus' taking on the frail human nature, which being common to that of us, is subject to being tempted in every way, just as we are (Heb. 4:15).

### The Resurrection and the Resurrected Body

We may recall at the beginning of first chapter on the definition of Christian Wholism that I argue that the full expression of this wholism will be culminated in the believer's resurrected body at the eschaton. Christian wholism begins here and now in our Christian walk but its praxis is a lifelong, ongoing process marked by progress and setbacks and re-starts. All along on this path to peace and joy, we are nurtured and cheered on by that resplendent hope promised by the One whose own resurrection forever redefines the reality of this universe. "I am the Resurrection and the Life." It is this hope and reality that St. Paul speaks of in 1 Corinthians 15:14-15, "And if Christ has not been raised, our preaching is useless and so is your faith. More than that, we are then found to be false witnesses about God...."or "misrepresenting God."

The Christian believer's resurrected body, patterned after Christ's prototypical resurrection body (pre/post-ascension body) shall assume a twin-mode with their perfection and wholeness: (1) a dominant mode with transformed, glorified, Spirit-ruled physical expressions incorporating our personal identity and continuity, operative in real spatiotemporal dimensions of Heaven and (2) an alternative mode capable of transphysical (transcending the physical) manifestations in ultradimensional reality of glory and splendor. A differentiation between Jesus' twin-mode resurrection body and that of the believer's is emphasized. On the basis of ontological Creatorhood and human creatureliness, this distinction is paramount.[27]

In Heaven, the believer of Christian wholism will have the choice to assume a materialized, physical, tangible body gloriously superior than our present one and truly a spiritual body in the sense that it functions according to spiritual laws and governed by the Holy Spirit and totally relieved of all the burdens of sinful flesh. Or as a viable alternative, the believer may also express itself as a nonmaterialized, transphysical (albeit limited ontologically because of our creatureliness), intangible, spiritual body not bound by space and time as are encountered in our physical universe. The glorious possibility is that we shall be able to exercise both of these necessary [28] choices at will or perhaps by just thinking it. At any time, at any place, the options can be modified and changed in however many times as we desire. This provision of options is guaranteed by the faithful God who has gifted us with the kind of freedom akin to His own. It necessarily follows then that in Heaven, at any time, there will be the possibility of redeemed humans in full physicality and wholeness participating in all the physical activities analogous to our own except with nth degree of excellence, beauty and perfection. In addition to this group of physicalized saints, there will also be the nonmaterialized faithful of God who rejoice in His presence with their transphysical state. [29]

## Christian Wholism and Religious Pluralism

As a theology and applied ethics, Christian Wholism must be examined in a public forum and argued against other religions and important philosophical systems. Of the myriads, I shall focus mainly on Confucianism, Taoism, Buddhism, Islam, Judaism, Marxism, secular humanism, New Ageism, radical postmodernism. This arbitrary selection is partly based on the number of people on this earth who have subscribed to these beliefs or are directly or indirectly affected by them down through the centuries.

1) **Confucianism**, which originates from the philosophy of Confucius in China (ca. 550 B.C.), strictly speaking, is not a religion but a political philosophy and an ethical system. It has influenced billions of people. It places great emphasis on moral standards, personal and social ethics, and an ordered society governed by *Li* (propriety and protocol). The ultimate pursuit in

life (the Confucian goal) is to become a superior person who is governed internally by *Ren* and externally by *Li*. .[30]

Virtues and principles taught in Confucianism include *Ren* (love, kindness, benevolence); *Yi* (justice, righteousness); *Te* (morality and moral power of a person); Lun (goodness, ethics, the heavenly principle); Zhi (wisdom); *Xin* (trust); *Li* (propriety, courtesy, rites, etiquette—how to comport oneself with grace and urbanity, also relationship between words, thought, and objective reality); *Wen* (learning, music, art, poetry, culture, the arts of securing peace); *Xiao* (filial piety, honoring parents); *Zhong* (loyalty and devotion); *Shu* (forbearance, considerateness); *Zhongyong* (Doctrine of the Mean, central harmony, balance, temperance); *Dao* (the way, the right behavior of person, ruler, community, nation); *Zhongshu* (Do not do to others what you would not want others to do to you), comparable to the Golden Rule "Do to others as you would have them do to you" (Luke 6:31). [31 32 33]

Confucius, a forerunner of virtue ethics, argues that the moral person is the standard for ethics. His concept of an ideal society is one in which there is hierarchical authority--a wise and moral ruler over the citizenry, parents over children, men over women (feminists beware!), the educated over the common people. Though he often referred to *Tian* (Heaven), he did not invoke a personal God. He himself never asked to be worshipped. For two millennia, Chinese have held him in great respect and adoration, and if this adoration is taken to be a form of religious sentiment, then Confucianism could fall into the larger context and loose definition of religion even though there are no formal ritual observances for him. Today, there are many Confucian temples, which are memorial buildings instead of places of worship. Confucianism has exerted its moral influence not only in China historically and in modern times, but to a large extent also in the Japanese and Korean cultures. [34]

Nowhere in Confucian philosophy, however, is there any discussion of a personal God, the origin and significance of the human body, or an afterlife in heaven or hell. Neo-Confucianists only speak of the "mind" of heaven and earth.

Confucianism, in light of its ethical and social thrust, contributes to the sphere of wholeness/order in society and government as well as ethical and individual moral perfection. But as a system of ethics and philosophy to address the comprehensive issues of wholeness in the context of a person's multiple dimensions, it does not seem to be adequate to the task.

2) **Taoism** (Tao or Dao means the Way, the essence, the nameless reality, the logos) is a native Chinese religion. It stresses love, compassion, moderation, humility, and recompensing injury with kindness. Its bible is the *Tao Teh Ching*. [35] It proposes a life of simplicity and harmony with nature. The recurrent theme in Taoism is that all human glory, achievements, fame, wealth, education, and political power are total folly and illusions. Some of the dominant themes are *wu-wei*—absence of striving toward worldly goals, a form of non-assertiveness, effortless action (effortlessness of moral action), acting through inaction, mastering through receptivity and yielding to the flow of rhythm. Taoism also introduces the concept of opposites *Yin* (feminine, dark, negative, passive, submissive, pliant, receptive, mysterious) and *Yang* (masculine, sunny, positive, constructive, active, open).

Taoism has two major branches. The intellectual Taoism embracing a mysticism according to which the eternal *Tao* is inexpressible but experientially available. The opening chapter of *Tao Teh Ching* states, "*Tao* can be talked about, but not the Eternal *Tao*. Names can be named, but not the Eternal Name. As the origin of heaven and earth, it is nameless; as the "Mother" of all things, it is nameable...The Mystery of all mysteries is the Door of all essence..." So the *Tao* is impersonal, a mysterious Force in the universe, a first Cause of everything thing there is. Scientists have used *Tao* in conceptual frameworks, *The Tao of Physics* being a recent example. A superstitious offshoot of Taoism which borders on magical religion is burdened with elaborate rituals. [36]

Taoism's contribution to our discussion of wholeness points to a form of metaphysical wholeness which embodies harmony with nature and touches our philosophical and psychological/emotional being. But it has little to tell us about our spiritual and physical interaction, and even less about a personal God.

3) **Buddhism** has several strands. The so-called noble truths in Buddhism state that all life is suffering, which originates from our human cravings or desires. Release from suffering is only possible by extinguishing these cravings and through the *Eightfold Path* to finally reach *Nirvana*—a state of eternal bliss and final release from the cycle of reincarnations. The *Eightfold Path* is the expression of a Buddhist's spirituality—through right speech, right action, right livelihood and effort, right mindfulness and meditations, right views, and right aspirations-intentions, based on the precept that all existence is unsatisfactory and impermanent, and that there is no permanent self—in other words misery, transitoriness, and non-ego. To these are added many specific abstinences and recollections. Thus, to a Buddhist, spirituality means engaging in moral conduct and above steps in mental discipline as preparation to receiving intuitive wisdom.[37]

Buddhism has several strands. Theravada (the way of the elders) branch is more conservative and presumably follows the original teachings of Buddha. Most of the followers are clustered in Thailand, Sri Lanka, Myanmar (Burma), Cambodia, and Laos. It has a basically atheistic approach with emphasis on individual efforts, meditation, and achievements to reach *Nirvana*—the blessed state of release from the endless cycles of birth, suffering, death, rebirth and suffering again. Theravada considers gods and prayers of lesser importance than effort on one's part. A Buddha (Buddha meaning the Enlightened One) to the followers of Theravada is nothing but a human who has discovered by his own efforts the way to Nirvana. [38]

The *Mahayana* variety, prevalent in China, Japan, Korea, Vietnam, has fused with Confucian and Taoist thoughts and practices. *Yana* means "vehicle," and *Mahayana*, the "Great Vehicle" which can help people cross over the river of suffering to the other shore, through countless rebirths, to *Nirvana*. The exemplary figure in this tradition is the enlightened and wise Bodhisattva, who helps people struggling with life to be free from suffering. Mahayana Buddhists worship multiple deities with incense-burning to make prayerful requests. The adherents believe that there are many Buddhas and Bodhisattvas. One of its sects is the intuitive Zen Buddhism, which distrusts reason and uses riddles and case studies *koans* to transcend reason in its path to enlightenment. Question such as, "…what is the sound of one hand clapping?" is used to confound sense and reason in order to encourage meditation leading to enlightenment.

The Vijrayana (thunderbolt) branch of Buddhism is most prominent in Tibet, China, Japan. It takes an accelerated path to Enlightenment by combining the wisdom and practice of both the Theravada and Mahayana traditions.

Buddhism in all its branches dwells on the same theme of suffering in life. Suffering can be eliminated by blocking out all human desires. Desires can be extinguished through the 8-fold Path, a system of human effort and rituals. This approach to life's realities, in my view, is negative and unsatisfying. After all, what is joy but the confluence of the hunger of a desire with the satisfaction of that desire, or the fulfillment of a void created by the desire. The desire for wholeness, joy and peace and perfect restoration to what is all good and right, planted by God for our ultimate good, must never be suppressed, let alone extinguished. Thus, Buddhism as a religion, in the context of Christian Wholism, is found wanting in major aspects.

4) **Islam** is a religion founded by Muhammad whose adherents are called Muslims (those who submit to God). The emphasis is on the Five Pillars: (1) Repetition of the Creed, "There is no God but Allah…;" (2) Prayer (5 times a day facing Mecca); (3)Alms to the poor; (4) Fasting in the month of Ramadan while eating at night only; A pilgrimage to Mecca during one's lifetime.[39] A person's salvation and final judgment depend on absolute submission to Allah's will and how faithful the five Pillars are carried out. [40]

In Islam, if there is such a concept of wholeness—spiritual salvation—it is based on human works-righteousness. There is no provision of grace to make up human deficiency. I shall argue that ultimate peace and joy are not obtainable unless they come as gifts of God who is the Creator of our person in all its dimensions and have the blueprint to reconstruct and make it whole again.

(5) **Judaism**: Speaking about wholeness, Judaism comes closest to the Christian concept of wholism under discussion here. After careful examination, Professor Green concludes that the Hebrew Bible provides no particularly "scriptural" vocabulary for

anthropological analysis when the words spirit, soul and body are used. Rather a common terminology of the ancient world was utilized to depict the human person as an integrated whole. [41]

The beliefs of Judaism include monotheism "The Lord is One." He is the omniscient, omnipotent, eternal, Creator God who revealed His law to Moses and other prophets and made a covenant with His chosen people. The requirements for this people are prescribed in the Torah (the five books of Moses) and the Talmud (Mishnah and Gemara, interpretations and commentaries of oral traditions). Humans can achieve holiness by observing the Torah, by offering sacrifices for their transgressions, and by doing good works since the destruction of the Temple in Jerusalem. The faithful are looking for the coming of a Messiah who will vindicate God's people. In the interim, emphasis is placed on communitarian life, preservation of identity and family, worship and observation of Sabbaths and festivals. There will be a judgment and a resurrection of the dead. [42] [43]

In our concept of Christian wholeness, humanity's spiritual void and human alienation from God cannot be remedied by animal sacrifices or good works. Spiritual wholeness can only be obtained by God's grace and healing through the God-man Jesus Christ, the Creator and Redeemer who was Himself broken and violated in all dimensions. He alone knows how to make humanity whole again. "...By His wounds you have been healed." (1 Pe. 2:24, Isa. 53:5). This is in contrast to Judaism, whose coming Messiah is still in the future tense. In Christian Wholism, we already have a living Prototype for the construct of wholeness. He not only has the blueprint; He has the power and intention to implement this blueprint of wholeness in our person, beginning now and continuing on to our resurrected body.

(6) **Marxism**: Karl Marx was influenced by Georg Wilhelm Friedrich Hegel's dialectic—a general historical law of thesis, antithesis, and synthesis, which the events of the world follow in the development of nations. As a nation becomes more powerful (this is the thesis), it produces opposition (antithesis), resulting in conflict and eventual resolution (synthesis). This synthesis itself now becomes a new thesis at a more advanced level, which in turn will develop its new antithesis, and conflict and resolution, and

through infinite repeated processes to reach a state of perfection. Hegel originally borrowed the idea from Zeno, Socrates, and Plato[44][45] who used dialectic (discourse/debate) as a logical process in argumentation—the method of contrary case.

Marx applied Hegel's metaphysical dialectic of nations to a historical, politico-economic material process reflecting the struggles and rivalries between different socio-economic classes. The employer-capitalists—thesis, controlling the means of production, will generate an opposing force—antithesis, from the employees (industrial workers in former USSR, farmers in China, oilfield laborers in the Middleeast, for example, resulting in predictable conflict, revolution, and resolution—synthesis. This synthesis, now a new, advanced thesis, prompts another antithesis, *ad infinitum*, eventually to reach a utopia of classless society. [46]

Designed as a definitive solution for human ills, Marx's and Friedrich Engels' political philosophy nonetheless excludes any discussion of a supernatural Being, spiritual composition of humans, and the reality of sin and fallen human nature. Its claim to restore political and economic wholeness to people has largely failed. The collapse of the former Soviet Union, the embrace of market economy and capitalistic ventures by China, the westernization of Eastern Europe, all testify to the deficiency of Marxist political and economic theories.

Marx speaks of self-alienation—a person's plight in the modern industrial and technological world when he or she is isolated from other people. This self-alienation is the result of humans' own making, because what technology was designed to give a person—leisure, comfort, security, cultural interaction— these are the very things the person is deprived of. People have become more like machines, and machines more like people.

For Marxists, the problem of alienation from our Creator is never addressed. Wholeness would be elusive if such an important part of a human's composition is missing.

St Augustine's famous reflection, "...Because You (God) have made us for yourself, and our hearts are restless until they can find peace in you...." [47] is no less true for Christians as for Marxists and Communists. "Man does not live on bread alone..." Mt. 4:4

speaks to the futility of economic and political solutions exclusive of God's domain and concerns of spiritual wholeness.

(7) **Secular Humanism** bases its philosophy on human interests and values. In the *Humanist Manifesto I and II and Secular Humanist Declaration, 1981,* [48] it is affirmed that the universe is self-existing without a Creator, that humanity has emerged from a continuous process, that dualism of mind and body be rejected, that a person is not immortal. Furthermore, there are no God-given values, and ethical norms are relative and situational, needing no theological or ideological sanction. The central humanist value is the preciousness and dignity of the individual. Reason and intelligence, not faith or passion, are the most effective instruments that humankind possesses. As non-theists, "we begin with humans not God, nature not deity...No deity will save us; we must save ourselves." Religion, to the humanists, is anything significant, interesting, or satisfying to the people. [49] "In the best sense, religion may inspire dedication to the highest ethical ideals; the traditional dogmatic or authoritarian religions...do a disservice to the human species." [50]

Secular humanism is anthropocentric, nontheistic, naturalistic and evolutionary in its worldview. Ethics and morals are relative and subject to change; there are no absolute moral values for the humanists. Self-sufficiency, human development, scientific and technological advances, complete realization of human personality in the here and now are the goals of human life. Such a philosophy, impervious to a person's spiritual needs and aspirations would fail to lead us to the pandimensional wholeness under discussion as defined at the beginning of the chapter.

(8) **New Ageism** has many varieties and appears in different forms. [51] The dominant theme is, "All is One." God, the Devil and devils, good and evil, angels, saints and sinners, animals, plants, the inorganic universe, each and every living and non-living entity are all in this oneness of reality. Most pantheistic New Ageism followers believe in an impersonal God, who exists from the necessity of His own nature. Creation is not from nothing but out of God. Everything in the universe is of the same substance as God. The universe and the world is God. The world is neither independent of nor distinct from God. By contrast, classical

Christian theism believes that this world is dependent upon but distinct from God.

Humans are divine, according to New Ageism. Since humans have the power and potential within, higher knowledge and mystical consciousness through illumination with an immediate, direct and intuitive experience can help one to reach his/her human potential and wholistic health. Logic is sometimes bypassed and language declared inadequate.

Knowledge is the key to overcome ignorance about the divinity within us. This ignorance is the source of all evil. Salvation therefore lies in enlightenment through our own effort that can be achieved in a number of ways. Any religion can help us to find the way to the truth, be it Jesus, Buddha, Krishna, Mohammad, or any god. Evil and suffering are, for most New Agers, illusions or lack of perceptions stemming from human ignorance of the true state of affairs.

Christian wholism presupposes a distinction between God and the human, the Creator and the created. Our existential experience affirms to us that our own effort is inadequate, our wisdom is limited, and our aim is far from the mark. Humans simply cannot pull themselves out from the downward spiral. Millions have tried, including the New Agers who are sincere in heart. We need the One who is both our Creator and Redeemer to point us the way to the all-encompassing wholeness, a gift not of human engineering but through the power of God.

(9) **Radical Postmodernism:** A definition of postmodernism is at times notoriously difficult because of the meaning of terms. In the words of philosopher Cahoone of Boston University, one is often unclear about authors' designation of what is meant "modern" and "postmodern" and "what it is whose obsolescence the term "postmodern" presumably announces." [52]

Postmodernism by definition is what follows modernism. But which modernism is it referring to? One option would be the 20th century movement which rejected the culture and tradition of Victorianism. Here postmodernism would then be the rejection of the ideals and style of that 20th Century movement. Another option takes modernism all the way back to the Enlightenment of the 18th Century with all those scientific theories, reliance on rationality, and confident cultural norms. Postmodernism in this sense has a much broader historical and ideological sweep, and a more radical denunciation of traditional beliefs and assumptions of Western churches and institutions. [53]

Postmodern thinking, in general, emphasizes openness, relativism, skepticism about truth, norms, meaning, knowledge, reason, authority, and rejection of absolutism. The concerns are persons, relationship, belonging, experiment, the "marginalized other, and consumer capitalism.[54] The postmodern worldview is essentially evolutionary, indeterminate, confronting a reality with an unfathomable mystery, and a process with dynamic relations.[55] [56] [57] [58]

Other concerns of post-modern theology are in the area of epistemology—theory of knowledge: Foundationalism versus Contextualism. Abandoning claims to knowledge in a universal discourse with alternative emphasis on timelessness, theories, generality, the anti-foundationalist camp stresses instead particular, timely, practical truth claims of specific, concrete, local worshipping communities as well as a narrative approach to Scripture.

In the words of philosopher Bernd Magnus of University of California, "Postmodern philosophy is…a complex cluster concept…includes…an anti-(or post-) epistemological standpoint; anti-essentialism; antirealism; anti-foundationalism; opposition to transcendental arguments and transcendental standpoints; rejection of the picture of knowledge as accurate representation; rejection of truth as correspondence to reality; rejection of the very idea of canonical descriptions; rejection of final vocabularies, i.e. rejection of principles, distinctions, and categories that are thought to be unconditionally binding for all times, persons, and places; and a suspicion of metanarratives of the sort perhaps best illustrated by dialectical materialism. Postmodern philosophy also rejects characterizing this menu of oppositions as relativism, skepticism or nihilism." [59]

Alister McGrath of Oxford and Millard Erickson at Baylor University both criticize the radical forms of postmodernism which argue that all interpretations are equally valid, that concepts such as self, truth and meaning should be abolished since language does not refer to anything and truth has no correspondence to reality. The deconstructionists would contend that the Bible contains no objective truth, that there are no absolutes. [60] Ethics has no norms; history no facts; language no reference; life and the universe devoid of meaning. "The distinction," in the words of Erickson, "between the truth and knowledge of the truth has frequently been neglected, with unfortunate results." [61]

As we can see from the discussions, there are valid, redeeming features in postmodern thinking which enlarge our vista regarding God's activity in leading us to the peace and joy in Christian Wholism. We are not to be bounded by centuries-old dogmatic teachings or learned interpretations of traditions and academia to constrict our reflections on this subject. We are free to challenge old "truths" based on past interpretations, which may well have been misleading and truncated. We are to put new wines in God's old wineskins, as it were, and see the transformations and surprises of Divine action on every turn. In such expedition, one must critically repel those radical, deconstructive postmodern thoughts that emasculate the Christian truth and existential meaning.

I argue that Christian Wholism must cultivate a robust intellectual discernment to set the boundaries that separate truth from falsehood, to preserve meaning from pointlessness, and to actively prepare us in God's work on earth in our journey to the promised land where eternal wholeness flourishes in our resurrected bodies.

# CHAPTER 3

---

# FAITH AND INTELLECT
# IN CHRISTIAN WHOLISM

The writer of Hebrews gives this definition of faith, "Now faith is being sure of what we hope for and certain of what we do not see." Heb. 11:1. Again this writer continues, "and without faith it is impossible to please God, because anyone who comes to Him must believe that He exists and that He rewards those who earnestly seek Him." Heb. 11: 6. That seeking, I believe, includes seeking to know Him better through our intellect. I shall argue that there can be no peace and joy in the context of Christian Wholism if there are too many unsolved intellectual conflicts standing between what the mind can perceive and what the heart believes.

Before we embark on the discussion on the interphase between faith and intellect, theology and science, let me make a digression. It is an intellectual, rational approach to provide a ground for the argument (not proof) for the existence of God. Rene Descartes (1596-1650) asserted that if one is to doubt everything, he or she must exist to do the doubting. He issued the famous Latin formula—*Cogito, ergo sum* (I think, therefore I am). Hence, there is at least one proposition which can withstand against the onslaught of the skepticism of doubt.

I argue that not only is it cogent and valid to state *Cogito, ergo sum*. I want to go beyond the Cartesian thought and assert that *Sum, ergo Deus est* (I am, therefore God is). The greatest certainty for me in the whole universe is the certainty that I exist, that I am self-consciously know and aware that I exist. Hence, by inductive reasoning, there is a probability that Someone greater than I am also exists. I am aware of my ability to think (my human thinking and its proneness to error notwithstanding), hence also the probability that a greater and more perfect Thinker also exists. Since self-consciousness and self-awareness are hallmarks of personhood, the awareness of my personhood inductively leads me to conclude that a greater person also exists. Similarly, all my creaturely attributes including love, justice, freedom, creativity, purposiveness, will, power, rationality, sociality, relatedness can be inducted and implied. Apologetics not being the main concern of our discussion here, we will take leave at this point.

What is intellect? It comes from the Latin word *intellectus,* meaning to understand.  In our common usage, by intellect we mean the capacity, faculty, ability, power of the mind by which we know, understand, and apprehend realities. It is cognition in contrast to feeling, emotions, and affective and volitional processes. Intellect is closely associated with mind, and is manifested by reasoning, critical thinking, memory, imagination, abstract thinking, judgment, perception, and synthesis. Without the mind, there is no intellect. Later, we shall also discuss that without the heart, there is no true faith. God is the greatest Intellect in the whole universe, because He is all-knowing (1Jn. 3:20) and all-wise (Isa. 48:3,5; 1Tim. 1:17; Jude 25; Ac. 15:18).

In answer to the question, of all the commandments which is the most important? The most important one, says Jesus in Mark 12:30, is "Love the Lord your God with all your heart and with all your soul and with all your mind (*dianoias*—a Greek word meaning understanding, intelligence, mind, thought*)* and with all your strength." You'll find the same saying in Matthew 22:37 and Luke 10:27. In 1Corinthians 2:16, Paul says, "But we [as Christians] have the mind ( *nous, intellect, understanding, mind)* of Christ."

Since Jesus is both the Author of our faith (Heb. 12:2) and our intellect (we are created in His image with mind, rationality, critical judgment, analytical function), it is only reasonable to conclude that there should not be any genuine conflict between these two aspects of our human constitution in the context of Christian Wholism.  In the secular world, intellect is identified with reason, logical thinking, rationality, science, mathematics;

whereas faith is considered as something bordering ignorance, superstition, fanatical thinking, abnormal psychology, believing in something without factual evidence, or a blind belief not grounded in knowledge.

I shall argue that Christian faith is not irrational nor blind. It is a faith, shaped by reason, based on evidence in Nature and Scripture, and supported, confirmed, and reaffirmed by factual knowledge as well as by personal experience. Let me suggest a dynamic structuring of our Christian faith by way of illustration:

Supposing I am starving and some stranger offers me something that looks like food, which he leaves on the table. I could say to myself: I believe that there is such a thing as food (I see it, I can smell it, I can touch it, I've read and heard about it). This is the first level of the meaning of faith. At this level, I believe there is a God, the Church is His appointed agency, and the Bible is His message to humanity—the source of doctrines and reflections which constitute our interpretations of God, His interactions with us, and our obligations to Him.

Now the second level of faith becomes evident when I believe (intellectually assent and agree to) the fact that the item sitting on the table will relieve my hunger. In other words, at this level of my faith, more than just information, I believe that God is important to a person, that Christianity makes sense, the Bible is a good book to read, the Church serves a useful function, and that the Christian doctrines are sound and defensible on academic and intellectual grounds. So far, the food is still sitting on the table, and I am starving and getting weaker.

The third level is when I reach out and start eating the item. First I start eating a little. Ah it tastes good, it relieves my hunger pain. I start to feel stronger; I can even think better. I not only believe that there is what looks like food on the table ($1^{st}$ level), not only believe that food can satisfy hunger (second level), but above all I trust in the efficacy of the item so much that I actually eat it. I am so committed to it that I am willing to stake my health and life on it for sustenance. In the same way, on this third level of faith, I take God seriously enough to act on His promises, to put my life under His guidance, to commit my heart for His safekeeping, to appropriate His forgiveness and love, and to rest my future in the hope of *parousia* and eternal life. This level of unshakable trust, the deep heart-commitment to God and His Word, this total response to God's grace from the core of my being, this experience of "Christ in me, the hope of glory" is the saving faith which is a gift of God that enables me to weather the storms of life and be carried to the eternal home.

This trust and deep abiding faith is the work of the Holy Spirit authenticating what we believe is true (Jn. 16:13, "When He, the Holy Spirit, the Spirit of Truth, comes, He will guide you into all truth." Now all three levels of faith dynamically interact with one another. As one knows more and more about God through study, research, reflection, such knowledge can further nurture the third level of heart-commitment faith and add to it assurance and affirmation in a feedback loop. The intellectual screening (the second level), makes the core belief more authentic and validating.

We see then that in this dynamic structure of faith, intellect is very much active in the building up of faith. At the first level of information, knowledge is dependent on the mind for reception and assimilation. At the second level, faith is critically dependent on the intellect for sorting out the incoming knowledge, information, and for analysis and evaluation of all the data.

Only on the third level of faith, however, intellect is not the most important factor. Here faith has to do with the heart, the willingness to trust that which cannot be physically demonstrated. "Now faith is being sure of what we hope for and certain of what we do not see" (Heb.11:1). Returning to our illustration and analogically speaking, at this level, by human reasoning, I cannot know for certain whether it is real food or just illusion or even poison. That is why some people call this willingness to risk trusting in Someone, something, a leap of faith. Nonetheless this center-core of faith is not blind, since it is first of all supported by the first two levels of knowledge and intellectual triage. Furthermore, it is authenticated by one's personal experience (eating a little of the food already inches me toward physical wholeness, i.e. less deprived nutritionally). That's how the psalmist metaphorically describes, "Taste (*ta`am*) and see that the Lord is good; blessed is the man (woman) who takes refuge in Him" Psa. 34:8.

There is a dynamic exchange between all these three levels of faith. As the deep heart commitment is nourished by the 1$^{st}$ and 2$^{nd}$ levels of faith, it itself can motivate one to search for more knowledge about God and evidences of His love and power (in our illustration trying to analyze what that food is—the food that I have eaten that gives me such satisfaction of physical wholeness). Recall when you first were converted to the Christian faith—it was a miraculous, exhilarating, personal experience, a gift from God who justifies you and even now is in the process of sanctifying you. Now you want to go back and analyze that experience and relive that moment of God's amazing and continuing grace.

There are Christians who are perfectly satisfied with the born-again experience and go on trusting God in spite of different challenges to Christianity in the secular world and academia. I have known of one professor-scientist, a devout Christian, who separates the faith and intellectual domains of his Christian life into two insulating spheres with no communication between the two. He told us that when he works on scientific research, he leaves God at the laboratory door. And when he worships in church, he leaves his scientific mind at home. He does not let his science training and scientific worldview interfere with his religious life. Faith to him is a form of surrender of his intellect to a higher authority, namely God.

There are on the other hand those who are troubled by rational challenges to our religious faith, which demand answers that are not satisfied by mere acquiescence, denial, or escape. I am in the company of this class. I believe that we are, first of all, commanded by God to give an answer. In 1 Peter 3:15, we are told, "Always be prepared to give an answer to everyone who asks you to give the reason for the hope that you have, but do this with gentleness and respect." Moreover, I believe that the Christian hope and beliefs are defensible and worth defending. To me, if my whole life is structured around this Christian faith, and my life depends on its validity for meaning and purpose, it would make no sense if my intellect cannot participate in it. My faith cannot be worth much if it is not worth defending or argued logically to my satisfaction. I cannot live a schizophrenic type of existence with my mind in one compartment and my religious faith and relationship with God in another totally separate sphere. My heart cannot long embrace what my mind consistently suppresses as dubious or rejects as untrue.

Now suppose we set "intellect" on a different trajectory, to the boundary of an ultradimensionality where our mind could only apprehend the reality that is there, where our reasoning could merely approximate the truth. This is the plane where faith and intellect intersect.

A common definition of intelligence, as we have already mentioned, is the capacity to learn, to reason and to understand with an aptitude in grasping truths, relationships, facts, and meanings. Or it can be defined as abilities for imagery, attention, comprehension, memory, imagination, judgment. Dr. Alvin Plantinga interprets reason to include perception, memory, rational insight, induction and testimony (inclination to believe what others tell us so as to learn from them).[62] For our discussion, I choose to define intelligence as including the capacity to perceive as many as possible dimensions of reality, their meaning, as well as our ability to interact and cope with these multifaceted realities.

With this definition of intelligence, I argue that faith is of the highest order of intelligence, because it is faith that enables one to perceive the many extra dimensions of reality, the highest and ultimate of which is God. The psalmist writes, "The fool says in his heart, 'There is no God.'" This statement makes sense, because the fool is the one with no intelligence. The fool does not have the highest order of intelligence we call faith to enable him or her to perceive the ultradimensional reality of God—a *sine qua non* of Christian Wholism.

Let me cite some specific issues that usually come up whenever there is the seeming conflict between faith and intellect.

1) Creation and evolution (discussed here in Chapter 3)
2) Science and theology [63] (Chapter 3)
3) Evil, suffering and a good God (Chapter 3)
4) Many gods and paths to salvation—religious pluralism (Chapter 2)
5) Resurrection [63a] and Christ's Divine nature (Chapter 2)
6) Psychoanalytic challenge—the concept of deity (Chapter 5)

(1) I have argued all along that God is the Author of both science and theology which are bound in one unitive reality. Thus any insights from science ought to illuminate the domain of theology.

(2) The current explosion of scientific knowledge has empowered us with unprecedented insights and information regarding the workings of the human body—its composition and complexity, its potentials, and its mystery.

(3) Through a greater understanding of our tangible human body in which reside no less than several layers of our unique human identity, a deeper appreciation as well as a better construct of the concept of Christian Wholism can be anticipated.

(4) In any attempts to harmonize the Scripture and Biblical teachings with scientific findings, one must be cognizant of the problems of bias, incomplete knowledge, participant's integrity, language, training and research competence and the noetic effects of sin

I define theology, *inter alia,* as a continuous human undertaking (or a discipline in academia) to portray our concept of God, His relations with the cosmos, and all the consequences thereof, in language and other communicative media understandable in our culture and for our time. *Science* for our discussion is defined as a systematized body of knowledge arrived at by a scientific method which includes observation of events; tabulation of data; positing theories or other higher conceptual schemes (principles and laws) in order to predict and explain a wide range of phenomena and to unify one's world views; and generally establishing models for testing, experimentation, universal confirmation, duplication. [64]

Before we delve into the issues, I want to acquaint the readers of the usual patterns of interaction between intellect—rationality, science, philosophy versus [65]faith—belief, theology, religion.[66] [67] Pattern A—Hostility, Exclusion, Warfare Model. Here scientism, scientific materialism, secular humanism claim that science is the only discipline that can provides all the knowledge there is in this universe. There is only one, natural reality and science has the monopoly of knowledge on this natural reality. These scientists want a total victory. They consider religion and faith as pseudo-knowledge with false conclusion of reality. The raging battle is often between scientific imperialism and ecclesiastical authoritarianism. There are scientists in this camp who do acknowledge the existence of something divine, but they are quick to add that the knowledge of that something comes from scientific research rather than from divine revelation and religion.

Pattern B—Isolation and Insulation Model. A demilitarized zone is established between science and religion keeping intellect and faith in two separate domains. Sometimes it is an enduring peace, other times it is an uneasy truce. The compartmentalized thinking is based on the assertions that science focuses on What is (fact) and why it works (theory) and how it works (applied science) whereas religion is primarily concerned with Who (God, Who), Why (moral and ethical reasoning, value, meaning), how (what difference it makes in life here and the hereafter). Science studies the age of rocks; Christianity believes in the Rock of Ages. Science can only ascertain what is, but not what should be in the context of morals and ethics and meaning.

Pattern C—Contact and Partnership Model. In this pattern, science and religion each acknowledges the other's value and contribution and seeks to build a bridge of understanding. Accord, harmony, humility and tolerance characterize the interaction in which each seeks to learn from the other.[68]

Pattern D—Complementary Enhancement Model. Each discipline believes that it can contribute to the other. Humility, cooperation, open-mindedness, and candor are hallmarks of this model.

## I. Creationism and Evolution

Let us now examine the contemporary image of warfare between Creationism and Evolution.[69] There are many subclasses in each category and nuanced analyses for each genre. I shall only paint the broad strokes as they relate to our discussion of Christian wholism.

In the creation/evolution models, one can separate the theistic varieties from atheistic, Darwinian evolution, a blind, random, purposeless process without God or higher Intelligence, characterized by long chronology (15 billion years for the universe and 4.5 to 5 billion years for planet earth and earliest life forms; 65 million years for mammals, thousands of years for modern humans).

The theistic models can be divided into long and short chronologies for the universe, earth, and life, and different combinations. The old universe, old life models include deistic evolution (God absents Himself after creation of life); theistic evolution (God uses evolutionary processes to accomplish His purpose in creating life on earth); progressive creation (God progressively creates at different stages and introduces through evolution greater and greater complexities of life forms culminating in the appearance of humans; day-age, cosmic time, metaphoric models, Satanic manipulation of God's initial creation of life models.

In the old universe and short chronology of life model there are sub-models depending on the interpretation of temporal gap between Genesis 1:1 and 1:2. There are long, medium, short, active and passive gaps with or without destruction of original creation and subsequent reconstruction.

Lastly, there is the most literal, young universe, young life (6000-10,000 years chronology) model with no gap, no evolution.

I propose here my own model which to me brings conciliation and consonance between science and faith, between evolution and the Bible. In my model, there is no raised fist, angry rhetoric, contrived manipulation of scientific data, illogical twisting of Scripture, or maligning God's character of love, justice, truth, and wisdom.

My Conceptual Model for the Origin of the Universe and Life on Earth is outlined here for further discussion.

**Basic Premises**

1.   God is the Creator of everything there is (*ex nihilo*--direct, immediate and/or through intermediate agencies and derivative means that He maintains*). He is the causation of all reality.

2.   No one knows for certain all the details and **when** and **how** God created.

3.   Anyone who claims to know for certain any specificity of Creation must at least prove himself or herself as a credible Bible scholar, hermeneutics and linguistics expert, theologian, anthropologist, astrophysicist, biochemist, physicist, molecular and cellular biologist, zoologist, geneticist, paleontologist, and archaeologist.

4.  It is well for the Christian to adopt a humble and open-minded attitude, to be willing always to listen and learn even from those with whom he totally disagrees; to be diligent in study, research, reflection; and to seek God's illumination in both Scriptural interpretation and evaluation of scientific data.

5.  One's presupposition and worldview largely determine how he/she interprets facts, data, and conclusions made by others. This is true for both scientists and theologians. None is immune to bias.

   Bias is defined as a particular tendency which hinders impartial consideration of a question or weighing a matter. There are different genre of bias—data collection bias, technical and inter-pretational bias, paradigm and presuppositional bias. In addition, the problem of incomplete knowledge, integrity of the theologian or scientist, the problem of language, individual's training and research competence, the noetic effects of sin, all play a part in the understanding and conclusion one arrives at on any given subject.

6.  Scientific interpretations and theories change; biblical exegeses also go through transitions and modification; and concepts are constantly in flux.

7.  True Christian faith, in my view, is not a blind, unexamined faith. It is a faith centered on God, His Word, and illumined by His Spirit; it is shaped by reason and reflection, seeking support from evidences open to public scrutiny and constantly looking for experiential confirmation and authentication by personal trust and heart-commitment.

8.  Fact versus truth: "The Lord is my shepherd"; literal specification versus metaphor.

9.  Most of us who are serious about creation and evolution are looking for some model that we can live with—with intellectual integrity while preserving our theological/belief system and our concept of God.

Theories of Origin of the Universe and Life on Earth: No one theory is without problem, scientifically or biblico-theologically. Two major approaches:

A.  Every non-living and living thing and all reality ultimately owes its being to God.

There are many theories on creation—fiat creationism, gap theories—big, medium and multiple small gaps; theistic evolutionism, progressive creationism, flood theories, age-day theory, ideal-time theory, pictorial-literary-framework theory, apparent age theory; other synthetic theories—old universe (8-15 billion years) and old earth ( 4 to 5 billion years) and ancient life evolved over eons or progressively developed under divine supervision; old universe, old or young solar system, young life on earth; young universe, short human life chronology on earth (6-10,000 years); other combinations.

B. Everything, animate and inanimate, comes by chance from "what-we-don't-know"; all life forms on earth are the consequence of blind-force evolution from the first life that arose from nonlife. This was accomplished by subsequent inherited variability, mutations, natural selection, and other mechanisms of microevolution acting together with environmental changes, over long periods of time (millions of years) , giving rise to trans-species macroevolution (from single celled organisms evolved into invertebrates, then vertebrate fish, then amphibians, then reptiles, then birds and lower animals, then primates, then man).

C. Major problems for young universe, young earth:
Arguments against: the most distant objects in the universe are 10-15 billion light-years from the earth; exploding stars; radiometric dating by various methods (potassium 40/ argon 40; strontium-87; rubidium-87; uranium-238/ lead-206; thorium-232 to lead-208) all seem to confirm long geological time; sedimentary rocks, geological columns (flood geology faces an enormous body of scientific findings that point to antiquity and the challenge as to why there are no higher life forms in the lowest strata—surely some animals and humans had been buried before the flood or the sick and disabled were left behind); coral reefs; evaporite varves; varves with pollens; cooling times of igneous intrusions. Admittedly there are counter-arguments against these scientific findings, but some of these arguments seem to besmirch God's character of trustworthiness.

D. Major problems for Theistic Evolutionism,[70] or progressive creationism:
Conservative view—This theory argues that the first 3 chapters of Genesis are a blend of history and allegory. But Adam and Eve were historical and the Fall was real. All life evolved according to

Darwinism. God picked one pair from the animal species and endowed them with spirituality. The pair disobeyed God and suffered spiritual death which was passed on to all of us. Thus we all need Christ's atoning sacrifice.

Liberal view—dismisses the first 11 chapters of Genesis as myths. God used evolution method to bring about men—evolving from the apes. "Sin" and imperfections are leftovers from animal ancestry and not because of the Fall brought on by Adam's and Eve's disobedience.

Arguments against: It is contrary to the OT & NT records. NT refers and Jesus alludes to Adam and Eve as historical (Mk 10:6). Jesus' genealogy traces back to Adam (Lk. 3:21-38). It is contrary to Paul's teaching (1Cor. 15:22, 49; Rom. 5:12, 17). The domino effect—if Paul's teaching of the first Adam and second Adam is undermined, so also is his argument and testimony concerning the Resurrection of Christ—this effect leads to the collapse of the whole fabric of Christian faith (1 Cor. 15:17). It is also contrary to Genesis "after its kind"—no trans-species evolution (dog does not become cat; cow does not become horse, frog does not become eagle. However, some would translate "after its kind" as "all kinds of," so this argument may be weak. The view is contrary to the plain language of Gen.2:7 and is a challenge to the conservative theistic evolutionists who accept the Fall as real but disregard all its detailed consequences such as punishment for Satan, Adam and Eve; painful childbearing for women, men's need to struggle in order to survive; alienation from God, and finally death.

E. Problems for Biological Evolution—the theory of blind natural forces through randomness and chance acting on non-living substances to bring forth simple cells resulting in more and more complex organisms through mutation and natural selection and small variations over millions of years (1) it does not reconcile well with the anthropic cosmological principle (things in the universe and the earth are so delicately balanced and fine-tuned as to make life on earth possible, e.g.: gravity and the weak nuclear force have to be tuned to each other with the astonishing accuracy of one part in 10,000 billion billion billion billion (theoretical physicist Dr. Paul Davis); (2) to date there are no significant intermediate fossils;  dating method and uniformitarianism could be challenged; (3) general adaptation versus specialized adaptation; (4) it is at odds with Genesis record and Jesus' acceptance of OT; seemingly contradicts the cross—the role of Jesus as the Redeemer, and also the resurrection hope as well as Pauline theology in Roman 5:12 ff.; (5) it does not comport well with the theological construct of fall and descent from a state of perfection in Adam as traditionally upheld by Christendom against the evolutionary ascent scenario from primitive to perfected beings; (6) it calls into question the moral structure and meaning of this universe and our existence; (7) Grasse, himself an eminent evolutionist and Europe's greatest zoologist, along with other evolutionists, rejects Darwinism as demonstrably false, and calls it a "pseudo-science"; (8) mutation, the result of copying errors in the genes, are practically always harmful, and seldom creative; a pathological process which may have little to do with evolution (Prof. C. Martin, McGill Univ.); (9) Evolution is challenged by the "design theory," mathematical probability theory, and irreducible complexity argument—the probability for the simplest living cell to emerge by random chance is one in 10 to the power of 100,000,000,000--about 500,000 pages of zeros after the number 1; complexity of blood-clotting mechanism and the human eye, adequately meet the challenge of Darwin (also see Michael Behe's *Darwin's Black Box).*

My own tentative model for the origin of this universe and human life on earth:

1) The universe and the earth are old (billions of years). In Gen.1:1 the terms *beginning, heavens,* and *earth* are not chronologically specified. Thus it is not unbiblical to postulate the antiquity of the universe.

2) There is a brief gap between Genesis 1:1 and the following verses. There had been a catastrophic event prior to Gen. 1:2, antedating the recent six-day creation, resulting in "vaporization" of the residues from destruction (thus no trace in the geologic column), ending in chaos (formless and empty—*tohuw, bohuw*) and darkness (*choshek*) as described in Gen. 1:2.

3) Satan, being one of the highest created beings and close to Christ, and wanting to be God who creates, "stole" the "blueprint" of creation. Using the primordial living cell which God originally

had created, he experimented and perfected a kind of "evolutionary process" (both micro and macro-evolution, thus bypassing intermediate forms) to make simple organisms evolve into complex forms, and over millions of years finally succeeded in evolving hominids (Australopithecines, Neanderthal, Cro-Magnon beings) through claw, blood and savagery. Deaths of animals and these hominids throughout the ages resulted in most of the fossils which we find today. Satan's intelligence supervised and guided the evolution.

4) God permitted Satan to carry out the experiments just as He has allowed evil and suffering to go on on this earth—to show all the other created beings the true character of Satan. If God had annihilated Satan right after he rebelled, other created beings in the universe might have doubted God's justice.

5) About 6 to 10,000 years ago, God intervened and "said" to Satan, "By evolving life forms, you think you are a creator. It has taken you millions of years to do it, but let me show you who the true Creator is. I will create Adam and Eve in a split of second from the dust of the ground—this God did and the record is what we read in Genesis.

6) Subsequent events could have taken different directions: (a) God had wiped out all of Satan's products of evolution before He created Adam and Eve 6-10,000 years ago. (b) Two separate and distinct human races appeared—the "God-race" whose members were made in God's image some 6-10,000 years ago, and the "Satan-race" whose descendants are without the image of God. The latter are the products of Satanic manipulation and evolutionary process, with a history of several million years. These two races have intermixed, intermarried, so that today we do not know what percentage of our ancestry is derived from the "God-race" or from the "Satan-race." Thus it is in a sense literally true that there is the angel in all of us and that there is the devil also in all of us. (c) The two races have never mixed down through the centuries. (d) Many or few from God-race have mixed with those from Satan-race. (e) Most from each race have intermixed but a pure God-race made in the image of God has remained. (f) Other possibilities.

7) Between Genesis 1:1 and Gen.1:2, prior to the cataclysmic event that destroyed the pre-Adamic creation, Satan had either

transported or shielded his counterfeit race from God's action and retransported them back to earth after Adam and Eve were created. Satan wanted to prove to God that he could even make the crowning work of God—Adam and Eve—to rebel against Him. So the battle—the great controversy between God and the Evil One—rages on.

8) According to my model, the Satanic descendants were cut off at the time of the Noahic Flood, and depending on the different scenarios enumerated above, either there was no contamination from Satan's race in Noah's line or the Satanic gene-pool had already been mixed in with that of the God-race in Noah's families. Alternatively, if the Flood was only a regional phenomenon (the once fresh water lake became salty Black Sea after it was flooded by the Mediterranean Sea through the Bosporus Straits about 7,500 years ago in the then known world as perceived by Noah),[71] Satan-race would not have been affected as they were clustering in parts of the unflooded world.

9) What about the 4th day of the six-day recent creation? I tend to argue that the solar system is as old as some of the other stars/galaxies, created within the time frame of Gen.1:1. However, when God initiated the more recent six-day creation starting in Gen. 1:2 ff., in order to make human life on earth possible (the anthropic cosmological principle of fine-tuning complex systems), He made two great lights...and the stars (prepared, adjusted, fashioned, programmed, dressed—all these meanings are not excluded in the Hebrew word *asah,* translated "made." *Asah* does not mean to create without the use of pre-existing materials). He did to the ancient solar system on the 4th day of His recent creation something like what He did to the formless and empty earth of Gen. 1:2, which, as I have stated, is also billions of years old, created during Gen. 1:1 time-frame.

10) My tentative model is not without problems. But it seems to me, it is a model that can accept the scientific findings seriously and honestly regarding the antiquity of the physical universe and the long ages of biological life forms including the counterfeit Satan-race with all the fossil record.

11) This model attempts to be faithful to the six 24-hour-day creation and the historical Adam and Eve. It argues well for the

character of God and preserves the redemptive role of Christ and Pauline teachings. The problems and implications of sin in relation to the fall of Eve and Adam are not psychologized away or mythologized.

12) Genesis 6:2 talks about the sons of God (here I interpret them to mean the ones from the "God-race") intermarrying with the daughters of men (I take them to mean the generic descendants from the Satan-race). Also, Gen. 4:17 speaks of Cain-the murderer, laying with his wife. Where did that woman come from? Cain's sister? We are not told specifically that at that time Adam and Eve had given births to daughters—perhaps later. So Cain's wife could very well have been from the Satan-race.

13) Jesus calls the Devil-Satan the father of lies (Jn. 8:44). What greater lie could there have been than to pose as the creator who can "create" humans (even though through evolutionary process)? Again Jesus said to some of the Jewish religious leaders, "You belong to your father, the Devil..."(Jn. 8:44). Is this a reference to the fact that perhaps these people were the biological progeny of Satan's genetic and biochemical sophistry? Since Satan is called the god of this world (2 Cor. 4:4) and the prince of this world (Jn. 14:30), it may be inferred that he has subjects who belong to him— subjects of his own biological making, subjects he can manipulate and enslave.

14) Satan is reportedly (Rev.12:7-9) the leader of the fallen angels, with the title Lucifer, Light-Bearer, the Morning Star (there are other variant interpretations of Isa.: 14:12-15 to be sure). His super-intelligence can be inferred and his hierarchical proximity to God's "headquarters" can be appreciated. Thus, the possibility of his access to God's creation secrets cannot be ruled out. In succeeding the evolving ("creation") of hominids, Satan intended to demonstrate to the whole created order in the universe that the sovereignty of Creator-God is legitimately challenged. It was time *(chronos)* for God to intercede. See under (5). This He did— beginning at Genesis 1:2.

15) Using this model, perhaps it would be easier to accept as God's doing when He ordered all the Canaanites, Amalekites, to be slaughtered, if these people were all from the Satan-race, who were like animals without God's image.

16) Let us continue to study and critique such a model or one similar to it while remaining reverently humble and beseeching God's illumination for understanding His truth regarding His Creation.

Since God is both the Author of science and theology, the Gifter of reason as well as faith, my hope is that we will arrive at a position where my heart does not have to embrace what my mind repeatedly rejects. I submit that on this side of eternity, even with our best efforts, we shall not understand to any great degree the mystery of His eternal purpose and creational methodology. Nonetheless, the fault is not in trying and failing. The regrets are rather our excuse, fear, sloth, our unrecognized intellectual and spiritual inertia.

### Reflection on the Controversy between Creationism and Evolution in the context of Christian Wholism

As stated in the first chapter, my concept of Christian Wholism is grounded in the Biblical doctrine of Creation and Redemption and our picture of who God is. His self-disclosure revealed through the God-man Jesus Christ portrays Him as love, justice, truth, wisdom, freedom personified. With such a picture of God, evolution as being God's way of creating humans does not comport well with a Being whose purpose is to make people and things whole.

Since bloodshed and death are normal occurrences and necessary processes in the evolutionary schema, if evolution is attributed to God's plan, they are at variance with the Biblical account of the origin of sin with its consequences of death. However, if evolution is a product of Satan's design, predation, blood and claw in Satan's evolutionary process is not a problem in my model. This is so because there had been no God's law for humanity before Adam's creation ("For where there is no law, there is no transgression" Rom. 4:15. Sin entered the world through Adam, and death [physical and spiritual] through Adam's sin, Rom 5: 12. Here death, I interpret it to mean, the death of the members of God-race, made in God's image 6-10,000 years ago, and not the death of Satan's life forms and counterfeit race during the evolutionary process). In addition, the Bible portrays man/woman started out as perfect beings and there was a Fall (a descent from perfection and sinlessness), whereas evolution depicts a gradual ascent to perfection over long ages. If Adam and humanity had not sinned, the Cross would be superfluous and man's need of a Savior (Jesus' incarnation, life, death and resurrection) would be open to conjecture.

If God used evolution for the creation of man/woman, was He guiding the process all along? If so, shouldn't He be responsible for those billions of years of pain, suffering, predator-prey bloody cycles of "tooth and claw"? Doesn't the ambiguous genetic inheritance and the unpredictable environment in combination make mockery of economic sense, efficiency, and intelligent planning? If God was not guiding the evolutionary process, it would appear that all these millennia of bloodshed and gore were outside of God's concern and providence leading to a theology that posits a disjunction between the pathetic human situation of brokenness, helplessness and lostness and God's goodness and divine intention to restore us to wholeness in Christ. Having said that, I am aware that theistic evolutionism is embraced by many sincere, well-informed Christians. The only difference between their view and mine is that I posit the evolutionary process as related to the work of Satan, and not of God—the Father of Jesus, who notices even the fall of a sparrow.

I want to conclude that my model is congruent with the findings of modern science, the biblical portray of the origin of the universe and humans, a comprehensive concept of the character of God and His interactions with the created order. There is harmony and coherence in this construct of a wholistic worldview that intimates not the uncertainty and savagery of evolution but the peace and joy of a world made whole by a loving God.

## II. The Problem of Evil [72] [73]

That there is brokenness and fragmentation on every level in our world is patently obvious. We only have to witness the events of this past century, especially beginning on September 11, 2001. Fear, uncertainty, lostness, despair, indescribable horror of first magnitude are diametrically opposite to peace and joy of wholism. The conundrum of a good God and the problem of evil, pain and suffering must be addressed.

In-depth analysis of the origin of evil, theodicy and the biblical concept of Satan is an exhaustive topic by itself. I will only briefly touch upon the blurred boundary of this subject.

The imago Dei, in my view, is a microversion of all God's communicable attributes. Since we are made in God's image after His likeness, humans are gifted with love, freedom, creativity, moral sense, justice, reason, truth, wisdom, purposiveness, goodness, and community (the Trinity is also a communitarian concept), albeit *in lower and limited degree* because of our creatureliness. In gifting genuine freedom to His creatures, including the freedom to go against God, the God of love incurs a risk—the risk of creaturely freedom to be used against His will and intentions. The alternatives to bypass such risk, *inter alia,* would be (1) not to create humans at all (which would be, I think, somewhat going against His nature, since the essence of love is giving, sharing and relationship. A Creator Who doesn't create? Like a teacher who doesn't teach? Or a singer who doesn't sing?) (2) to create the kind of humans who either cannot rebel against Him or always will make the right choice to follow Him—a programmed robot that can say 'I love you' but not 'I hate you, or I choose not to go your way." God's fellowship with such clones would be meaningless since genuine relationship can flourish only with beings who have genuine personhood and love grounded in authentic freedom.

The risk so incurred by God is stupendous, for it entails the emergence of evil and suffering which require the atoning death of His Son. Had God instantaneously annihilated the Evil One as well as Adam and Eve at the moment of their rebellion, the other created beings, angels and all in this vast universe, would have doubted God's justice. All the living creatures up to that "initial time," as can be determined from the Biblical record, had had neither the experience of rebellion against God nor the knowledge of the diabolical consequences of evil. The aftermath of sin could not have been envisioned by the heavenly host who did not understand Satan's guile.

God knows the end from the beginning (Isa. 48:3-5) and knows exhaustively all things (1Jn3:20).Though He foresaw and foreknew the devastating effects of sin and the enormity of suffering, in order to continue to honor the human freedom He had graciously accorded, (without which we cannot be responsible, moral beings capable of genuine and loving relationship with the Creator), in pain God allowed evil and sin to continue until Satan's deception and the ugliness of sin could be totally unmasked.

Evil, tragic as it is, must run its course. Ultimately the created beings will be convinced of God's justice and they must also secure a guaranteed antidote not against the possibility but the probability of a second rebellion. The redeemed will be sealed with such abhorrent aversion toward sin—separation from and going against God's intended purpose for our well-being and fulfillment—as to never freely desire a rerun of evil's ravages. Since there will be a multitude of free people over infinite time, the possibility of sin's reemergence is always there. But should that happen, this time God's justice will no longer be challenged even though the renegade is forthrightly dealt with. The created beings will be both the judge and jury who have personally experienced the senseless, self-defeating usurpation of God's prerogatives.

While we are on the subject of evil, "Where was God on September 11, 2001?" Lurking behind this question, and screaming louder is the more indicting question, "Why does a good God, if He is all-powerful, allow such unspeakable horrors?" Of course, such a question would compel us to refocus our discussion on the problem of evil—its genesis, manifestation and final resolution. Theologians, philosophers, ethicists and men and women of all ages have wrestled with pain over this conundrum for centuries.

Let me posit a construct with some degree of coherence that makes sense to me.

Some 15 billion years ago, God created the universe. From eternity till then, the Triune council had met numerous times. The agenda had always centered on: "Let's do some creating." Creativity is part of God's nature. That urge is so strong that its suppression is impossible. To an infinitely small degree, asking God not to create would be like asking Augustine not to think of God or Mozart not to compose music.

Why were there so many meetings and hesitations about creating, especially about creating free human beings, on the part of the Triune members? The "problem," if we can call it that, was

God's foreknowledge. As soon as the subject of creating the universe and humans was conceived, all the implications and consequences were before God's "eyes."

The members of the Trinity foresaw all: love, freedom, its abuse, evil, sin, rebellion, suffering, damage control, the plan of rescue and redemption, the temporary reconfiguration of the Godhead and its incarnation and the unbelievably destabilizing God-challenge. Before them were the death of God's grandson Abel, the Flood, the death of Jesus-the-Incarnate, the lions' devouring Christians in the Coliseum, the Black Plague, the millions dying in the French Revolution, the American Civil War, World Wars I and II, the Holocaust, the Nanjing Massacre in the Sino-Japanese War, and the Twin Towers of the World Trade Center crumbling to the ground. More vividly, divine foreknowledge saw the millions of clenched fists and wrenched hearts pointing to Heaven with the question, "Where is God?"

Each member of the Triune Council at various times had repeatedly tabled the vote. Eons went by. But the urge to create could no longer be contained, even though the Triune fellowship was all sufficient and its members were not lonesome, lonely or feeling any need other than the desire to create. But a breakthrough came when the Second Member, who previously had deferred to further discussion along with the others, now voted to go ahead with creation. Immediately they heard a "Big Bang."[74] Or did they see it?

More discussions followed and 10 billion years went by. The earth, which humans were eventually to inhabit, was brought into existence. More discussions followed, especially during the creation of the pre-Adamic scenario (see my creation-evolution model). About 10,000 years ago, planet Earth was adjusted and made suitable for human habitation according to the "Anthropic Cosmological Principle."[75]

Behind the Triune struggle are these issues: God is love. He is the most free of all free beings. He is the Creator, and the urge to create, which is a part of His nature, is irrepressible. God's love desires nothing but the best for His created beings. Nothing but the best includes what He Himself is and has, namely love, freedom, and creativity among other attributes.

Genuine love cannot be coerced. It must be expressed on the basis of freedom. Among other things, genuine freedom includes the possibilities of loving as well as hating and rejecting the one who loves. Thus freedom entails the risk that beings who reject love and things other than those that are lovely and ideal can happen. These non-loving beings and non-ideal things in the temporal-spatial dimensions occur as moral and natural evil.

I believe that God, with His omniscience, foreknows all the morally and eternally significant choices we will make with our God-given freedom right down to the end of our lives. This includes the terrorists' decisions. Without encroaching upon our freedom, or acting contrary to His own character and attributes, God does everything in our favor by lining up positive elements that point toward love and goodness under His sovereign control to make the ultimate choices of free beings realizable, the choices He already foreknows.

I posit such foreknowledge on the basis that God knows all the details of the infinite situational factors of this universe: life and non-life, organic and inorganic; time, space, energy, matter, and their infinite possible alternatives, combinations, and outcomes; order, complexity, or chaos whether Newtonian, quantum, or Heisenbergian, as well as all the eliminatable dead options. Because He knows all the live options that are open to us in addition to our past behaviors and patterns as well as those patterns of behavior of others, which are based on our genetics and whatever in the matrix, all of which He also knows to an infinite degree, there is then not much of a mystery for God as to know what choices we will make.

I believe that God's omniscience is compatible with limited, yet genuine human freedom. I have no problem in positing that God limits His power for the sake of honoring human freedom, a gift He lovingly bestows upon us. To think, however, that He limits His omniscience, that He chooses not to know what choices humans will make, is quite another matter.

As I understand Him, our God is not a dichotomous, split-minded deity whose "right mind" does not know what His "left mind" does or think. Anything God does not know, whether it be our choices or anyone or anything or any situation in the universe, is potentially a threat to His ontological being. This unknown factor potentially has an upper hand over God.

It is not enough to say that God with His infinite resources can cope with any situation. That would be like saying that someone has all the resources necessary to cope by picking up the pieces after the twin towers of the World Trade Center in New York City have been brought down. The God who knew that the towers would be demolished independently of His will to prevent or allow this destruction is surely greater than a deity who is caught by surprise.

Assuming that such a scenario is putatively valid, I maintain that God even knows what He chooses not to know. Why? Because a God who knows what He chooses not to know is greater than a deity who doesn't know. And by definition, as Anselm puts it, God is a Being than which nothing greater can be conceived. I prefer to think of Him as the One over whom nothing and no one in all reality can prevail. Absolutely nothing!

God is not only omniscient and omnipotent, He is also the freest of all free beings. There is no possibility, probability or actuality, including the events of September 11, 2001, in which He is not free to be involved or to know. Logically speaking, there are a few things God is not free to do. God cannot will Himself out of existence, to be God and not-God, to do evil, to be illogical and absurd, to be anything contrary to His character as we know it from His revelations, such as to renege on the gift of freedom He gives even to the terrorists.

God is free to limit His power and in so doing He need not impinge on neither His omniscience nor the creaturely freedom with which He has gifted us. As long as God refrains from interference or imposing any kind of control, direct or indirect, His knowledge of the future alone would not compromise human freedom, which at most, however one defines it, is a limited freedom.

For theology to make sense in our lives and thinking, it ultimately has to come down to a personal and existential level. To be sure, we picture God and His attributes in anthropomorphic terms. But how else can we do it? Between the extremes of a "process theism"—God whose being and fulfillment are dependent

on a material world of some sort, which to me is not the God
portrayed in the Bible, and a narrow theism which declares that
God who has ordained and predestined every event in the physical
world, as well as every detail of the lives of His created beings,
thus making history just a forward replay of His finished product,
where do we find the significant human freedom that we cherish?

Somewhere in human history and in our own lives we find the
markings of God's dynamic interactions with us. Deep down in our
existential struggles, in the face of the evil and sufferings in this
world, our souls cry out for a God who, we can be confident, has
the power, will, and goodness to vanquish evil with certainty. Any
God less than that is too effete.

Made in the image of this God, here and now, we want the gift
of genuine creaturely freedom to be authenticated. Yet, staring at
us bloody and raw are the horrors which are a consequence of
unprincipled uses of freedom. God is in the same dilemma as we
are, so it seems.

A contingency, philosophically speaking, is neither an
impossibility nor a necessity. This means that a contingency is a
possibility. A necessary condition, being, or proposition is one
which depends on nothing else. By contrast, a contingent condition
or being is one which is dependent on something or someone, as
yet uncertain, in order to occur. Thus, God is a necessity. Our
world, humans, the future are all contingencies, because they all
might not have been or might not have occurred, from our human
viewpoint.

A contingency is an event that might or might not actually
occur. As such, contingencies are inherently uncertain. From this
point of view, future events are contingent because it is uncertain
whether they will or will not occur.

As brought out in other discussions, we all believe that God is
omniscient but we have different understandings of what this
means. I tend to think that there is nothing that is uncertain to God.
This is contrary to the Whiteheadian and Hartshornian views that
the future cannot be known in detail even by God. I believe the
uncertainty is with us.

I hold that even Heisenberg's uncertainties are known by God's
omniscience. Mathematicians, it is said, can use calculus, high

math, and computers to map out the exact pattern a certain drunk will walk, taking into consideration of millions of facts (such as the thickness of the heels of his shoes, the thousand minute variations of the surface of the road, the direction of the wind, the condition of his hip joints, etc, etc). If there are one trillion possibilities that might shape a certain event, God knows them all. If there are ten trillion, trillion, trillion possibilities as how an event might turn out, He knows them well. Let that number take the infinite regress or progress, and He is on top of all of them.

Nonetheless, even if certain events or choices by free beings will lead to tragedy, individually or globally (how more relevant and graphic could the tragedy of September 11 tragedy be?), God may or may not interfere because of His respect for our creaturely freedom. He knows who is going to respond to His grace and who will reject His love. I've come to think that He knows who will be saved. We are the ones who do not know.

With this belief, I finally came to a solution (satisfactory to me at least in the context of Christian Wholism) as to whether those who lived before Christ's incarnation will be saved, or whether those infants or children who died before the age of decision, or the ones buried in the rubbles of New York and Washington, D.C., will also be saved. Love and justice demand that salvation be equally offered to everyone who might want to accept it. Thus, those born before Christ, as well as the hijacked passengers, the inhabitants of the Twin Towers, even those who masterminded the September 11 attacks, will be judged according to the light they had in their circumstances. God knows how they would have responded had they been presented with the truth and the gospel. Based on that knowledge, God will either grant them salvation and wholeness or allow them to experience eternal separation and loss.

It is that some people, particularly those whose freedom to love or not love, whose essential humanity, was prohibited by others from developing, will be as if they had never been. I believe such a stance allows a more wholistic approach to the problem, because it portrays God as having a more personal and caring touch with His creation and His interest in restoring wholeness to as many as possible.

To the Panentheists in the Whiteheadian and Hartshornean camp, one of my questions is this: If contingent future events are outside the purview of God's omniscience, and therefore outside His power to plan and cope for in advance (sure, some will say He is able to cope once the event has occurred—like the mop-up job once a bomb has exploded), does that uncertainty not control God?

For example, if the uncertain future is forever out of God's grasp, what guarantees there are against and coping mechanisms for, the possibility of second or third rebellions against God? Given the millions of the saved with their freedom exercised over infinite stretches of time or eternity, the possibility of a repetition of Adam's Fall cannot be ruled out. I myself would not like to relive the saga of "The Great Controversy between Good and Evil" and all the pain and suffering of humankind.

Given my concepts of God's omniscience and omnipotence, I do have an answer addressing the possibility of second or third rebellions against God, should they occur. I acknowledge in the meantime that any relentless push toward any form of determinism, indeterminism, self-determinism, absolute divine sovereignty, human freedom, and degrees of openness of God and reality, God's omniscience and foreknowledge, lands us in the realm of mystery.

I would feel uncomfortable, actually with great apprehension, about leaving my eternal destiny in the hands of these so-called free moral agents over stretches of time and eternity. Who can be ever sure that one of these free beings might not abuse the agential freedom again and again and again! I would rather put my trust in the goodness, justice and love of an omnipotent Creator. I know that deep down in me (I can only speak for myself), there is that longing for closure and wholeness—personal and cosmic.

Might it not be necessary for God to act should rebellion repeat? I would like to think that we, the veterans of sin, suffering and redemption, would be assigned to the role of judge, jury and penal administrator for anyone involved in the second, third or any subsequent rebellion against God. At that point someone would say, "I have been there, done that and had enough." We could play the "videos" of human history, individual and corporate. I am absolutely certain that we would have a sure verdict for that "wayward" member,"—a verdict without a reasonable doubt. No coercive force need be employed. That wayward member would beg for a state of non-being after marshaling any kinds of evidences in defense and being granted any witnesses and testimonies as desired. The trials could last as long as necessary while the effects of the rebellion are contained. God would just "sit there" and enjoy the whole scene.

That, perhaps, would be His crowning glory: to see free, moral beings deciding on what is best for them without any of His help. In deep satisfaction, the Trinity could then univocally sigh, "Ah, our creation was not in vain, as we have known all along! We knew it when we first decided to create free beings. We know it now."

For the redeemed, the will to enforce a collective aspiration for a universe at peace and in harmony and ultimate wholeness would find its grounding in the law of Heaven set up and subscribed to by all heavenly inhabitants. This enforcement of a commonly shared will would not be coercive to the wayward who, by virtue of their membership in the heavenly abode, would have personally sworn to uphold the "Heavenly Constitution."

One's freedom, when encroaching upon another's freedom, is in itself a passive form of coercion. I want to retain my freedom to be what I want to be, to live in wholeness, peace and harmony and perfect relationship with God and His created order. I have the freedom not to be robbed of this freedom or not to have it disrupted by someone else's abuse of freedom. Should disagreement and unresolved issues come up as is often the case among free beings, we can always refer them to the "Living Constitution," and its unerring interpretation, whose name is God.

**Now let us return to our discussion of love, freedom, evil and suffering and the Triune struggles for creating free moral beings, including Satan who can bring on evil and horrors on a massive scale, such as those of September 11, 2001.** How many of us have said in times like these "If I were God, I could probably do better."

It has dawned on me that only love can authenticate love, only genuine freedom can guarantee the exercise of genuine love while risking the expression of genuine hate. Love, however, being the essence of God, is such a strong attraction that it will be genuine freedom's ultimate choice and resting ground. That reality is what will guarantee against second, third or any subsequent rebellions by free beings. God knows no defeat. Abuse of freedom and the consequential evil is only a detour. God's ultimate intention for His creation cannot be thwarted.

On an existential level, the human carnage and inexplicable sufferings of September 11 demand justice by the cosmic Ruler. After touring the rubble site, Senator Hillary Clinton said it seemed she was standing at the edge of hell. Except, of course, the people in that hell had not freely chosen it to be their abode, and neither did they deserve it. Cosmic justice must be meted out in the form of resurrected bodies for a life eternal. In comparison to whatever remaining temporary life they would have enjoyed to the fullest for those who died on September 11, the glory and reality of the resurrected life will be worth far exceedingly, abundantly above all one could think.

Trying to arbitrate all the tensions amidst the reflection of love, free will, evil and human suffering, one might arrive at the tentative proposition that what happens in the world is the best that could happen in the context of God's character, human freedom and a fallen world. But we tend to recoil by asking ourselves, "Was what happened on September 11 the best that could have happened?"

A "yes" answer provokes more questions on God's goodness, justice and power. Yet, if the answer is "no," a ghost haunts us in the form of the accusation that God somehow is less than all-powerful, all-perfect and all-knowing. We are left with the impression that God is not in total control of what goes on here on earth. Therein lies the mystery of evil. I maintain that the only one who can explain evil is God. We shall look forward to hearing that master lecture by Him with a question and answer session!

The Archbishop at St. Patrick Cathedral, quoting Aquinas, says that evil is nothing, non-being. How then can one fight against nothing? Many speak about evil, but few have identified the Evil One in public discourse. Even a staunch evangelical Billy Graham did not cite Satan, Lucifer, the Devil, the Evil One by name in the Friday Memorial Service. Is evil really the faceless and nameless one? Evil in its abstraction does not bother us. It is only poignant when it touches our own personal lives, individually and as a community. Thank God, evil and the Evil One does not have the final say. God has the final word, and it's going to be nothing but good.

**So where was God on 9-11-01? I believe He was no farther from the world and all of us on that day than He was when Adam and Eve rebelled, during the days of the Flood while the world perished, in the Colosseum where Christians were food for the lions, during the days of the bloody American Civil War, World Wars I and II and Pearl Harbor and Nanjing Massacre, and when Jesus was nailed to the cross. God was no nearer to us on 9-11-01 than on V-Day in 1945, in the early hours of Sunday after Jesus' death, and finally on the glorious resurrection morning, Hallelujah.**

**When we consider what we should do in the aftermath of September 11, 2001, our thoughts turn to what is doable in the real world.** From a Christian perspective, in different degrees we do as we always do in the face of tragedy, whether personal, national or international. We pray, seek God's guidance, comfort and sustaining power and study His Word. We open our hearts to the love and support of Christian and other communities. We grieve mostly in private, we sometimes act irrationally, we have a "funeral," literally and figuratively speaking. We pick up the pieces, with courage, hopefully now wiser and humbler, and move on. We do so not aimlessly, but reminding ourselves that every happening that outrages our senses of justice and love reinforces the reality of this world's fallenness. We look heavenward and toward resurrected life for the ultimate resolution.

Regarding what we should do in response to the events of September 11, I am more persuaded by just war theories than by pacifism. It is my observation that pacifism works only if there is an overwhelmingly large number of other people who are willing to arm themselves and die for the causes pacifists espouse.

At a minimum, especially for Christians, the Ambrosian-Augustinian concept of just war with all its subsequent modifications, in my view, demands that whatever we do must be: (1) for a just cause—to eradicate terrorism; (2) with the right and competent authority—United Nations resolution and proper authorization from the United States Congress; (3) with the right and defined intention—to achieve a peaceful world free of terrorism for all people; (4) in proportion to Christian and democratic values—war acts with their attendant violence must not have even worse effects, such as causing indiscriminately injuries and deaths to untold numbers of people and the unraveling of the international community; (5) in line with our utmost concern for the innocent and most vulnerable of society; (6) weighed against the foreseeable outcome and probability of success if war is undertaken; and (7) the last resort and unavoidable option open to deliberation and implementation. A scenario rendering this last resort to war unnecessary would be that if all the terrorists were truly converted to Christian love and voluntarily surrendered themselves, asked for forgiveness, restitution, and submitted themselves to deserved punishment.

To see the oppressed and suffering people, especially women and children in some parts of this planet earth, caught as they are in the midst of the moral and natural evils of this world, is to want to shun war at all costs, unless we have no other option.

Ultimately, national and international tragedies break down into individual and personal tragedies, albeit in different degrees. That is where the struggle rears its head. We should be thankful that in our existential struggles and pain we can still hear that distant refrain: evil and the evil one do not have the final say. God does. Hope beckons. Life in our resurrected bodies with the peace and joy of wholeness is not just a vision, it is a reality. It is the cry from our hearts.

# CHAPTER 4

---

# CHRISTIAN WHOLISM AND THE BODY

## The Human Person

In Christian Scripture, the main texts that speak of human nature, its origin, and composition are recorded in Genesis 1:26,27. "Then God said, "Let us make man in our image, according to our likeness; let them have dominion over...all the earth. So God created man in His own image; in the image of God He created him; male and female He created them." The NRSV renders the 27th verse as "So God created humankind in His image, in the image of God, He created them; male and female He created them." [76]

In Genesis 2:7, the record goes on, "....the Lord God formed (Hebrew *yasar*, to mold, to fashion, to carefully shape) the man from the dust of the ground and breathed into his nostrils the breath of life, and the man became a living being (*nephesh hayyah*). [77]

In Genesis 2:15, the creation account continues, "The Lord God took the man and *put him in the Garden* of Eden *to work it* and *take care of it*. And the Lord God commanded man, "*You are free to eat from any tree in the garden, but you must not eat from the tree of the knowledge of good and evil, for when you eat of it you will surely die*" (emphasis mine). From this OT text, it may be deduced that the human ideal environment is one approximating a garden-like ambiance, surrounded by mountains, lakes, trees, birds, flowers and butterflies. Despite many human achievements and progress, jungles of concrete, metropolitan habitation, windowless

schools, fluorescent ceilings, shopping malls wired to a bombarding cacophony, are a far cry from that creation model.

All these texts inform us that humans are created to work [78] and
to assume responsibility, to be stewards, to take charge of nature
and to care for God's created order. They are given freedom, albeit
freedom with limitation and definitive boundaries. The Scriptural
passage also clearly delineates the consequence of the abuse or the
knowing misuse of that freedom.

Psalms 8: 3-8 declares, "When I consider your heavens…What
is man that You are mindful of him, the son of man that You care
for him?  You made him a little lower than God (the heavenly
beings; Hebrew *Elohim*) and crown him with glory and honor.
You made him ruler over the works of your hands; You put
everything under his feet…"(later quoted in Hebrews 2:5-8). Here,
under inspiration, the psalmist David assesses the worth of the
human with balance.  In the vastness of God's starry heavens, man
is puny and seemingly an insignificant speck of dust.  Yet in God's
creation hierarchy, he/she stands tall and preeminent among all.
Looking at the stars and entertaining the question, the psalmist
places the evaluation right where it should be. It is humans who
contemplate nature. And nature, though real and independent from
the human family, casts in God's design often as the passive object
of human thought or the perception in the mind.  Nature, as best as
one can infer, does not ponder humanity.

This Biblical portrayal of man/woman with lofty status and
individual dignity is a flat refutation of the shadowy origin of
humankind propounded by atheistic evolutionists. Ernst Heinrich
Haeckel, the noted German biologist and philosopher of evolution,
describes man as a mere placental mammal which has no more
value for the universe at large than the ant, the fly of a summer day,
the microscopic infusorum, or the little bacillus. With such meager
assessment of human worth, meaninglessness of life and despair
for living are everywhere a daily encounter.  Nowhere in Scripture
are there evidences of such debasement of human nature and abject
appraisal. [79]

Crowned with glory, honor, and wholeness, man and woman
were destined for greatness and nobility. Interrupted by sin and
rebellion notwithstanding, God's telos for the human, I shall argue,

cannot be thwarted. In our resurrected bodies, that glory and honor of reflecting God's power and goodness, will find their full expression. This is what I have consistently maintained that absent our glorious, transformed resurrected bodies, God's original human creation would have been a failure, an unredeemed failure.

Psalm 51:3-14 depicts the human as sinner. From the potential of dignity, wholeness and perfection described in the foregoing paragraph, man has descended to the moral pit with brokenness at every level. "For I know my transgressions, and my sin is always before me.... Surely I was sinful at birth, sinful from the time my mother conceived me.... Save me from bloodguilt...."

Philosophers, theologians, ethicists, anthropologists, social scientists, psychiatrists, psychologists, and Christian scholars have all debated on human nature's evil dispositions whether by inheritance and/or by social conditioning, with equivocation and at times denials. But the Old Testament witness and human history do not equivocate on this subject. One finds ample confirmation, upon principled reflection, that sin is endemic in all cultures and walks of life. In truth, one of the distinguishing characteristics of human nature is its sinfulness. In his dedicatory prayer, Solomon states, "There is no one who does not sin..." (1 Kings 8:46). In Ecclesiastes 7:20, it reads, "There is not a righteous man on earth who does what is right and never sins." This Old Testament theme of human sinfulness carries through to the New Testament period in which we find the author of 1 John 1:8 summing up the debate succinctly and with authority, when he declares, "If we say we have no sin, we deceive ourselves, and the truth is not in us." Paul reechoes, "For all have sinned and fall short of the glory of God" (Romans 3:23).

The New Testament concept of the human is patterned after the life and teaching of Jesus and the Pauline preaching of man's need for grace and redemption—a process toward wholeness.

In Matt. 1:21 the Angel of the Lord proclaims, "you are to give Him the name of Jesus, because He will save His people from their sins." Men and women are important enough for Jesus to "empty Himself (*eauton ekenosen*, Phil. 2:7) of all but love," to die for fallen humanity. "The Son of Man came to seek and to save what was lost" (Lk. 19:10). For His disciples and for all believers, weak and prone to error, He treasures them nonetheless. "Father, I want those You have given Me to be with Me where I am...," Jesus pleads (Jn. 17:24). For every life situation, He always places the person above the letter of the Law. "If any of you has a sheep and it falls into a pit on the Sabbath, will you not take hold of it and lift it out? How much more valuable is a man than a sheep!" (Mt. 12:11). And in Matthew 10: 30, 31 Jesus assures His disciples of their inherent worth as the objects of God's protective concern, "And even the very hairs of your head are all numbered. So don't be afraid; you are worth more than many sparrows." Luke 12:24 expresses similar sentiments.

Turning our attention to Jesus' disciples, we find in John 1:12,13 the God-intended dignity accorded to "all who received Him (Jesus, the Word), to those who believed in His name, He gave the right to become children of God—children born not of natural descent, nor of human decision or a husband's will, but born of God" (parenthesis mine). The ultimate divine intention for the human to become God's very own is expressed in the vouchsafing of Jesus' embodiment--"The Word became flesh and made His dwelling among us. We have seen His glory, the glory of the One and Only, Who came from the Father, full of grace and truth" (Jn.1:14). Professor McDonald argues that "It is against the perfect humanness of Jesus that the dignity of every man is to be measured.... By uniting Himself with man, God's Son has made it clear for always that being human is no mean condition." [80]

Further along, the Apostle John reaffirms the exalted potential of human destiny by describing, "How great is the love the Father has lavished on us, that we should be called children of God! And that is what we are!" (1 Jn. 3:1). The Apostle James also echoes the Old Testament witness for man's constituent, "....men, who have been made in God's likeness...," while the author of Hebrews writes, "Both the One who makes men holy and those who are made holy are of the same family. So Jesus is not ashamed to call them brothers" (Heb. 2:11).

The New Testament view of humanity is complemented by Pauline theology on the sinfulness of human nature and its desperate need for divine grace. The portrayal of this "beastly nature" in humans is held in tension with the "angelic God-like" potential of human destiny. In redemption, one implies the other. Paul minces no words when he states in Romans 5:12, "Therefore, just as sin entered the world through one man (Adam's fall), and death through sin, and in this way death came to all men, because all sinned...." To this universal sinful nature in doomed men and women, Paul's affirmation brings hope: "...all have sinned and fall short of the glory of God, and are justified freely by His grace through the redemption that came by Christ Jesus" (Rom. 3:23). Elsewhere Paul speaks of the human as bearing the moral image of God; being possessive of a conscience (1 Cor. 15, 1 Cor. 8:7-12); is constituted of spirit, soul, flesh, body, mind, heart with at various stages an old nature, new nature, outer nature and inner nature residing in a natural man, a spiritual man (Eph. 3:126, 4:24; Gal. 6:5, 4:23; 1 Corin.2:15, Rom. 8:5-7, 12:2). Our later discussion will elucidate some of these terms used by Paul in his conception of humanity now and in eschatology.

## The Image of God in the Human

The image of God in humanity as a Christian doctrine is grounded in the traditional key Biblical texts in Genesis 1:26.27, 5:1, 9:6; 1 Corinthians 11:7; Colossians 3:10; James 3:9. Ray Anderson cites additional texts including Romans 8:29; 2 Corinthians 3:18; Ephesians 4:24; 1 John 3:2; Apocrypha Wisdom ii 23 and Ecclesiasticus xvii3. [81]

Gen. 1:26, 27, "Let us make man in our image, according to our likeness; let them have dominion over...all the earth.... So God created man in His own image; in the image of God He created him, male and female He created them."

Gen. 5:1, 2, "When God created man, He made him in the likeness of God. He created them male and female and blessed them."

Gen. 9:6, "For in the image of God has God made man."

1 Cor. 11:7, "A man ought not to cover his head, since he is the image and glory of God."

Col. 3:10, "....the new self, which is being renewed in knowledge in the image of its Creator."

Jas. 3:9, "With the tongue we praise our Lord and Father, and with it we curse man, who have been made in God's likeness."

The early church fathers and theologians such as Irenaeus (ca. 130-200 AD),[82] Tertullian (155-220), Clement of Alexandria (150-215), Origen (185-254), Athanasius (296-373), Ambrose (340-397), Augustine (354-430),[83] all made a distinction in meaning between "God's image" and "likeness of God." The prevalent idea then assigned image to mean bodily traits, human characteristics, free will, reason, power to have dominion over the earth. Likeness of God for some denoted or connoted the spiritual nature, original righteousness or qualities non-essential to man. The controversy was far from being settled.

Catholic theology [84] on the whole has held that natural endowments such as spirituality, freedom and immortality constitute the natural image of God (*justitia naturalis,* a state Adam was created with, without sin, but also without positive holiness, subject to concupiscence, the tendency of the lower passions to rebel against the higher powers of reason and conscience).Original righteousness (the original state of God-likeness; *justitia originalis*), the supernatural gift (*donum superadditum supernaturale*), was later added to the original constitution of the human. Though this gift (likeness) was forfeited after Adam's fall, the essential nature of man (imago Dei) was kept intact in fallen humanity, much like Adam before the fall and prior to the gifting of original righteousness, with now a stronger tendency toward evil and alienation from God.

During the Reformation, most Protestants expurgated the Catholic formulation and propounded a different interpretation. To the Reformers, *image* and *likeness* were synonymous with identical meanings in the context of Hebrew parallelism. Between Luther and Calvin, opinions differed in the group meaning of image and likeness (Hebrew: *tsalem* and *demut;* Greek: *eikon and homoiosi*s; Latin: *imago and similitudo*). Luther applied image and likeness of God exclusively to original righteousness which was forfeited when Adam and Eve disobeyed. Calvin was more inclusive in that he grouped original righteousness and "everything the nature of man surpasses that of all other species of animals" as constitutive of the image of God and likeness of God.[85] What was lost through sin was only the original righteousness (God made man upright and morally good [Gen.1:31; Ecl. 7:29]). The essence of human nature, reason, moral judgment, integrity, sympathy, fairness, self-control, power to subdue nature have been preserved through "common grace."

Pelagians, rationalists, evolutionists accord to humanity no primitive holiness but a state of naïve innocence and moral neutrality. Free will alone equips men and women to decide among a variety of options, relying on reason and experience to choose the best alternative.

Many interpretations of the imago Dei make use of a model, mold or pictorial analogy. Philosophers and theologians argue that whatever the human possesses in himself/herself is what is modeled after, molded according to, or copied from, to a lesser degree in perfection and extent of course, the image of God— whatever attributes He has and what ontologically He is. But there are other "novel" approaches on which we shall now focus our attention.

Reformed theologians by and large interpret the image of God in man as consisting in his/her rationality and moral competency.[86] Others consider the imago as expressing certain characteristics through one's personality or in one's sonship which was lost by Adam's Fall and which can only be restored in Christ.

As early as 400 AD, Augustine theorized that being in the image of God implied not only unique intellectual powers but most importantly a correct posture, the posture of obedience. To him, "….the true honor of man in the image and likeness is of God, which is not preserved except it be in relation to Him by whom it is impressed." Thus a relational element is introduced to the concept of imago Dei.[87]

Friedrich Schleiermacher (1768-1834), the father of liberal Protestant theology, equates the image of God in the human with his/her dominion over nature.[88]

Soren Kierkegaard (1813-1855), the Danish theologian and founder of existentialism, posits that the image of God does not exist in man; man exists in the image of God only whenever he consents "to be nothing through worship." [89]

Emil Brunner, the Swiss Reformed theologian (1889-1966), seems to have resurrected the old distinction between image and likeness and couched it with modern terms. Irenaeus, as discussed earlier, among the early church Fathers, distinguished the image from the likeness of God, which most Catholic tradition had followed until it was rejected by the Protestant Reformers. Brunner initially used the term "formal" (the essential structure of man's being, not greatly affected by sin) to distinguish it from the "material" imago Dei (that aspect of the image which was lost after the Fall). [90] This terminology, though later renounced by Brunner, sheds some light on the traditional understanding of the substantial imagoDei consisting of reason, will, imagination, value perception, intelligence, judgment, power to think and to do) versus the relational concept of imago Dei. In the thinking of this neo-orthodox theologian, the formal, the substantial imago Dei, the natural endowments of humanum, are powerless to save the person. Only through a redemptive relationship with God through His grace and man's faith, is there hope for the emergence of health and salvation for humanity. Brunner seems to situate relatedness in humans primarily as a functional quality and not as ontologically based.

Karl Barth (1886-1968) also speaks of the relational aspect of the image of God. He considers the imago Dei as concrete human existence in the form of co-humanity so that the ontic *is* the relational, and also as man's appointed position vis a vis God and his response to God. [91] In addition he conceives of it in terms of male and female and that only in relation to Christ can there be a true understanding of man. [92]

E.G. White (1827-1915), a religious writer, capsulizes the image of God in these words, "Every human being, created in the image of God, is endowed with a power akin to that of the Creator—individuality, power to think and to do...." [93]

Paul Ramsey argues, "the image of God is rather to be understood as a relationship within which man sometimes stands, whenever like a mirror he obediently reflects God's will in his life and actions." [94]

Carl F.H. Henry, writing from a conservative evangelical perspective, issues a warning against the neo-orthodox theology of imago Dei as propounded by Barth and Brunner as well as liberal theology by others. He declares that "Neo-orthodoxy not only rejects in common with Protestantism generally, the Roman catholic exposition of the image in Thomistic terms (of analogia entis, a "being" which Creator and creature share in different degrees), but also sets aside the traditional Protestant confidence in the Genesis creation narratives as a scientifically relevant account of origins." [95] Henry's concern and its wider implication can be interpreted to take on the essence of a few condition-result statements.

Some may argue that if the imago Dei is simply a relation, to the exclusion of ontological attributes, and no more than a standing toward God as some theologians claim, and not a state (Adamic purity and righteousness before the Fall and residual common grace of reason, judgment, intellect, moral sense, creativity, freedom), Adam could be thought of merely as a type of man with a mystical status and without a historical nexus as depicted in the Bible. If Adam is not historic, one is free to introduce into one's theology certain atheistic or agnostic evolutionary scientific dogmas of the origin of the human. Is this what some theologians have unwittingly fallen into or even taken pride to assert? The logical pathway for such a theological enterprise, as argued by some, would be a journey to a watered-down version of human creation by God. The implication is a predictable negation, ever so subtly, of God's lawful and authoritative claims of the moral "oughts" in and Creatorship over one's lives.

There are other theologians who think of the image of God as a human function—what one does, how one exercises dominion over God's creation. This view is primarily based on Genesis 1:26, "...let them rule over the fish of the sea and the birds of the air, over...,over all the earth, and over all the creatures...," and Psalms 8:5-6, "You made him a little lower than the heavenly beings and crowned him with glory and honor. You made him ruler over the works of your hands; You put everything under his feet...."[96]

Ray Anderson has carefully examined and discussed the four aspects of the imago Dei. As encounter and relation, freedom in dependence, responsibility in hearing the Word of God, gender differentiation in sexual unity, he posits that the image of God is thus best expressed through personhood and humanity. [97]

The views in the preceding discussions are helpful, but not exhaustive. I contend that the imago Dei is multifaceted and polydimensional in the context of Christian wholism.

### The Unique Multilayered Personal Identity

Jesus says in Mark 12: 30, "Love the Lord your God with all your heart (*kardia*) and with all your soul *(psyche)* and with all your mind (*dianoia*) and with all your strength *(ischus)*. This multi-dimensionality of human composition is also reflected in Pauline writing as recorded in 1 Thessalonians 5: 23: "May God Himself, the God of peace sanctify you through and through. May your whole spirit, soul and body, be kept blameless at the coming of our Lord Jesus Christ." In Genesis 2:7, it is recorded "…the Lord God formed the man from the dust *(aphar—earth,* ashes, dust) of the ground and breathed into his nostrils the breath *(neshamah)* of life, and the man became a living being *(nephesh—*soul, creature). The inert earth, acted on by the life-giving breath of God His Spirit, comes alive with soul. In Job 33:4, it is stated, "The Spirit of God has made me; the breath of the Almighty gives me life." **The soul** in my definition is an aggregate word encompassing ideas of life, consciousness, self-awareness, thought, will, intellect, cognitive capacities, memory, imagination, reason, judgment, emotion, personality, temperament, sense perceptions, freedom, creativity, and everything that makes a human human. The soul then is related to identity-information and the individual's salvation history, to be explained later. A simple analogy would be electricity (the Spirit of God) acting on a light bulb's tungsten filaments (the inanimate earth and dust particles) giving rise to heat and light (the soul as defined above). The soul, therefore, does not have an independent existence. [98] [99] At death, when the Spirit, carrying as it were the person's identity and salvation history of the Divine-human encounter—the responses to God's grace—is returned to God, the soul is extinguished along with the demise of the body. [100] "If it were His intention and He withdrew His Spirit and breath, all mankind would perish together and man would return to the dust" (Job 34: 14, 15). The soul ceases to exist when a person dies, just as the light and heat from the bulb disappear when the electricity is switched off.

Having said that, I acknowledge that there are many sincere, scholarly, and devoted Christians who have a different belief and conception of the "soul," while arguing forcefully and cogently with biblical texts and Christian tradition. But the different interpretations of "soul," in my opinion, would in no way undermine our discussion of Christian Wholism. The concept of wholeness and perfection awaiting the believers is commonly shared no matter how "soul" is interpreted. What is of prime importance is that the wholeness concept must locate its ultimate development in that perfect state represented by the imagery or reality of soul in all its richness and beauty.

Made in the image of God (Gen. 1:26), we are gifted with most of His attributes to a lesser and inferior degree. I would suggest that ontologically we are also a Trinitarian entity with spirit, and "soul as defined above," and body; all three components in one person. Ordinary life experience and general reflection tend to confirm the truth of *the biopsychosocial unity in a person.* For Christians, there is, in addition, a spiritual dimension overarching this complex unified whole. A human is born with a body whose development together with the soul as defined above largely follows the genetic code's preprogramming while being impacted by environmental factors. A person is created as a social being with needs for relatedness and interpersonal interaction. Christians who have been touched by the grace of God find awakening in themselves a spiritual life which affects the core as well as the peripheral concerns of the person's being.

I would argue then that a person's identity is multidimensional in view of our human composition as described in the preceding paragraph. This identity begins its scripting from the beginning of personhood in a mother's womb (or mechanical womb should that be a reality) until death separates the Spirit of God from the corporeal body.

Our identity is first of all determined and sustained by God (See Ch.7).[101] [102] What God does not want to remember cannot be our identity. "I (the Lord), even I, am He who blots out your trans-gressions, for my own sake, and remembers your sins no more."

(Isa.43:25) This leads to my claim that in His unfailing love and faithfulness in keeping promises, only what God will be proud of remembering is worth preserving. The saga of our individual fallenness and the cosmic controversy between good and evil with all the gory details are only on record as something that have been overcome and redeemed. **The most important dimension of a Christian's identity, the core identity, which is to be preserved for Heaven is his/her moment-to-moment response to the grace of God. This particular level of identity—the individual salvation history—is absolutely unique, even for identical twins.** This spiritual identity embodies one's character as well as the history of good works performed out of a heart overflowing with gratitude for God's love, and not from a sense of self-righteousness, duty or merit-earning. Another dimension of identity resides in the genetic code given to a person by God at the time of conception. Together with the history of the body's 'soulish' manifestation, the identity of such is preserved and imprinted as it were on the Spirit of God at the moment of death when the Spirit is returned to whence it came.

On earth our identity, based on the composition of our human nature as discussed in preceding paragraphs, is encased in several concentric layers. On a superficial level, one is often socially known and identified by what one does, what one possesses, what and whom one controls, and with whom one is associated. On a deeper level, one is known by his or her character; by one's education, life work, accomplishment; by one's family, loved ones and friends, who know about all our weaknesses and failings. There is a structure of interpersonal and transpersonal relatedness which I would categorize as our *objective, extrinsic identity.* The *subjective extrinsic identity* would be my awareness of what people think of me in addition to my own visual and kinesthetic sense of my body parts.

On the deepest level at the center of our being is what I like to call our *intrinsic identity.* There are *objective and subjective components* to this identity.

*Objectively*, it is known perfectly by God and imperfectly by me. This is where my salvation history is daily in the making—**my continuous moment-to-moment response to God's grace either**

**positively or negatively.** The totality of the response involves my spiritual life, my 'soulish' aspect of my person (defined earlier), and my physical body wherein is found my genotype, phenotype, the DNA's and RNA's, the enhancer genes and suppresser genes.

*Subjectively*, I know about this identity through my consciousness, my self-awareness "I know that I know," and through my memory, imagination, intuitive reflection, careful thought, study and investigation. Descartes' *"Cogito, ergo sum*—I think, therefore I am" dictum helps foster such subjective identity. However much one doubts one's identity, he or she must exist, otherwise he or she could not doubt. And this indubitable realization of one's existential life in turn authenticates one's identity.

In sum, this *multilayered personal identity* [103] distinguishes each one of us as absolutely unique in all of God's creation. It defeats duplication and falsification. It is a dynamic process being shaped, added on, deleted, marred or refined continuously between the two ends of our existential continuum. It is at once fragile and enduring: fragile because of the contingencies of life and human proclivity; enduring because it is determined and sustained by God. It can withstand temporal gaps and physical deprivation. When one loses consciousness in a car accident or under anesthesia or suffers amnesia, the subjective intrinsic identity is lost, but the person's objective intrinsic identity and all the extrinsic identity markers remain intact. Through disease, cancer, accidents, surgery or congenital malformation, body parts including the brain may be deprived or need severing. Memory may be impaired; neurosis and psychosis may set in. But the objective, intrinsic and extrinsic, identity endures. I shall argue that a Christian identity having been "purged" by God's love and forgiveness is what is going to be preserved in our transformed resurrected body. As a corollary, the unbeliever's identity is sealed by his or her rejection of God's love and grace.

The preservation of our identity is safeguarded by God's power, His integrity and faithfulness. It is, as it were, stored on the hard disc of a computer to which only God and the individual have the keys for access. For the Christian, this unique personal identity, begun at the commencement of meaningful life, grows and blossoms throughout our earthly sojourn. Stamped with God's supererogatory care, it is intimately tied to our physical body intrinsically and extrinsically. It finalizes at death and is destined for Heaven, waiting to be fully expressed in all its splendor in our resurrected body at the Parousia.

In discussing identity and all its implications, it is important to add that a Christian's salvation is on an individual basis. In other words, we are saved first of all as a person, and not as a member of a saved church or a redeemed people of God. The parable of the lost sheep (Mt. 18:12-14); the prodigal son (Lk 15:11-32); "…whosoever believes in Him shall not perish but have eternal life," (John 3:16) all suggest redemption on a one-to-one basis. This truth is brought out most poignantly by the Apostle Paul when he declares, "…The life I live in the body, I live by faith in the Son of God, who loved *me* and gave himself for *me*" (Gal.2:20, emphasis added).

Whether one subscribes to the doctrine of God saving only His predestined elect or saving whoever accepts His gracious invitation, it remains the case that the person of faith among the elect or the unchurched  member of the "invisible church of God" receives atonement first and foremost as an individual in his or her unique identity before he or she joins the faith community.

## Christian Anthropology Supports
## Christian Wholism

The image of God in humans with all its dimensions is relevant to any discussion on Christian anthropology. Let us examine its mosaic under the following categories:
A) Origin: The concept of the image of God in humans is biblically grounded in Genesis 1:26, 27. Image and likeness are synonymous in Hebrew parallelism. This image derives from God's creation, dependent on and sustained by His power.[104] Thus it parts its way from notions of intrinsic divinity and certain versions of evolutionary thought.[105] The doctrine of imago Dei recognizes the Genesis account of the Fall and the effects of sin which tarnishes the image.[106] Anderson states, "Humans were created in a spiritual relation to God, not only as moral agents.  Breaking of a moral law

leads to guilt, while severing a spiritual relationship leads to death. That there were moral consequences to the sin which severed the spiritual relationship between God and the humans themselves, is obvious...." [107]

B) The Contents of the Image: Christian scholars and philosophers have hotly debated whether the human bearing the image of God is fundamentally a trichotomous (tripartite), a dichotomous (bipartite) or an ontologically monistic creature. [108] If trichotomous, a person would be composed of a spirit, a soul, and a body of flesh. If dichotomous, he/she has a spirit/soul and a body/flesh. In ontological monism, body and soul are indivisible and inseparable; they are two aspects of the human life/ personhood/ human nature. In modern terminology of unified embodied human existence, it is often said that a man or a woman does not possess a spirit, plus a soul, plus a body; rather he is human only as body and soul and spirit; or she is human only as body and soul or body and spirit/soul as an integrated whole. [109]

Christian Platonism and Greek dualism have had enormous impact in shaping the Christian theology of the nature and composition of imago Dei. Several temptations stalk our path as we seek to explore this aspect of the image. The linguistic urge would be to plumb the etymological depth and find out exactly what these words in their original language mean:

**Spirit** (Hebrew *ruach;* Greek *pneuma*; Latin *spiritus*)
**Soul** (Hebrew *nephesh;* Greek *psyche*; Latin *de anima*)
**Body** (Heb.nearest equivalent *basar;* Gk *sarx / soma*; Latin *corpus*)

Another temptation is to preload our established theology and ask ourselves what these words must mean in order to make our theology as we understand it consistent and defensible.

Joel Green warns us on both these pitfalls since conceptualizations of human nature (here the image of God in the Christian context) are not necessarily tied to particular vocabulary (etymologically speaking); and biblical writers did not develop a highly specialized or denotative vocabulary for describing human existence. [110]

Quoting from Eve Sweeter's *From Etymology to Pragmatics: Metaphorical and Cultural Aspects of Semantic Structure* (Cambridge Press, 1990), Green suggests that the question to ask in the face of the words spirit, soul, body, flesh, heart, mind used by the biblical writers, should be, "How would this word be understood given the literary co-text and socio-linguistic context within which it has been communicated?"

After careful examination, Green concludes that the Hebrew Bible provides no particularly "scriptural" vocabulary for anthropological analysis when the words spirit, soul and body are used. Rather a common terminology of the ancient world was utilized to depict the human person as an integrated whole.

If our assumption is that Scripture is the word of God and that God is eager to reveal the truth about Himself in Scripture, in nature, in science, through the Church and our own experiential knowledge, we can know something about the imago Dei. The human image of God will become clearer as we focus on the person of Jesus--"His Son...who being the express image (or the exact representation of His being, Greek *charakter tes hupostaseos autou)* of His person" (Heb.1:3); "of Christ, who is the image (*eikon tou Theou) of God*" (2 Cor. 4:4); "the kingdom of His dear Son...who is the image of the invisible God (*eikon tou theou tou aoratou)*" (Col.1: 13-15). The apostle Paul assures us that "for those God foreknew He also predestined to be conformed to the image of His Son (*tes eikonos tou huiou autou) (*Rom. 8:29).This last verse, I believe, adumbrates the human image as a process in the making toward the telos of full conformity to the image of Christ who in turn is the true and express image of God.

The trichotomists of human nature argue their position from the Bible where in addition to the material body, words such as spirit and soul are used (see the Greek, Latin and Hebrew equivalents of these words in preceding paragraphs). In addition, in 1 Thessalonians 5:23, the apostle Paul writes to the believers, "May God Himself, the God of peace, sanctify you through and through. May your whole *spirit, soul and body* be kept blameless at the coming of our Lord Jesus Christ" (emphasis mine). Again in Hebrews 4:12, we find these words, "For the word of God is living and active. Sharper than any double-edged sword, it penetrates even to dividing *soul and spirit*, joints and marrow; it judges the thoughts and attitudes of the heart."

The dichotomists cite the same passages in the preceding paragraph but maintain that the words *spirit and soul* in the Bible are used interchangeably. In Revelation 6:9, "When he opened the fifth seal, I saw under the altar the *souls* of those who had been slain because of the word of God and the testimony they had maintained." And Revelation 20:4, "I saw thrones on which were seated those who had been given authority to judge. And I saw the *souls* of those who had been beheaded because of their testimony for Jesus and because of the word of God...." [111] Other Biblical texts cited are Deuteronomy 6: 4, 5 "The Lord our God, the Lord is one. Love the Lord your God with all your heart...soul...strength"; Matthew 10:28 "Do not be afraid of those who kill the body but cannot kill the soul"; Mark 12:30 "Love the Lord your God with all your heart...soul...mind...strength"; Luke 1:46 "My soul glorifies the Lord, my spirit rejoices in God my Savior"; 1 Corinthians 5:3 "Even though I am not physically present, I am with you in spirit"; Hebrew 6:18-19 "We have this hope as an anchor for the soul" and James 1:21 "the word planted in you which can save your souls"; 1 Peter "...through whom also He went and preached to the spirits in prison...." Other cited texts to support the soul's distinct entity and conscious existence, which are at least arguable, include Luke 23:43; 2 Cor.5:1-9, 12:2-3; Phil.1:20-24; Heb.12:23 [112]

The proponents of bipartite, dichotomic human nature use these foregoing texts to argue against the monists by pointing to a distinct and separate non-material, non-bodily entity described by the Biblical writers—the entity named soul or spirit. And on the same grounds, they disclaim the trichotomic concept citing the synonymous use of the words spirit and soul. Man or woman then possesses either body and soul or body and soul/spirit. In either combination there is a duality in the composition of human nature.

The monists who subscribe to human ontological monism [113] counter the trichotomists and the bichotomists by calling attention to the unity of the human in every sphere of his being. Biblically, it is that "the Lord formed the man from the dust of the ground and breathed into his nostrils the breath of life, and the man became (*hayah*, always emphatic) a living being (or soul, nephesh) (Gen. 2:7). It is not, by a crude analogy, that the hardware (the physical body from the dust) of a computer is all prepared and then the program software (the soul) is inserted by God when He breathed the breath of life (electricity turned on) and the computer goes into action ready to show the world what it can do. Rather, the Genesis account gives the impression that both the hardware and software are all in place only to jump into action with all the soulish manifestations (consciousness, self-awareness, will, personality, intelligence, thought, freedom, creativity, emotions, relatedness, language, religiosity, and every characteristic that makes a human human) as soon as the electric current (God's breath) is operative.

In the OT, the Hebrew word *nephesh* is translated as "soul' or "being." According to Anderson, *nephesh* designates all that has life and breathes, is applied to both humans and animals, separately as well as collectively in Genesis chapters 1 and 9.This OT concept of *nephesh* determines the content of the NT *psyche*. Contrasting with the Greek view, the soul (whether *nephesh* or *psyche*) is the concrete life of the creature. That is, it is the life of the body and therefore intimately belongs to the body.[114] The word 'soul' (nephesh) is never used to refer to something external to a person, states Anderson. "The soul refers to either the whole person, or some aspect of the person…thoughts, feelings, energy, spirituality, the subjective viewpoint, mind, personality…. But the soul could never exist outside of a person….The concept of an immortal soul is thus without clear biblical support." [115]

Although some of the cited passages can be argued to support a dualistic nature of the human *non obstante,* one searches in vain to locate a definitive biblical text which indicates that the soul survives the body to assume a conscious, independent entity.[116]

In the Septuagint (the oldest Greek translation of the OT, 100-200 BC), the translators used the Greek *soma* to convey a range of Hebrew concepts denoted by the Hebrew word basar (flesh), signifying human individual corporeality, bodiliness. There is no Hebrew equivalent in the OT corresponding to the Greek idea of soma. A different Greek word, *sarx,* is used to portray human creatureliness or humanity. There is a differentiation between body and flesh in that body can be transformed but not flesh. Soma stands for man in the solidarity of creation, as made for God; while sarx (flesh) stands for man in his/her distance from God. [117]

The translated Greek *soma* is used for a corpse (1Sam. 31:
10,12), dead body (Deut. 21:23, Isa. 5:25), the back (Isa. 38:17).
According to Siegfried Wibbing of Germany, *soma* in the OT has
the basic meaning of the body in the sense of the whole person (not
personality).[118] However, Robert Gundry argues that in the LXX
(Septuagint), no matter in what form the underlying Hebrew word,
be it basar or any other word, *soma* is used to denote the physical
body alone and that there is no convincing support for *soma* as
equivalent to a whole person.[119] In Job 19: 25-26, *basar* is used, "I
know that my Redeemer liveth....In my flesh *(basar)* I shall see
God."

*Nephesh* and *basar* are often used in parallel but never in
contrast. [120] In other words, *nephesh* and *basar* are at times almost
synonymous (body = flesh) but not used as contrasting terms such
as body versus soul. H. Wheeler Robinson claims that "the Hebrew
idea of personality is that of an animated body, not (like the Greek)
that of an incarcerated soul."[121] In Gen. 2:7. "the Lord formed
*(yatsar)* man from the dust *(adamah)* of the earth and blew into his
nostrils the breath of life, and man became a living being *(nephesh)*
or living soul." [122] God is seen here to have performed two actions
(fashioning and inbreathing), rather than superimposing one entity
the "soul" onto another, the body. Just as God is One (Deut. 6:4),
so is His created image a psychophysical unity.

Derivative of the Hebraic concept, there is, it appears, little
support for an independent existence of a soul (or the concept of an
immortal soul).The soulish manifestations of a person, described in
previous paragraphs, are extinguished at the time of death when the
Spirit returns to God and thus is separated from the body, which
lies low and undergoes decay.

The New Testament records 101 times of the word *psyche* with
37 occurrences in the Synoptic Gospels, 10 in the Gospel of John,
15 in Acts, 13 times in the Pauline Epistles, 7 in Revelation, 6
times each in Hebrews and 1 Peter, twice each in James, 2 Peter,
and 1 John, and once in 3 John.

*Psyche* is described as the seat of life, or life itself, the whole
natural being and life of man, numbers of people, inner life of man,
equivalent to the ego, person, or personality, the fact of being alive,
that which has to do with willing and emotion, that which

completes the unity of the body of Christ, all that characterizes the living person of God in the OT, as being destined for eternal life and victory over death, as something to be preserved for eternity (consistent with my concept of identity-information-soul).[123]

In the NT, *soma* can mean a corpse (Matt. 27:52), the body of Jesus (Matt. 27:58), a metaphorical depiction more than merely a physical organism (Matt. 6:22, 25), and Jesus' total giving of Himself. However, for Paul, according to Bultmann, *soma* has a specialized meaning in the sense of person. And it would be un-Pauline to think of the body merely as a figure or form.The Pauline concept of *soma* then is not merely an outer form but the whole person (Rom. 6:12 "Let not sin reign in your mortal *soma"* or Rom. 12:1 "to present your *somata* as a living sacrifice"). The only human existence that there is—even in the sphere of Spirit—is somatic existence. [124]

Elsewhere soma denotes members of a body or organs (Rom. 4:19 "Abraham's body as good as dead"); in connection with sex (1 Cor. 7:4); or warning against sexual immorality (Rom. 1:24, 1 Cor. 6:13-20); a corporate body (body of Christ); the meaning of "self"—desires of the body equivalent to desires of the flesh or sinful nature (Rom. 6:12, Gal. 5:16- 24).

Paralleling the Hebrew thought on "soul," Bultmann concludes that man does not have a soma; he is soma; man, his person as a whole, can be denoted by soma.[125]

After some analysis, including the Gnostic influence, Bultmann states that where the contrast with *pneuma* is not involved, Paul uses soul (*psyche*) altogether in the sense current in the OT-Jewish tradition; viz. to designate human life, or rather to denote man as a living being. He continues, "*psyche* is that specifically human state of being alive which inheres in man as a striving, willing, purposing self. And even where *psyche* is depreciated in contrast to *pneuma*, it does not mean mere animal life but full human life—the natural life of earthly man in contrast to supranatural life. The natural man is not just a person with biological needs but one whose life is directed toward, and limited to, the earthly.[126]

Regarding the Greek and Descartes' dualism and the controversy among theologians, Barth admits the futility of searching in the OT and NT for a theory of the relation between body and soul. Instead, he emphasizes man's encounter and relation with God.[127]

Pannenberg claims that the soul is the life of its body and that "it is not another component part of a human being over and above the body," as in Cartesian or Platonic dualism.[128]

By now one may conclude that there is much overlapping in meaning and thus ambiguity in the terms spirit, soul and body as employed by the biblical writers and as interpreted by theologians. Such is what it should be and must not be a surprise when one realizes that the human is a unity, an integrated whole, an inseparable entity of spirit, soul, and body. For those who insist on thinking in compartmentalized spheres, I would propose the following, based on Scriptural teaching and our contemporary understanding of human nature in the context of Christian wholism.

**Spirit**—the human spirit, derivative of God's Spirit, the highest level of the function of the human mind in cognition, reasoning, apprehending, intuition, which acts as the contact point by which a person interacts with God's Spirit. (It is close to what Paul describes as the mind of Christ [*noun Christo* 1 Cor.2:16]).

**Soul**—reason, imagination, abstract thinking, memory, projection into the future, judgment, will, moral sense, "heart" in Biblical terminology, temperament, personality, speech, language, consciousness, self-awareness, instinct, intuition, desire, emotions, sexuality, sociality, biological drives, relatedness, in sum what makes a human human. (See later discussion of soul as information-core identity-depository of one's salvation history and Divine-human encounter).

**Body**—the physical constitution with all the anatomical parts consisting of cells, tissues, organs, systems, flesh (*sarx),* bones, blood, lymph, taxonomically belonging to the species *Homo sapiens,* of the genus *Homo,* of the family Hominidae, of the order Primates, of the class Mammalia, of the phylum Chordata, of the kingdom Animalia.

**Human person**--unitive, integrated whole of spirit, soul and body.

From the foregoing discussions, it is evident that arguments can be made for any of the theories of the constituent elements of human nature and the composition of the image of God. I contend that only one thing is certain in this controversy. It is that there is a tangible, material, physical aspect of our human nature which is accessible to observation, verification and confirmation with objective criteria—i.e. the physical body and its ordinary manifestations which are solidly within the purview of scientific investigation. But in addition to the body, there is just as certain in our nature a component part which is intangible, immaterial, paraphysical and transphysical. The latter component is undifferentiated and escapes any definitive descriptive vocabulary and often eludes any human scrutiny and fruitful probing—falling under the category of soul, spirit, "heart," mind, consciousness, self-awareness, moral sense, conscience, thought, intuition, inspiration, certain kinds of emotions, personality, individuality, imagination, creativity, memory, volition, will, purpose and purposiveness, intentionality, spiritual affinity. The list is by no means exhaustive.

The problem when deciding conceptually or functionally how to group these elements is that there is a wide range of ideas controlling the classification. For example, if one believes there is such a category called "soul" but not "spirit" in humans, then most of the foregoing entities may be classified under soul or soulish manifestation. If the soul has an independent existence apart from the body, how much of the total person would belong to soul and what remainder is claimed by the other? To a trichotomist, perhaps the entities may be divided among our nature Godward (the spirit), our nature earthward (the soul), and our nature selfward (the body). For a materialistic-reductionist, who believes in neither spirit nor soul, all the elements would be grounded in the body. If at death, the spirit returns to God, where did the spirit reside when the person was still alive? Would he/she not be the "host" for the spirit?[129] And what would be the relationship between the spirit and the soul, assuming they are not synonymous terms? [130] There are yet many other combinations which would pose interesting questions on this subject. I should, however, focus now on a new construct of body, soul, spirit that is consistent with Christian Wholism.

Contemporary science, philosophy, psychology, medicine and some theological circles all seem to point to a materialist-physicalist, monistic paradigm of human nature and a unitary, wholistic view of the human person.[131] Existentially, a common experience shared by reflective people is that when they sin, usually their whole person as an integrated entity sins. When we are redeemed, God redeems our whole person—spirit, mind, body, thinking, attitudes, life style, worldviews, our wills, our interests, our loyalties, and ideally every sphere of our personhood. In medicine, the notion of the interrelatedness between the mind and the body, the psychosomatic theories, have been undisputed for many years. From the neuroscience and neuropsychology laboratories have come the findings of the significance of physical substrata in explaining many of the human phenomena. In the field of genetics, scientists have probed not just the hereditary diseases but human traits. Genes are linked to temperament, risk taking, introspection, openness to God (religious conversion may fall under such a category?). One's temperament is said to greatly influence what type of theology one embraces, as well as the kind of worship atmosphere one prefers. The recent success in cloning sheep, other animals, human stem cells invites the possibility of cloning of human being[132]—which might envisage a technical kind of physical immortality. The question may be asked, "Should human cloning become successful, could one's religious experience be carried forward with the cloned body? What about the "soul" for those who believe in it? What would be the cultural earthquake to the secular society if all of a sudden, there would be a thousand Billy Grahams (assuming the clones carry some of Billy's religious fervor) calling sinners to repentence? Or conversely, again assuming the cloning carries forward some determinant characteristics, what might one encounter if every community were populated with hundreds of militant atheists or anti-religionists? Discussion of such religious subjects as soul or spirit or God might possibly be curtailed or met with persecutory sneer.

Brushing aside all such metaphysical and hypothetical questions for the moment, I shall now proceed to suggest a new definition of soul in the wholistic context.

I argue that a multidimensionality of human composition is reflected in the OT, in Jesus' statement in Mark 12:30 among others, as well as in Pauline writings. I suggest a definition of **soul** as an aggregate word embracing properties, functions, and expressions of life, consciousness, self-awareness, reason, thought, will, intellect, memory, freedom, creativity, emotion, personality and every characteristic that makes a human human.

From all the discussions up to this point, a summary statement may include that a man/woman is a physico-mento-psycho-socio-spiritual unitary being acting and being acted on as a whole person in totality. At death (see analogy of the electric current being turned off when the Spirit returns to God [Eccl. 12:7; Job 34:14-15]), the body (the tungsten filament in the light bulb) remains and decays, and the soul (all the manifestations of life and functions including consciousness, self-awareness, will, memory, judgment, language, emotions…) is extinguished as far as the body is concerned  but the person's identity is preserved by God.

Here I like to incorporate one's core identity with its subjective and objective components into the concept of **"soul."**  In life, all the soulish manifestations listed above are the means by which one's core identity is established—moment-to-moment positive, negative, and neutral responses to God's grace  in the God-human encounter—along with the other dimensions of individual and social identity. This plenary identity is commenced at birth, sustained by Him, made glorious by His forgiveness (all sinful memories purged), safeguarded and preserved as one's information code at death.

Carried by His Spirit, this identity-information-**soul** will find its ultimate expression in the transformed, glorified, resurrected spiritual body as the complete image of God. The "soul" by this conception is the Christian believer's whole salvation history in the making (or could be the unbeliever's indicting record in progress), completed at the end of our earthly life, sealed for eternal bliss or ultimate doom on Judgment Day. This "identity-soul" does not possess an independent life; it is that, however, which gives meaning and identity to our resurrected body. It is what accords our image of God its individuality and establishes the continuity and linkage between this life in groaning and the next for glory. [133]

To propose such a novel concept of soul (novel in the sense that I know of no theologian or philosopher who has officially spoken or written about this notion), it is required of me to answer some anticipated questions from the perspective of Christian Wholism under discussion.

For those theologians, human ontological monists or others who do not believe in such an entity as soul, my concept should pose no difficulty. I only use the word soul to designate that whole constellation of non-material, intangible, but nonetheless real and reason-correlative, common experience of our reflected life. That constellation includes our unique individual identity manifested through our thoughts, personality, judgment, emotions, conscience, beliefs, freedom, creativity, moral sense and every other characteristic and activity that distinguishes us as human. This identity-soul does not have to answer to the so-called "intermediate state, disembodied soul" problem in Paul's 2 Cor. 5:1-10 posed by the dichotomists (see discussion preceding), i.e. what happens to the person between the time of death and resurrection? My concept would claim that this identity-information-soul is preserved by God for safekeeping awaiting[134] the resurrected body to complete its glory while the body lies in decay. (The physicalist-ontological monists must surmount the difficulty in postulating how one's self-identity is preserved intact through death and the same unique person emerges in the resurrected body. We can all agree that this takes a miracle of God's omniscience and power. I simply furnish a possible mechanism in the conception of the event that is describable and understandable this side of eternity. The human ontic monism, based on my model, is left intact. During life, this identity-information-soul is an integral part of the whole person. It and the physical body are one. Neither one without the other would have a meaning or *raison d'être* by itself.

For those dichotomists who believe in the bipartite nature of humanity (a human possesses a body and a soul and at death, the immortal soul is freed and goes in bliss back to God, waiting for the eventual reunion with the body), I want to point out that our area of disagreement lies not in the content of the soul. Surely most dichotomists would subscribe to the soul having an identity, individuality, with an earthly redemptive history which is the basis for its final abode. My concept includes all these informational data and identity markers. Our difference situates at whether the soul has a conscious life of its own. The bipartitists argue that the soul has an independent, conscious, immortal existence in the presence of God. My concept emphasizes life being determined and sustained by God alone, whether here on earth or in the Resurrection when this non-living identity-information-soul is again programmed into the resurrected body. It takes a different trajectory from the dichotomist view which argues for an inherent, indestructible, immortal life in the soul which is released from the physical body at the time of death.

To the trichotomists, my concept and theirs both subscribe to the reality of Spirit (God's) and/or spirit (human). If the former, it is never ours to possess, so that it is logical to think that it would return to God when a person dies. If the latter, i.e. a human spirit, my interpretation would link it to the very central core of one's identity-information-soul where the deepest Divine-human encounter occurs. It should present no difficulty as to wherever the trichotomists want to place the human spirit. For others, spirit and soul are just synonymous, words to be used interchangeably. Regarding the soul, my answer to the tripartitists is the same as to the bipartitists.

### The Wholistic Concept of the Image of God

To examine this aspect of the image, we must return to Gen. 1: 26-28: Then God said, "Let us make man in our image, in our likeness, and let them rule over...all the earth, and over all the creatures.... So God created man in His own image, in the image of God He created him; male and female He created them. God blessed them and said to them, "Be fruitful and increase in number, till the earth and subdue it. Rule over...every living creature...."

(1) Genesis 5:1 and 9:6 repeat the same motif that the human was created in the likeness of God, in the image of God. Nowhere

in the biblical record does it state that any other of God's created beings were made in His likeness.[135]

Since God the Father, the Son and Holy Spirit are three Persons in One Trinitarian Essence,[136] the human, having been created in God's image, reflects a relational element.

(2) From the Genesis record, it can be inferred that human relationships include one vertical dimension toward God and three horizontal dimensions: to oneself, to other fellow human beings, and to the earth. This relational concept of imago Dei was presaged by Augustine as far back as 400 AD. After analyzing the thoughts of Brunner, Berkouwer and Barth on this subject, Anderson concludes that to a varying degree, these three reformed theologians, while affirming the ontic reality of the human person in the imago, all stress the relational aspect of the image as primary.[137] Karl Barth has often been quoted, "For the meaning and purpose of God at His creation were as follows. He willed the existence of a being which in all its non-deity and therefore its differentiation can be a real partner; which is capable of action and responsibility in relation to Him; to which His own divine form of life is not alien; which in a creaturely repetition, as a copy and imitation, can be a bearer of this form of life.... In God's own being and sphere there is a counterpart: a genuine but harmonious self-encounter and self-discovery; a free co-existence and co-operation; an open confrontation and reciprocity." [138]

To claim that the imago derives its distinctiveness from its capacity for relation with God, others, and self, needs some qualification. Animals, perhaps less knowingly, also stand in relationship to their Creator, us and themselves. Much of modern-day New Age philosophy pares down the distinction between humans and other animals. To its worshippers, the whale stands equal in worth and position with the human, since all is in god and god in all.

(3) I shall argue that humans are distinctly unique on this earth. They alone are commanded to rule over all the earth and all the creatures, to have dominion over them and to subdue them, as well as to till the earth, to work it and take care of it (Gen. 2:15).

(4) There is that implicit duty of a steward, a protector, an administrator, an organizer, with all the delegated sovereignty to

oversee and care for, in modern terms, the ecological health and well-being of this planet. Yes, God's viceroy on earth!

(5) Man/woman is given that reasoning power, intelligence, the freedom and creativity, self-awareness and imagination, and the ability for abstract thinking, memory of the past, projection for the future, and above all, the affinity for the spiritual and the restlessness for God.[139]

Questions can be raised as to whether Adam had received the full share of God's communicable attributes, and therefore the complete image ontologically speaking, before Eve was created? That humans are created as social beings needing interaction with others for self-identity, fulfillment, and meaning is a conclusion to be drawn from Genesis 2:18 when "The Lord God said, 'It is not good for the man to be alone. I will make a helper suitable for him.'" Is the sociality of humanity reflective of the Trinitarian interrelatedness and distinctly of a different hierarchical plane than that of the other animals?

(6) Man or woman is fully reflective of God's image only from where he or she stands in relation to God. Either male or female is potentially a true image of God but not a complete one. Let me illustrate: supposing Jesus were here on earth today in His physical form and we took an antero-posterior (front to back) X-ray view of His body, it would be a true view from where I stood. Then we took a lateral, side view; again it would be a true view of His body. But neither one, though complete in its own dimension, is complete for His whole body. Two views, complementary to each other, would reveal more of Him. And suppose we took a MRI (magnetic resonance imaging, a relatively new diagnostic modality with multiple axial rotation views) of Jesus, more of His physical body could be known. Each of these many views is complete in itself but not sufficient for a comprehensive picture of His body.

By analogy then, the Apostle Paul, whose marital status is perhaps uncertain; Pope Paul and Mother Theresa, the celibates; Billy Graham, who is married; Beverly Harrison, a feminist Christian social-ethicist, presently divorced; can each in his or her gender be the potential true image of God. **But man and woman together in whole, make a better image-bearer for God!** By extension, it takes not one, but male and female, the whole family, the church, the whole world of Christian communities to reflect the multifaceted, sublime image of the character of God.[140] I submit that the tarnished, defaced post-Fall images of all the believers are as yet a far way off the total picture God has in mind in His creational and redemptive purpose.

(7) A religious visionary of the 19th century also pointed to the multidimensional composition of the human reflecting the image of God in us, which is in the process of preparation for eternity.[141]

(8) Finally, my strongest argument for a wholistic concept of the imago Dei is that this selfsame image which perfectly reflects the Creator-God, Jesus-God-Incarnate, without whom nothing was made that was made (Jn.1:3), came to bear. Truly, He is the "Christ, who is the image of God" (2 Cor.4: 4). Jesus, the Bearer of the sin-corrupted image, who has overcome lostness and brokenness with wholeness, shall one day restore wholly this image in the believer's resurrected body. One must sense both the wonder and mystery of this imago Dei in all its glory.

Summary: The Biblical concept of the human seems to describe a person with different dimensions of expression and multiple levels of complexity in dynamic interaction within oneself, with others, and God and the universe. In its action mode, the person is a soul with self-consciousness, reason, will, judgment, imagination, language, freedom, autonomy, emotions, relational and social extensions with others as well as the environment. In its inactive mode, it is a record which preserves one's minute to minute response to God's grace—positive, indifferent or negative. Thus, to use a crude analogy of computer terminology, the person as soul is analogous to a floppy disc which holds the salvation history of the person. It is a finished product at death that has been purged of what is not considered desirable by the person and by God. It is then safeguarded and preserved by the Creator for re-creation at the Resurrection.

The person reflected in the soul as defined above has an absolute unique identity, which can be differentiated between identical twins, even separable between cloner and clonee, should human cloning become a reality. This is so because of the unique and innumerable life's responses to God over different time and space.

## Physical Health and Christian Wholism

From time immemorial, the specter of illness has always posed as a most dreadful threat to humankind. It is often the harbinger of death. It strikes without warning, it inflicts pain and suffering without mercy, and its causality forever remains mysterious and unpredictable. Before the scientific age, people were made to believe that malevolent gods or evil spirits brought on sickness. Humanity needs a good God to fight off the illness-producing agents. Thus divinity and illness and healing were naturally linked in people's mind. The priests, the tribal leader, the chanting magicians, and some modern faith-healers garnish all the prerogatives of healing. Dispensing it at will constitutes power over life and death. It was no accident that the root words for physical healing and salvation (spiritual healing) are the same.

Ambroise Paré (1510-1590) the noted French physician and surgeon with humility and insight states, "I dress the wounds and God heals it." Such proclamation from an educated class and revered profession legitimized the healing ministry with its spiritual dimension. From Pare to Claude Bernard to the Nobel Laureate Alexis Carrel (1873-1944), down to our contemporary world, the relation between health of body and the state of the "soul" has become increasingly more evident.

To set the background of contemporary American society as a reference to what we consider relevant as religious and spiritual beliefs and practices in relation to health issues, let me cite the following statistics:

95% of Americans espouse a belief in God when questioned about their religious beliefs; 80% of Americans believe that the Bible is the actual, or inspired, Word of God; a near 75% of Americans say that their religious faith is the most important influence in their life; 42% of Americans describe themselves as being "born-again."; almost 40% of Americans attend worship services on at least a weekly basis.[142] No survey is needed to demonstrate that 99% of Americans would consider health as one of the most important assets in life and that its preservation is on the top of a list of priority. What is the correlation of a person's religious belief with his/her health?

Dale Matthews, MD, a professor of Medicine at Georgetown University School of Medicine, has compiled a four-volume annotated bibliography of clinical research on spiritual subjects, and written sixty peer-reviewed scientific articles, book chapters in this field. Numerous research studies have furnished evidence that religious involvement and spirituality can improve the chances of being able to stay healthy and avoid life-threatening and disabling diseases like cancer and heart diseases; recover faster and with fewer complications if one does develop a serious illness; live longer; encounter life-threatening and terminal illnesses with greater peacefulness and less pain; avoid mental illness like depression and anxiety; and cope more effectively with stress; steer clear of problems with alcohol, drugs, tobacco; enjoy a happier marriage and family life; and find a greater sense of meaning and purpose in one's life.[143]

Stories after stories, Dr. Matthews told how religious involvement helps people and his patients prevent illness, recover from illness and most remarkably live longer. Statistics from 91,909 individuals showed that those who attended church once or more a week had significantly lower death rates from coronary disease (50% reduction), pulmonary emphysema (56% reduction), liver cirrhosis (74% reduction), suicide (53% reduction), also significant reduction in the incidence of vaginal infections, sexually transmitted disease and precancerous cervical lesions. Of course, religious involvement with attendant healthy life-style of less smoking, drinking, and sexual behavior must be factored in. [144]

Dr. Bradley Wilcox, a professor of Geriatric Medicine at Harvard University, attests to "the power of lifestyle over genetics." "In our work, we've found that lifestyle accounts for about two-thirds of life expectancy; one third is due to genetics." Dr. Wilcox's study correlates with the research on 34,000 men and women over a 25-year period by Gary Fraser, MD, PhD, Professor of Medicine and Epidemiology at Loma Linda University. Dr. Fraser has shown, as reported in the *Archives of Internal Medicine* of July 2001 that Adventist men lived 9.5 years, women 6.1 years longer than other Californians because of their lifestyle and diet. Dr. Wilcox says he considers spirituality and having a support system to be essential in a healthy lifestyle. "We look at it as four legs of a chair—diet, exercise, psychosocial factors, spirituality— and each leg has to be in balance." [145]

## Emphasis on Whole-Person Care

In 1980 a whole-person medicine international symposium was organized largely by the Christian medical Society in America. Participants included Professor David Allen, a psychiatrist from the school of Medicine at Yale University, Dr. Lewis Bird from McGill Univeristy, Dr. John Brobeck from University of Penn- sylvannia School of Medicine, Dr. Edmund Pellegrino, philosopher and ethicist from The Catholic University of America and Georgetown University, Dr. Robert Hermann, a biochemist and several other ministers. [146] Loma Linda Health Sciences University School of Medicine, the only medical school in the United States which publicly professes its Christian faith and practice has over the years placed great emphasis on whole person care in the training program for physicians. Its motto is "To make man whole."

The symposium stresses a whole-person perspective that is grounded on the Judeo-Christian faith and philosophical wholistic paradigm. It argues for a medical education that emphasizes rigorous scientific approach as an integral part of wholistic medicine in the care of patients; that the physician must have an awareness of his/her own need for wholeness, and a conceptual training the Christian physician. Integrated biblical models of medical care, church health-care clinics, care for the terminally ill, marriage and family life, were proposed. The ministry of medicine in the care of the whole person and clinical view of the Gospel were also discussed.

Ethical responsibilities of the health-care professional in a wholistic context include knowing the facts, mastering the body of knowledge pertinent to one's profession, good clinical training followed by continuing education, and involvement in research, all preparatory to good ethical decision making. [147] In addition, wholistic approach to medicine encourages the healthcare professional to gain an informed perspective of all the factors that could impact the patient's life and illness, including an understanding of how the patient perceives his/her pain. Dr. Allen emphasizes the dynamic principle of "empathic caring" by identifying with others and treating them as one would want to be treated. This principle of reciprocity in biblical terminology is the Golden Rule, spoken of by Jesus in Luke 6:31, "Do to others as you would have them do to you." Its mirror image is the Confucian's Silver Rule, "Do not do to others what you would not want others do to you." A word of caution here. These rules must be used in conjunction with other biblical principles when they are employed in ethical and moral decision-making. Just because Louis Pasteur was willing to subject himself to testing of an untried rabies vaccine with probable fatal consequence in light of his research passion, it does not mean he should subject everybody to such risky procedure without violating the principles of freedom, autonomy, privacy, individual rights to refuse treatment or experimentation.

For the healthcare professional to remain whole, healthy, and strong to face challenges in this broken world, I argue that prevention of professional burnout be seriously considered. Roderick Firth's model of an ideal observer in being disinterestedly interested and dispassionately passionate might serve as a guide.[148] The acknowledgment of our own limitation and God's sovereign will and purpose for humankind can help assuage our sense of failure in spite of our best efforts. Dr. Allen suggests a multi-disciplinary review committee in difficult decision-making process. In such a committee, I anticipate members from the chaplaincy and clergy, physicians, ethicists, nurses, social worker, hospital administration, legal representatives, patient advocates, laypersons particular interests and passions are diluted and balanced by those who hold opposing views or perspectives. In addition, such multidisciplinary committees can offer broader-based advocacy and insure informed consent. Besides an added benefit from a mutual educational experience, the committee provides a communication channel leading to greater trust and openness in the doctor-patient relationship, and thus better and more comprehensive care.[149]

Other qualities which enter into this fabric of a wholistic approach in healthcare are: (1) Being innovative in seeking out all the possible treatments for the particular patient with different degrees of dysfunction and fragmentation in the multidimensional composition of personhood. This applies especially to the physically challenged, learning disabled, economically deprived and culturally disadvantaged. Christian wholism is forever mindful of the Christian principles of love, forgiveness, justice, freedom, equality, human dignity, human value, rights and responsibility, truth-telling, protection of the vulnerable in society, and walking the second mile. (2) Self-introspection and reflection on the part of healthcare professionals and balancing between the popular, social, utilitarian dictum—the greatest good for the largest number of people and the individual's claim to his/her belief, God-endowed rights, resources, liberty, autonomy, and destiny.

Dr. Arthur Dyck of Harvard Divinity School and professor of population ethics at Harvard School of Public Health challenges the criteria and practice of Yale University's Duff and Campbell to make decisions as to which infant should or should not receive life-saving medical intervention. Basing on support from Joseph Fletcher, Richard McCormick and others, Duff and Campbell conclude that very defective individuals are considered to have little or no hope of achieving meaningful humanhood. One needs to intervene to save only those who have potential for human relationship. Medical intervention ought not to be given to those below the threshold of humanhood who have little or no capacity to love or be loved.[150]

Christian wholism must not confine itself only to human life and living. It ought to address issues confronting us at the very beginning of life and at the end of one's existence—"Live whole and die whole." Wholism as defined earlier examines all the dimensions of personhood or humanhood, their relative significance, their relationship to one another as well as their competing values oftentimes held in tension. For example, at what point is wholistic medicine deemed futile therapy, mere technological heroics, procedures only prolonging suffering instead of prolonging meaningful and qualitative life? In the wholeness assessment, competing priorities, human values and sensitivity of individual patient and family must be respected and carefully balanced. Christian wholism opts for wholistic living that promotes peace and joy. But should not the emphasis also be given not only to living wholesomely but also dying well and dying whole?

Dying whole includes dying with dignity, in control of the kind of medical intervention given and received, retaining the right to refuse futile therapy and procedures for oneself and one's minor children. For Christians, this earthly life, precious as it is, is not necessarily accorded the highest value. Death is not the be-all and end-all. Christian wholism is an eschatologically forward-looking concept and practice that finds its ultimate realization in the believer's resurrected body. As such it is adequate to meet the challenges posed by some of the most dilemmatic ethical issues of both ends of the spectrum of life as well as issues arising from modern genetics and technology. These issues will be discussed in the chapter under wholism and ethics.

**Two Worldviews for Whole-Person Health Professionals**

Since medicine, dentistry, public health, nursing and other health-related professions are science-based disciplines, students and practitioners who embrace Christian beliefs and Christian wholism face two seemingly opposing worldviews. One is represented by Jacques Monod, a Nobel Laureate molecular biologist. His purely mechanistic, irreligious worldview places man alone in the unfeeling immensity of the universe, to which he came without meaning and purpose, solely by chance. The only compensation is to be free from deceitful servitudes and to be able to live authentically. This scientific presupposition refuses to admit the possibility of a supernatural intrusion into the closed system of our known time-space-matter reality. This philosophical and scientific exclusivism mandates that only scientific statements are valid, that scientific statements are impersonal, that only scientific method is valid as a means to discover truth, that personal choices, subjective experiences, states of mind...are intrinsically meaningless. [151]

Then there is the other perspective framed within the Christian worldview. Dr. Robert Herrmann, a biochemist, formerly from Boston University School of Medicine and Massachusetts Institute of Technology, now of Templeton Foundation, quotes Donald McKay as saying, "We know we are on our Father's business no less when investigating His handiwork than when engaged in formal acts of worship. In place of jealously secretive gods we have One whose very nature is Truth, and Light, Himself the giver of all that is true, who rejoices when any of His truth is brought to the light and obeyed in humility. Oxford physicist Dr. Charles Coulson once commented, "The practice of science is to be seen as a fit activity for a Sabbath afternoon."[152]

There are other scientists of international stature such as Professor Roger Sperry, a Nobel Laureate in Medicine and Physiology, who challenges the mechanistic, deterministic and reductionist materialism. For example, on the subject of consciousness, he asserts, "Consciousness is conceived to be a dynamic emergent property of brain activity, neither identical with nor reducible to, the neural events of which it is mainly composed.... We do not look for conscious awareness in the nerve cells of the brain, nor in the molecules or the atoms in brain processing." [153] In other words, Sperry is admitting to another level of reality besides the merely physical time-space-matter-energy dimension.

Michael Polanyi, an eminent British scientist-philosopher at University Manchester shows that the search for scientific truth does not have the infallible, impersonal objectivity generally attributed to it, but that unavoidable nonobjective components in science have a significant bearing on our truth seeking. [154]

I shall argue that for those health professionals who subscribe to Christian wholism with all the multifaceted dimensions of personhood, science and technology are no impediments to rendering whole-person care. On the contrary, scientific progress only reveals to us the power, wisdom, intricacy and complexity of God's creation. We are to be God's co-workers, representatives on earth, to bring healing and wholeness to those lost and broken in this fallen world. There is no greater task in bringing glory to God than the complimentary, harmonious working together between the divine and human agencies. God is the author of both science and Scripture. Genuine scientific truth with the correct interpretation must find its correspondence with the principles in God's Word. Through the telescope and microscope, we see God's handiwork reflective of His genius in perfecting the prelapsarian human body in beauty and wholeness. On earth, even the best whole-person care falls short of the ideal. It is powerless to thwart death and decay, which is certain and impartial. Christian Wholism thrives on the hope for eternal life with its attendant ultimate wholeness in the Kingdom of God that knows no tears, nor disease, nor death.

**Christian Wholism and Education of Christian Physicians**

To spread the concept and practice of whole-person care, it is crucial that physicians and surgeons be educated on the principles of Christian care-giving. Jesus' own healing ministry while He was on earth is the prototype and model.

Medical education in the United States historically owes its success to some of the intellectual giants and visionaries such as President Charles W. Eliot of Harvard University, Dr. William Osler, Johns Hopkins, the benefactor of Johns Hopkins University, John D. Rockefellers Sr. and Jr. and their Foundation. The Flexner Report of 1910 served as the wake-up call for reform and revolution.[155] The goal was scientific medicine at its best with its integration into a university program, strict admission standards, well-trained faculty in basic science and clinical medicine and well-equipped laboratories and research facilities. Today medicine is solidly grounded in science and to a large degree cast in a non-religious worldview and philosophical and materialistic humanism. Universities with their medical schools which started as church-affiliated institutions with Christian beliefs and Catholic or Protestant denominational support have all become secular universities with no religious orientation for their students. The notable exception is California's Loma Linda University and its Health Sciences Center which operates the only Christian medical school in America with an annual 150 incoming Freshmen medical students and granting many professional degrees including MD, PhD, DDS, DPH, D. Psych, D. Pharm, and others. The University also operates a Dental School, a Nursing School, School of Pharmacy, Graduate School, School of Public Health, School of Allied Health, with a Faculty of Religion interacting with all the schools and departments. The annual budget for the University and its Medical Center which is internationally known for infant heart transplants and proton beam for cancer treatment is $850 millions for year 2002.

The School of Medicine at Loma Linda University includes in its bulletin a mission statement, which reads, "To continue the healing and teaching ministry of Jesus Christ, to "make man whole." Luke 9:6. "The overriding purpose is the formation of Christian physicians, educated to serve as generalists or specialists providing whole-person care to..." through education, research, and service, "ministering to the physical,, mental, emotional, and spiritual needs of patients...," by developing the whole person, and reaching the world by providing whole-person care wherever the opportunity arises...sharing the good news of a loving God as demonstrated by the life and teachings of Jesus Christ...." The medical curriculum and other professional curricula for the students include required courses of religion in the areas of biblical studies and theology, biomedical ethics, and relational studies courses.

In our multicultural, morally and religiously pluralistic society it is fair to ask whether whole-person care must be of a Christian variety. By definition, whole person care incorporates a spiritual component. But must that component be exclusively Christian? My answer is yes and no. This question is of a genre similar to the question, "Are Christians the only ones who are going to be saved?" It is my belief that in the ocean of God's love and justice, His omniscience and omnipotence, all those sincere seekers after truth and practitioners of virtue before and since Christ's incarnation, within and beyond individual Christian or corporate Christian' reach, according to the light and circumstances of their life, will be saved if they genuinely live up to what their consciences or Holy spirit tell them, even in the absence of overt confession and profession of faith in light of one's existential circumstance. To be saved by the name of Jesus Christ (Acts 4:12) embodies the meaning that Christ is the only means by which human salvation can be secured. Recall at the beginning we discuss the linguistic roots of salvation, healing, and wholeness. Christ is the Creator as well as the Redeemer-Forgiver who by His life, death, and resurrection, is able to make humans whole here on earth and there in eternity. To be saved by His name is to ascribe to and live by what that name symbolizes—*inter alia,* love, justice, wisdom, truth, humility, forgiveness, freedom, creativity, faith, and hope.

Returning to the original question whether whole-person care must necessarily be of the Christian model, the yes answer would argue that only the true Christian God can render a person genuinely whole—both the healer physician and the healee patient. Authentic whole-person care ought to touch the healthcare professional's bruised body and spirit as much as the one needing to be healed. The health concept underscored by Christian wholism, as I have repeatedly stated, is multidimensional aimed at healing all the broken and fragmented spheres of our existential life.

But if the Christian God is the only true God, might He not also work through other religions to make it possible for the created beings to receive the whole-person care? To deny such a possibility borders not only on gross spiritual arrogance, but in this context is also a denial of God's wisdom, mercy, freedom, and omnipotence. Having said this, it remains true that scientific medicine is largely Western medicine and that there is only rare models of whole-person care available from other than a Christian variety. This fact attests to the uniqueness of Christian wholism as defined earlier in the first chapter of this book.

Dr. Edmund Pellegrino, physician, philosopher, ethicist, former president of the Catholic University of America, Professor at Georgetown, Yale, State University of New York, admits the difficult challenge of fusing being Christian of faith and compassion and being a physician trained in secular humanism and scientific materialism. The unprecedented success of scientific methodology and therapeutics has engendered "an understandable hubris." [156] Science is proclaiming that it can heal not just the body, but also the mind. What else can the physician of faith bring to the theatre of the healing science and arts?

Central to the physician-patient relationship and the obligation of the physician is the fundamental and irreducible concern that *"this* patient, *now*, with *this* set of needs, arising out of *this* particular illness" is in need of help and healing. I argue that in the best interest of the patient, a decision can be made as to how best to reach a diagnosis, formulate a plan of treatment, outline alternatives and practical options, implement the therapeutic modalities, and offer realistic outcome and risks, and yet not withholding assurance and hope.

The moral and ethical dimension of medicine casts the physician in the role that he or she promises to undertake the healing responsibility within a special set of human relationship inn which the healthcare professional confronts another human being in "a state of special vulnerability, the state of illness." In the words of Dr. Pellegrino, "persons who are ill are human beings in a state of compromised or wounded humanity. They have lost to varying degrees the distinctly human possibilities of free and rational decision-making about themselves and their bodies." In today's world, however, where patients' rights and autonomy are doubly underscored by societal expectations, patients in general have or are given more decision making powers regarding their health, treatment options, and every aspect of the care of their bodies.

For a Christian physician whose goal is to bring to the patient whole-person care, a higher principle and dimension beyond moral medicine must be in place alongside scientific competence. That higher principle is the justification of a faith commitment anchored to a source "outside and superior to humankind...that higher dimension is revealed in the gospel of Jesus Christ, whose irruption into human history redeemed humanity, fulfilled the prophecies of the Old Testament and forever altered the meaning of human relationships. All who follow Christ must love God as Father; all human beings are potential brothers and sisters...The Christian is committed to a special way of love and charity exemplified by Christ. That way must illuminate the Christian's every action and thought. He or she must become a partner in Christ's ministry to the world. With the church, the Christian is called to evangelize, witness, teach, and announce the good news... If they are to follow Christ, healing for Christian physician cannot never be anything other than ministry. It cannot ever be merely science or even public service. Physicians heal insofar as medical knowledge allows. But they must also care for and feel for the sick, whether medical means are adequate or not. Christian compassion means to "suffer with" those who suffer." [157]

But what and how should Christian physicians be taught about giving whole-person care with the higher dimension discussed above? For Christian institutions such as Loma Linda University Medical School, Dr. Pellegrino suggests first of all teaching by example and behavior. "If the student is to be convinced of the probity of the Christian ministry of healing, he or she will expect that the search for God and Christ will be taken seriously, that faith is sustained and deepened, that a concern for justice and mercy is manifest and that a dedication to religious and moral values enters into each clinical decision. To be authentic as Christian physicians, teachers must demonstrate that we care for the patient, that we place the patient's needs above our own convenience and comfort, that we wear our authority and knowledge humbly, that we teach, explain and be patient and sensitive to every nuance of behavior which might introduce even a trace of humiliation for the vulnerable person who is ill." In today's practice of medicine in the environment of HMO's PPO's, high patient volume and limited clinical time, government bureaucracy, insurance company interference, liability threats, litigious society, federal and state control, patients' high and at times unreasonable expectation, the determination to live out the Christian ideals has become even more challenging. I argue that without the strength and wisdom that can only come from on high, the task of upholding the Christian standard and aspiration would be well-nigh impossible. Christian physicians who have been made whole by His grace are God's new creations, empowered to more than overcome real and potential obstacles while sharing the richness of wholistic care to patients.

Besides precept and modeling in a Christian medical school, formal instruction of ethics, philosophy and theology should also be taught to the future physicians (representative of the whole class of healthcare professionals), so recommends Pellegrino. I might also add biblical studies and spiritual formation seminar under the category of theology. A course in relational psychology and cross-cultural studies, in my view, would also help.

In a secular medical school, Christian physicians, teachers, and students are called upon to seek support from the Campus ministry, to witness to the secular world their own Christian life and belief, to fuse the fire of faith and reason, and work with other Christians to clarify and deepen their idea of what it means to be both a Christian and physician.

## A Physical Wholeness Model

The World Health Organization gives health a definition which reads, "Health is a state of complete physical, mental, and social well-being and not merely the absence of disease or infirmity." Based on the accumulated research by many over the past 50 years, let me propose a model for physical health. I shall use an acrostic device to link the praxis of health to the word WHOLENESS:

**W**—stands for water and weight control. Plenty of water intake and copious amount for external cleansing of our body. Weight control through temperance in food intake and regular aerobic, cardiovascular, muscle building and muscle conditioning exercises.

**H**—represents hope, humor and hearty laughs; hope that is based on our Christian faith and looks forward to eternal life in our resurrected body. Humor and hearty laughs are good medicine since life cannot be lived in constant tension and seriousness. By all means, laugh at our own follies and life's incomprehensible mystery knowing in faith the assurance of God's love and forgiveness.

**O**—is oxygen and plenty of clean, fresh air and negative ions near oceans, forests, mountains, and lakes.

**L**—stands for love—love to God and love for people. Love is not a cure-all in this fallen world, but if love does not work, few other things would, ultimately or eternally significantly. Jesus was the embodiment of love, yet He did not solve all the problems while He was on earth. Love is about what we do while in hope we await for the final consummation of God's plan and purpose for our lives as well as for the unfolding destiny of this universe.

**E**—goes for exercise, enthusiasm, endless forbearance. Enthusiasm (*en theos* meaning God within us) gives us the energy, motivation, joy of service in sharing a wholistic life with others. Empathy and forbearance release the blocked energy in our life channels obstructed by the demons of hatred, jealousy, resentment, pride, greed, unforgiving spirit, revenge, sloth, and covetousness.

**N**—stands for nutrition and needed sleep, rest, relaxation, recreation. Avoid a high fat, high sugar, red meat diet and sweetened, caffeinated, carbonated drinks. Opt for copious amount of fruit, natural fruit juice, vegetables, nuts, legumes (beans), grains, food with high fiber content, complex carbohydrates. Include moderate amount of vegetable oils, judicious amount of vegetable, dairy, fowl, or fish proteins; vitamins, antioxidants, minerals, and liberal amount of water. Avoid tobacco, alcohol, drugs, caffeine, highly processed food, food with preservatives, artificial coloring, artificial flavorings including MSG. Allow sufficient sleep and regular periods of relaxation and diversion as well as vacations for renewal and recreation.

**E**—stands for effort in disciplining one's natural tendency of taking the easy road and in establishing good health habits. E also means continuing evaluation of the factors which hamper one's goal to wholeness, healing and health.

**S**—this first S represents searching for a balance between work and rest, between God-dependence and self-reliance, between financial security and philanthropy, between self-sacrifice and self-nurture; between relational-social needs and quiet, reflective self-intro-spection, between spiritual concern and earthly necessities, between love and beauty versus lust and vanity, between time-conscious mode versus person-oriented disposition. The list goes on.

**S**—the second S stands for spirituality and the spiritual mindset, which capsulizes all the above. It is through the spirit of man, the highest level of our mental/intellectual faculty that God communicates with us. Christian wholeness first begins as wholistic thinking in the mind and in the heart. Thoughts translated into actions and behaviors through empowerment by the Spirit of God will effect changes and transformations. Bodily and emotional healing will in turn move us toward wholeness in peace and joy.

And what is spirituality? In my view, the ideal Christian spirituality in the context of wholism includes the following, among other elements:

1) It is theocentric and Christocentric—not egocentric.
2) It must involve our whole being—spiritual, mental, emotional, physical, psychological, and social.
3) It is an authentic experience on the heart level—a natural outflow of our sincere desire to seek God, and in humility to acknowledge our gratitude that He also seeks us, and that our efforts to seek Him please Him and will not be in vain.
4) Christian spirituality links oneself to God the Father, through His Son, by the Holy Spirit, in a process beginning now with joy and love and in faith and hope extending to the eternal future.
5) It presupposes diversity and spontaneity in expression beyond the basic Christian disciplines of prayer, Scripture reading, church attendance, community fellowship, introspection, study and reflection. Few attempts are flawless in this life; failure and disappointment also stalk the sincere in heart in their spiritual quest.
6) It is mere works-righteousness if not based on acceptance of God's grace and awareness of our inability to do anything spiritually significant without His help.
7) Here on earth Christian spirituality is a process of being remade in the image of God, which calls forth faith and action, trust and effort.
8) Expression of our Christian spirituality changes as our concept of God, of ourselves, of the world deepens and widens, and as science and Scripture—both instrumentalities of God—open new vistas in our understanding of the Universe and what God has in store for us.
9) Christian spirituality is ultimately validated by our desire and concrete action to serve others—anything less is merely a self-centered rehearsal of our attempted acceptance by God.
10) Thus, Christian spirituality is an experience with a purpose: to glorify God by being what He intends us to be, and by doing what He expects of us, namely, to be involved in His created order, His people, their salvation, their service and needs.

# CHAPTER 5

## CHRISTIAN WHOLISM IN THE PSYCHOLOGICAL SPHERE

In the context of Christian Wholism, what does it mean for a person to be psychologically whole? Human personality and its pathological features have occupied a major emphasis in the study, research, and therapy by psychologists and psychiatrists. To discuss pathology, one must often refer to what is not pathological. Though psychologists do not ordinarily use the words "whole" or "wholistic" or "wholeness," terms such as mature personality, healthy personality, self-actualization, congruence, authenticity are common parlance.

If personality can be qualified in a continuum at one pole as pathological, unhealthy, mid-range, and the other pole as healthy, mature, self-actualized, authentic, transcendent, then whole and perfect personality would belong to the latter cluster.

Freud speaks about the development of the ego,[158] Maslow discusses characteristics of self-actualizers,[159] Allport describes the six aspects of a mature person,[160] and J.D. Carter outlines five basic criteria of a mature personality,[161] or whole personality in our context.

I shall argue how these personality maturity criteria are congruent with the wholism under discussion.

(1) Realistic View of Self and Others. We have asserted all along that the human person is created in the image of God to be a unitive, whole person with all the varied dimensions in a dynamic interaction with our environment. A serious internalization of this belief is the key to understanding the human psyche and social relations. This means a person has an accurate and objective

evaluation of the strengths and weaknesses of oneself and of the gifts and talents endowed by God. It is important to know what he can do best in his own assessment as well as that of others, or whether her interest measures up to her ability. How she views others' ability, talents, spiritual gifts, and potentials in comparison with her own is also important in the profile of a mature personality which aspires to wholeness and "perfection," ultimately realizable in our resurrected bodies. "Love thy neighbor as thyself," is best implemented when a realistic self assessment and others' needs are appropriately understood.

From a biblical perspective, humans have fallen from the ideal state and are encumbered with a sin nature which is in need of redemption through the life, death, and resurrection of Jesus. In addition, Scripture informs us that we are all creatures of the same God who is no respecter of person. "I now realize how true it is that God does not show favoritism but accepts men (women) from every nation who fear Him and do what is right (Acts 10:34). "God so loved the world that He gave His one and only Son, that whoever believes in Him shall not perish but have eternal life" (Jn. 3:16). We are sinners, yes, but as brothers and sisters in God's human family, we are also God's crowning work worthy of His redemption and our mutual caring. An honest, balanced self-understanding of this fundamental truth, in my view, is one of the hallmarks of a mature Christian on the way to experience the peace and joy of wholeness.

(2) Acceptance of Self and Others: Included in this aspect of personality are allowing, believing and recognizing that there is something real and worthwhile in one's own life and others' even though there are imperfections. Realizing that all humanity are objects of Christ's redemptive offer and that we all are in need of acceptance and forgiveness by God and by others would change one's paradigm of social interaction and tolerance. Accepting what is another's right and legitimate need prompts a mature, whole person to want to meet that need. An unwholistic approach makes one reject another because of prejudice, habit of thought, ingrained attitude, careless thought, or one's own unresolved conflict.

(3) Living in the Present: Christian Wholism recognizes that life and time are gifts from God and that humans are placed on this

earth with a purpose—to be stewards of this earth's resources and trustees of nature's bounties. We are to diligently attend to our work on a daily basis while aiming at long-term goals informed by past experiences.

This world being fallen, humans must be resourceful in facing and coping with adverse circumstances. Anchored by the assurance of our creaturely worth in the eyes of God, we are to have a balanced evaluation of our own worth, career, family, church, and country, the world. Aware of the transitoriness of life, we work hard to accomplish what needs to be done, but always with the belief that a more perfect day is yet to dawn. Living in the present delivers one from just daydreaming and unrealistic fantasies. It helps one to appreciate life one day at a time with all its richness and potentials while admitting that whatever is at the present is not all that could be. Self, others, nature to be made whole by God is forever the vision of one who has a mature and wholistic approach to life in the context of Christian Wholism.

(4) Having values: Psychologists, psychiatrists, and counselors speak of "the will to meaning,"[162] "Unifying philosophy of life," "choice and the courage to decide how one is going to live," "self-chosen values."[163] But what kind of values should one have as one aims at the praxis of wholism?

Values are defined as guidelines emerging from one's life experience that serves to guide that person's thoughts and behavior in the future. Secular psychologists believe that it is inappropriate to base moral education on transmitting or imposing an external set of values. Distinctions between personal preferences, tastes, social/cultural values, religious, moral/ethical values are often blurred resulting in moral and ethical relativism. Current research on values clarification generally proposes the following criteria for values: Values must be freely chosen among alternatives. They should be something a person is positive about and cherishes and willing to publicly affirm or associate. Values ought to be chosen and repeatedly and consistently acted with full knowledge of the consequences.

Christian Wholism calls for internal coherence and congruency between one's belief system and his/her actions. The reality of one's fallenness in need of redemption by a Creator whose love impels Him to seek to restore us to wholeness must be the grand imperative value guideline for Christians. An existential encounter with this loving and gracious God sets the stage for further experience of wholistic living. As argued earlier, humans have been gifted with genuine freedom, so that the Christian values are freely chosen among alternatives of other religions, philosophies, and gods. There is "prizing," "cherishing," and passion in embracing the values of wholism in that the latter leads to peace and joy. There is the mission to make it public and to extend the good news of God's redemptive wholeness and healing to others because wholeness' compass is wide enough to circumscribe all those in need. From a heart overflowing with grace and spiritual wholeness, there is that constraining love to make others whole. The consequences of Christian values of wholeness are peace and joy, which are self-authenticating and value-affirming.

(5) Having Goals: This psychological criterion for a mature personality is amply congruent with the Christian ethos. The Apostle Paul declares, "...But one thing I do: forgetting what is behind and straining toward what is ahead, I press on toward the goal to win the prize for which God has called me heavenward in Christ Jesus" (Phil. 3:14). In the praxis of Christian wholism, goal-setting unifies all the subspheres of a person's life dimensions. In a fallen world with all the pain and suffering, moral and natural evil, the Christian needs the cheering chorus from that realm afar beckoning us to persevere in peace and joy toward that grand consummation. In that resurrected body made glorious by His grace and power shall Christian wholeness ultimately find its fulfillment.

(6) A mature person in psychological description and the Christian who has been made whole relatively in all the dimensions of personhood, in my opinion, ought to possess a sense of belonging. I am speaking of belonging to God, loved ones, friends, church, community, society, nation, the world, the universe. He or she is warmly sustained by a balanced sense of worthiness (between pride and false modesty)—worthy to be saved, loved, given attention to, to be a recipient of God's grace, honored as a citizen of a country, race, and counted within the brotherhood and sisterhood of the human family. In addition, he or she must also

possess a reassuring sense of competence in whatever he/she undertakes in career, caring, and service to others. Finally the praxis of Christian wholism challenges the person with a purpose, meaning, and the impetus to make a difference in life. Sharing wholeness is wholeness acquired.

In the context of Christian wholism, all the spheres of a person's life are interrelated and interdependent. Insights and knowledge into the interaction between psychology and theology/religion can contribute to the understanding of wholeness.

Psychology is defined as the science of mental states and processes, studying among other things, motivations, emotions, and behaviors. Psychologists and philosophers discuss twelve fundamental human emotions (affective states, conscious or vague awareness, feeling tones). The pleasant variety includes love, joy and awe. The unpleasant and generally destructive emotions are anger, jealousy/envy, fear, shame, sorrow, pain, disgust, emptiness, confusion.[164] These descriptive words change as the emotional state alters its intensity and duration. For example, when anger becomes intense and lasting, it borders hate.

Since emotions have their important impact on wholeness living, it is well for us to examine some of the destructive emotions that can easily rupture the mosaic of peace and joy.

(1) Anger (resentment, hate, at times masked in cynicism, sarcasm, distancing): Resentment is unexpressed anger, and hate is intense anger usually prolonged and tending to aggressive behavior. Psychologists have posited several theories about anger.

In the hydraulic model,[165] anger is viewed internally independent of context as an instinct which requires periodic discharge and healthy expression in an appropriate setting. Christians generally teach that anger becomes a sin when it is inappropriately expressed towards the wrong object or person.

The frustration model links anger to a discrepancy between one's expectations and achievement/reality, personally and societally. Unrealistic expectations and demands on one's self and others result in frustration, loss of self-esteem, anxiety, loss of equilibrium of wholeness in one's living.

Anger has also been considered as a socially learned behavior through internalizing perceived effective behaviors. Anger in modern psychodynamic formulation is a particular response to arousal, which one can constructively re-channel or direct to socially acceptable behavior and creative work. Such redirection of angry feelings with all their explosive power can be a learned skill as part of a conflict management protocol. Christians who aspire to be whole must learn patience, engage in reflective listening, adopt communicative strategies and engagement in the context of Christian sensitivity and compassion.[166]

In the totality of Christian Wholism, nothing disrupts the fragility of peace and joy faster than anger with its explosive outburst. I shall argue that there is a way out from this threat to wholism. First, one must recognize that self-control is one of the fruits of the Spirit promised to those who are spiritually whole. By implication, God's power and grace are sufficient for those who humbly submit themselves to imploring for divine provision. Second, one must keep in mind of the overall picture in which one would ask whether his or her angry outbursts are worth the consequences (relational, financial, social, physical, spiritual, one's career, reputation, community acceptance) to oneself, others, now, or in the future. Third, one must recognize one's particular vulnerable areas that trigger anger manifestations in addition to the general factors such as fatigue, hunger, loneliness, insult, injustice, failed expectations. Fourth, a useful psychological skill to adopt is imaging—actively visualize one's success in handling anger and the satisfaction thereof. Fifth, trying to set up some control mechanism of accountability—to God, to another person, as a further safety valve in case of relapse. Sixth, Christians are called to trust in Divine power and forgiveness, the former to sustain one in quest for wholeness, the latter to retreat to in our existential imperfection and proneness to failure.

(2) Jealousy, Envy: Though jealousy and envy are terms often used interchangeably, there is a distinction to be made. Jealousy usually involves three parties and envy only two. In jealousy, there is the self, a loved object, and a rival, whereas in envy, there are only the self and the other to contend with. Jealousy's psychodynamic root is fear—fear of losing the love and affection of another person, or the exclusive possession of a thing in competition with a rival.

God declares Himself as a jealous God (Exo. 20:5) in anthropomorphic and anthropopathic language. God the Self will not tolerate any diminution of the exclusive loyalty and devotion by His created possession—the human family—against any idols people worship, which are His "rivals." Where does divine jealousy stop and where does sinful jealousy start? Are His creatures permitted some degree of divine jealousy of their loved ones to signify the intensity of their love for the love object in the same manner as God for His human family?

Envy is feeling sad because of what one does not have or what one cannot be in comparison to another. Jealousy is frantically wanting to hold on to what one already has against a threat of loss and deprivation in the context of a competitor who comes to rob one's self-esteem, identity, and *status quo.*

I argue that a Christian approach in the context of wholism would be to think of the biblical reminder, "Return to your rest, O my soul, for the Lord has dealt bountifully with you" (Psa. 116:7). "But whatever was to my profit, I now consider loss for the sake of Christ. What is more, I consider everything a loss compared to the surpassing greatness of knowing Christ Jesus my Lord, for whose sake I have lost all things. I consider them rubbish, that I may gain Christ and be found in Him..." (Phil. 3:7). A Christian's joy and peace finds its source in gratitude for what one has been gifted by God and contentment even in a threatened loss of possession and love in the presence of a rival. A Christian can be assured, in the midst of fearful thoughts and situations, of God's loving care and His purpose for his/her life in the intricate web of existence. He rests his hope in the resurrected body—the ultimate fulfillment of everything good and desirable. Having a proper perspective on the transitoriness of this life with all that is perishable against the permanence implicative of eternal life must ever be the grand theme in Christian wholism.

(3) Fear, anxiety: anxiety is free-floating apprehension in the face of perceived or imagined threat whereas normal fear (versus irrational fear which is phobia) is an adaptive and protective response to real danger. Fear and the triad of peace, joy, trust in wholism cannot coexist for long without the submersion of one to the other. Fear and the perception of the consequences of the threat

arising from the identifiable person, object or event are always linked. The physiological response is a preparation for withdrawal, escape, recoil. Moderate amount of fear is constructive and salvific for the physico-psychologico-spiritual being.

Fear of God is in such a category even though fear here denotes in addition reverence and respect for God's sovereignty, holiness, and power. "The fear of God is the beginning of wisdom" (Prov. 9:10), "The fear of the Lord leads to life..." (Prov. 19:23).

The hallmarks of wholism are peace and joy and by implication the absence of excessive, destabilizing fear. Christian Wholism is realistically tough in facing the thing feared most by resting on a God, the Creator of this universe, the great I AM. He is able to prevent as well as make whole what poses as a threat to our wholeness, for He says, "So do not fear, for I am with you; do not be dismayed, for I am your God." (Isa. 41:10).

The apostle John states, "God is love. Whoever lives in love lives in God, and God in him. In this way, love is made complete (*teteleiotai* has been perfected, made whole) among us...There is no fear in love. But perfect (*teleia)* love drives out fear, because fear has to do with punishment. The one who fears is not made perfect in love" (1Jn.4:16-18). And before His ascension, Jesus who holds the prototype of Christian wholeness reassures us, "Do not let your hearts be troubled. Trust in God; trust also in Me..." (Jn. 14:1).

(4) Pain, suffering, sorrow: Pathophysiologically pain is any unpleasant sensation localized to a part of the body resulting from tissue-destructive process, or mechanical stimulation of hollow viscera in the presence of inflammatory mediators.[167] Pain is usually accompanied by an emotional and psychological response. Suffering refers to the subjective, cognitive, evaluative, meaning-laden component as experienced by the one who endures pain. Sorrow is a form of psychic and spiritual pain brought on by disappointment, despair, loneliness, separation, loss, shame, and a constellation of other internal and external factors impacting an individual and may or may not be associated with physical pain. The intensity, threshold, and perception of pain in different individuals and under diverse circumstances are modified and culturally conditioned.[168] The secretion of enkephalins, endorphins,

dynorphins [169] which are opiate-like narcotic substances in the pituitary gland of the brain, is modulated by emotional states, and may be related to acupuncture analgesia.

Pain signals disease or human brokenness. It can have a useful function in detecting, localizing and identifying where wholeness is lacking. I submit it is good Christian virtue to courageously attack whatever the problems as identified by pain while utilizing all God-given means and resources including medical science, psychological counseling and spiritual empowerment. For chronic, recurring or unrelenting pain beyond medical management, Christian wholism dares to proffer acceptance, acquiescence, courage, and trust in the ultimate healing with wholeness in our resurrected bodies. There is no earthly sorrow which Heaven cannot cure.

(5) Pride, arrogance: Though pride is basically an ontological state, an attitude, a posture of an unrealistic self-assessment, it too has an emotional content. One is saying to oneself subconsciously or consciously that he or she is more whole than the other and looks with contempt those who are less whole and perfect. Or as an abnormal defensive mechanism of overcompensation, the person is unable to accept his own lack of wholeness and desperately trying to compensate the inferiority and inadequacy by pretending more whole than he really is.

Christian wholism presupposes our dependency on God for wholeness in our human dimensions. Pride is antithetical to this acknowledgment in humility. Pride, as the genesis of sin, can also have its origin in egocentric wild ambition to aspire to what ontologically is God's attribute or possession. The biblical portrayal of Lucifer's fall falls under such a category.

I argue that the concept of wholism predicates its fulfillment on the sustaining power of God. And such an understanding and dependency should preclude pride in all its manifestation.

**Psychology and the Christian Faith**

The relationship between psychology as a science and Christian faith as a belief and worldview can be inimical, irrelevant, parallel, complementary, convertiblistic, and integrational. The conflict model sees irreconcilability in light of the differences in presuppositions and assumptions.

Christian Wholism seeks to focus on the integrational model by capturing psychological insights and theological illumination to enhance our human journey toward peace and joy. Let us examine some of the contact points at which these two disciplines and human dimensions intersect.

(1) God Concept: Psychologists speak of the unconscious, the preconscious and conscious layers of the God concept. The first two categories are emotionally laden representations of God from childhood and adolescent days of interpersonal experiences with parents and other emotionally significant authority figures. Added to this milieu is the individually created God concept according to the child's psychological needs.

The conscious layer of God concept represents a more intellectual view of God based on rational thought, serious reflection, religious tradition, certain momentous life experience.

The experiential God concept is a particular type of object representation, which refers to a relatively enduring schema or image of another person based on an organization of all experience in relation to that person. The relationship with another person is psychologically taken in, or internalized, and becomes a permanent though malleable part of the psyche. Each God representation is connected to a particular sense of self by associated emotions at any given time. The experiential God concept is relatively enduring organization or cognitive schema of God bound to a particular sense of self by feelings that were experienced in relation to him.[170]

Psychologists believe that this God concept functions as a type of template that governs to a large degree one's wishes from, beliefs in, expectations from, and fears of God. Such a revisable God concept is always receptive to new acceptance or further rejection according to the psychological needs of the person. The development of the God concept corresponds well to Jean Pieget's cognitive developmental stages. [171]

A God concept as postulated by psychologists emphasizing love, intimacy, interpersonal dialogues, acceptance, forgiveness, healing, affection, self-esteem, trust, dependability would be helpful to define Christian wholism's components.

(2) Psychological Perspectives of Religion: William James (1842-1910), who completed his medical training at Cambridge University, was for many years a professor at Harvard. Besides his contributions to philosophy and religion, he was also credited as the father of psychology in America. He authored *The Principles of Psychology*, which for many years was a standard text in universities, here and abroad. James' pragmatic approach to religion puts every religious belief to an experiential test whether the belief leads a person to better behavior than if that person had acted on unbelief. His position comes close to the Psalmist statement, "Taste and see that the Lord is good...." (Psa. 34:8). James discards any religious beliefs which fail to work experimentally in one's life. He emphasized religion's function as a way of knowing life and that psychological insights are useful to explain religious experience.

William James made effort to justify religion by his empathic-descriptive exploration of religious experience and an explanatory account of it. He believed in the healing that comes from a spiritual power within one's deepest being. His scientific and academic background notwithstanding, James was convinced that physical and psychological healings did take place as a result of the teachings and practices advocated by the mind-cure movement.[172] James believed that there are potential forms of consciousness entirely different from our typical waking consciousness, including the "subliminal self" which connects us to the regenerative energy of the spiritual world, a dimension of reality experienced at the truest level of our selfhood while at the same time analytically and objectively distinct from our conscious personality.[173]

Following James' radical empiricism, there is today much current interest among empirical psychologist in developing tests for correlating religiousness, spirituality, mental health, and other alternate measures of religiosity. Research on religious development at various stages of life, conversion, meditation, mysticism, and coping process can all help toward a greater understanding of Christian wholism as it impacts one's religious life at different levels.

James speaks of the other forms of consciousness, other dimensions of reality, and the complex intertwining of the psyche and the spiritual. His approach and perspectives through his psychical research, even though at times very similar to those of New Age thoughts, point to a wholistic realm where all these "realities," "dimensions of life" intersect and fuse.

Carl Gustav Jung (1875-1961) was a Swiss psychiatrist and psychologist, who founded analytical psychology. He came from a Lutheran Christian background, and his father as well as many of his uncles were clergymen. His fascination with the unconscious and psychopathology led him to formulate the archetypes—typical, primordial patterns of energy and behavior. There are the archetypes of the collective unconscious, which is deep and universal. They stand in contrast to the contents of the personal unconscious—the shadow with repressed, forgotten memories and emotions—which are superficial and individual and consist of feeling-toned complexes.

The collective unconscious "has contents and modes of behavior that are more or less the same everywhere and in all individuals. It is, in other words, identical in all men and thus constitutes a common psychic substrate of a suprapersonal nature which is present in every one of us." [174] The archetypes of the collective unconscious, according to Jung, are inborn images and symbols pointing to the basic themes and fundamental motifs of our existence. They reside in the deepest stratum of the human mind and as such remain unmasked and hidden from us. However, representations of these archetypes can be discerned through symbols, fairy tales, folklore, legends, myths, esoteric teachings, in different religion and culture throughout human history.

Carl Jung's depth psychology (emphasizing personality in terms of unconscious processes) sees religion as inextricably and vitally bound up with essential human dispositions. These dispositions are derived from the "collective unconscious," whose archetypes represent the forms and patterns of experience of countless human generations and their pre-human ancestors, preserved in the form of various mythical images and ideas.

Jung differed from Freud on the psychology of the unconscious by going beyond Freud's emphasis on infantile sexuality to a person's general and religious history. Jung also emphasized the reality of the soul and incorporated it in his discussion of analytical psychology and religion. The Bible, to Jung, is a book to be respected for those stories and symbols which touch upon the meaning of life and death, evil and suffering, sin and guilt, love and healing, as well as forgiveness. Christ is the divine model of the intersection between the divine and the human and the psyche and soul is where such interaction takes place. The cross which is the ultimate symbol of the interaction between the divine vertical and the human horizontal, is where the ego needs to die so that the soul and psyche can more abundantly live.

Jung found the archetypical concept mentioned in the writings of Philo, Irenaeus, Augustine's *ideae principales,* and Plato's *eidos.* Of interest, the God archetype for the Christian is the *imago Dei,* the image of God imprinted in the unconscious mind of every human being. He believes that humans must learn how to harness the conscious and the unconscious aspects of the psyche. He makes a distinction between ego and self—the former is the center of consciousness whereas the latter is the center of one's total personality which consists of both the conscious and the unconscious. Individuation is the developmental process by which the center of personality shifts from ego to self. As a person proceeds in individuation, he/she becomes more whole and able to find healing through creative solutions for their problems.[175] Individuation is the lifelong process of striving toward psychic balance and wholeness. It is accomplished through the progressive differentiation of the unconscious contents and their integration into consciousness. [176]

According to Jung, the self is the totality of the psyche's conscious and unconscious components in the archetype of wholeness. It comprises the full scope of a personality from its most individual traits to its most generic attitudes and experiences, actual as well as potential.[177] The archetype of wholeness or of the self can be regarded as the dominant of psychic growth.

A crude analogy would be the model of our computer with which the text of our discussion is being typed. There is that original text, the conscious component as it were, but there are also the "markups," corrections, formatting, deletions, additions in red or blue ink representing the unconscious (unseen, i.e.) that go to making up the final product of this text. Clicking the view icon for the original text with the markups will reveal all the hidden corrections. Psychologically it may be useful to view the hidden markups to trace the journey of what it takes to arrive at the final text, to learn past mistakes, to change the existing text which has incorporated the markups, in order to achieve an even better text (a more wholesome, healed life with harmony in all dimensions). Thus wholeness is a process, a progressive ongoing revision of the existing text taking into consideration both the conscious as well as the unconscious elements of our psyche. The inner unification that Jung speaks about is the fusing of the "conscious" existing text with the "unconscious" hidden markups to result in a better life, the final text.

Besides the concept of the collective unconscious, Jung elaborated on personality types of extroversion versus introversion, feeling versus thinking, intuiting versus sensing. According to Jung, intuition (*L. intueri*—to look at or into) is a basic psychological function which mediates perceptions in an unconscious way. Everything, whether outer or inner objects or their relationships, can be the focus of this perception. The peculiarity of intuition is that it is neither sense perception, nor feeling, nor intellectual inference, although it may also appear in these forms. In intuition, a content presents itself whole and complete, without our being able to explain or discover how this content came into existence. Intuition is a kind of instinctive apprehension, no matter of what contents. Like sensation, it is an irrational function of perception. As with sensation, its contents have the character of being "given," in contrast to the "derived" or "produced" character of thinking and feeling. Intuitive knowledge possesses an intrinsic certainty and conviction....[178] He argues for inner unification through active imagination; creative expressions through painting, sculpting, writing, dancing as means to integrate the unconscious as part of the human healing process; and also the symbolic value of dreams in psychotherapy.

Jung discusses the religious function of the soul (*psyche)* in Psychology and Alchemy. He states, "I have been accused of 'deifying the soul.' Not I, but God Himself has deified it! I did not attribute a religious function to the soul, I merely produced the facts which prove that the soul is *naturaliter religiosa,* i.e., possesses a religious function... For it is obvious that far too many people are incapable of establishing a connection between the sacred figures and their own psyche: they cannot see to what extent the equivalent images lie dormant in their own unconscious." [179]

In the context of Christian wholism, one can detect certain concurring statements when Jung speaks of the psyche's drive toward wholeness. [180]

## Psychology of Religion and Christian Wholism

Psychology of religion, historically, referred to the scholarly "analysis of psychological meanings, origins and patterns in religious ideation and practice," through the application of psychological theories and methods. It has become a broad intellectual discipline seeking to explore and interpret the cultural phenomenon of religion as it keeps pace with advances in metapsychological, experimental, empirical, phenomenological, humanistic, transpersonal, socio-biological, and nuerocognitive approaches. It has integrated with sociology, anthropology, political theory, and other academic enterprises that examine ethno-feminist and other cultural issues.

Sigmund Freud theorized religion as an attempt, in moments of weakness, to reclaim the protective care of the seemingly all-powerful father of early childhood. Caught in the Oedipus complex of fantasies of incest with mother and parricide accompanied by fear of castration, the child experiences castration anxiety and murderous hatred for the father, and abandons the Oedipal fantasies in a renunciation that Freud considered the first moral. The superego, according to Freud, is derived from the memory of the father's forbidding voice connected with castration anxiety, which sets the pattern for later moral interaction with other paternal figures including God and social authorities. Freud concluded that the female equivalent to castration anxiety is penis envy, which generates a weaker form of morality and a weaker connection to civilization. Women...show less sense of justice...more often influenced in their judgments by feelings of affection or hostility. Such androcentric language would sound very offensive to our contemporary culture.

Freud's views of religion and morality have been the subject of criticism and frequently becoming themselves the subject of psychological analysis.[181] More positive views of religion have been championed by British object relations theorists Guntrip and Winnicott who argue that religion by offering a sense of cosmic connection and validation serves as a kind of psychotherapy that—as long as it resists neurotic distortion—promotes better and more satisfying interpersonal relationships. In addition to Freud's two realms of human ideation (an infantile, autistic one to which religion belongs and a mature, reality-oriented one, predominantly the world of science), Winnicott posits an illusory, intermediate area of experience, the contents of which help all of us bridge inner and outer realities. Adults cope with life through continuing elaboration of the intermediate sphere, in the diverse forms of human culture, including religion. Viewed from such a perspective, religion is not something to be outgrown as an infantile experience, but a potentially vital resource for the fullest realization of human ideals. Psychologists here come very close to say religion is a path to wholeness.

Carl Gustave Jung in 1913 took exception to Freud's view in psychoanalysis as referred above when he published *Psychology of the Unconscious.*

Ego psychologist Erik Erikson locates the ontogenetic origins of religion in the early mother-child relationship. Erikson argues that these origins testify not to religion's immaturity as theorized by Freud, but to its association with the most fundamental needs and longings of the human species. Not only does religion universalize the first stage of personality development in trust and mistrust but also confirm the most basic virtue, hope and its mature derivative, faith. Religion also provides support for the attainment of wisdom, the vital virtue of the last of Erickson's eight stages, that of old age.

Humanistic psychologist Erich Fromm returns to authoritarian religious traditions which enjoin obedient submission to a reigning transcendent power, foster feelings of diminution, guilt, sorrow. He describes the humanistic religious traditions, which center in humankind and its strengths, as promoting self-realization and a corresponding attitude of joy. Rollo May contrasts religion that functions as refuge for weakness with religion that serves as a source of strength. Abraham Maslow distinguishes "peakers" who have intensely personal, religious, or peak experiences and use them for personal growth and fulfillment and those "non-peakers" who repress such experiences. Maslow advocates a new humanistic psychology of self-actualization that would promote such peak experiences.

Gestalt Therapy—an existential-humanistic form of psychotherapy, which is based on the assumption that individuals have within themselves all they need to achieve personal wholeness and to live effectively. Therapy focuses on living in the present and acting on awareness to finish an unfinished business resulting from failing to act on important past awareness—unexpressed feelings of anger, guilt, pain, hatred, jealousy and other negative emotions. The completed experience is a Gestalt.

Unless a person is aware that he/she lacks wholeness (harmony in life and peace and joy in living), no action is forthcoming, and therefore no change is anticipated. Gestalt therapy stresses action rather than talk or analysis or understanding or intellectual rumination. Questions take the form of "What is your guilt?" "How do you experience your guilt?" and not asking "Why you think you have this guilt?"

Gestalt excludes the reality of a supernatural power that makes personal wholeness possible. It downplays the cognitive dimension of a person and deemphasizes one's responsibility to others even while speaking of one's responsibility to self for making necessary changes. Specific techniques include experiments in dialogue, completing unfinished business, playing the projection, reversals, exaggeration, guided fantasy, and dream work.

In the context of Christian wholism, human lostness and brokenness are major unfinished business both for the individual as well as for God. What is needed is a divine Gestalt.

Psychologist Wulff is wary of any disposition to reduce religion to some simple formula to be explained away by psychological mechanism. On the other hand, psychologists who are frequently disdainful of religion, view with suspicion of any theory or study that tends to valorize or promote religion. Wulff admits that psychologists of religion are rarely disinterested investigators—

they act to promote or demote religion, based on their own experience and sensibilities and prior judgment about the nature of religion.

Contemporary pluralism may be evident of health and potential creativity for the field of psychology. One needs a closer look at a number of fundamental issues, such as assumptions, methods and goals in the context of today's religious pluralism and postmodernism. We should ask for clarification of the role of personal religious perspectives and agendas that shape one's evaluative work in the field.

Diane Jonte-Pace of Santa Clara University, editor of *Religious Studies Review*, in her essay "Analysts, Critics, and Inclusivists—Feminist voices in the psychology of religion," includes feminist critical responses to Freud's theory of the gendered origins of religion and morality. In her responses to Jung's approach, she also quotes literature's recent criticism that although Jung valued the feminine, he did not value women, that his model of God despite incorporating feminine and masculine, material and spiritual cannot transcend its foundations in androcentricm, gender essentialism, and ideologies of female inferiority.

Bonnie Miller-McLemore, Professor of Pastoral theology at Vanderbilt University Divinity School speaks about feminist transformations in pastoral theology in the context of shaping the future of religion and psychology. Psychology is considered as a tool for the enhancement of the faithful care of others. It is also a cultural force that shapes moral ideals and spiritual hopes and hence requires critical evaluation. In the two-way interaction between psychology and religion/theology as scholarly disciplines, "religion is not simply an object of study, but rather a body of beliefs and practices about ultimate and mystical dimensions of life to be encountered, experienced, tried, and perhaps followed." There has been a reassessment of the core functions of pastoral care. In addition to the traditional functions of healing, sustaining, guiding and reconciling, four additional practices have received recent attention. They include resistance (confrontation with evil, contesting violent behaviors), empowerment (advocacy of and giving resources and means to the vulnerable and those deprived of power), nurturance (passionate and dedicated proclamation of love that creates the possibility for difficult change) and liberation (escape from unjust affliction and release into new life and wholeness as loved people of God). As mentioned earlier, here is an example of how psychology has integrated with sociology, feminism, and political theory as it enters dialogue with religion.

William Barnard of Southern Methodist University summarizes his reflections on "psychology as a religion". It is interesting to note that he defines psychology as a humanistically oriented psychotherapy which helps one become more whole, fulfilled, congruent, and aligned with depth. Religion does not refer to a church's preoccupation or institutionalized religious practice or a set of authorized theological dogmas, but to "spirituality" that explores the depth of reality and consciousness, and traces the source; heals, enlivens and fulfills.[182]

Barnard raises the question of who the legitimate players are in this sub-field of "psychology as a religion." He includes Carl Jung, transpersonal theorists Abraham Maslow, Ken Wilber, David Levin, and probably William James. What about the mesmerists, theosophists, neo-pagans, and New Agers? Do they count as part of the 'canon,'" asks Barnard. "Or is their thought too 'low-brow' to be seriously considered?" Barnard's answer to the canon question is an emphatic "yes." It is his hope that since many academics have embraced postmodernism with its suspicion of rationality's hegemony, and its belief that we all understand the world through the lens of our particularity, New Age thought might get a fair and respectful hearing in the overall exchange between psychology and religion.

Can psychology collaborate with religion in promoting mental and spiritual wholeness? A more pragmatic question might be: How can psychology collaborate with religion/theology in providing resources for coping with modern-day life? There is a growing body of research pointing to religion's potential role in being such a crucial resource for life's struggles in the face of ill health, intense suffering, life-threatening crises, and brokenness at every level.

Theologians and religionists tend to assert that theology and religion are not reducible to psychological dynamics. God is not simply our projection in our infantile stage of development.

Psychological insights, methods and theories can indeed illuminate religious faith and practice. Theology and religious knowledge, on the other hand, can facilitate psychologists' understanding of clients in their clinical work. Both scholarly disciplines of religion (specifically Christian theology) and psychology, with their respective presuppositions and concerns, have unique contributions to make toward humanity's wholeness. They can join hands in freeing the souls and psyches from the grip of sin and despair by encouraging dialogue between, and integration of, psychology and religion toward the goal of Christian wholism.

## Psycho-Neuro-Endocrino-Immunology

The last two decades have seen an exponential growth of knowledge in the field of molecular biology, genetics, biochemistry, neurochemistry, neurophysiology, endocrinology, immunology, pharmacology, psychology and psychiatry. What started out as a science called psychobiology to study the interdependence of behavior and biological determinants has widened the search for pathways linking the human nervous systems and the immune system. Since the central nervous system including the brain, the substrate of our mind, has everything to do with "spirit/soul," and the immune system being crucial to our health, the significance of their interactions is readily apparent. Brain, of course, is not mind, but without the brain, there is no mind. The mind is where the human spirit dwells and through it God and humans communicate. See my discussion under Christian anthropology earlier in this chapter.

I argue that the concept of Christian Wholism which stresses the interdependence and harmonious development of all the dimensions of personhood is further validated by scientific research and application that address the biological foundation of psychoneuroendocrinoimmunology. A bold attempt has begun to unlock the "mysteries" of the anatomic structures, pathways, the biochemical substances, the physiological processes, the signalers and receptors involved in the mediation of psychological states and human behavior. Research in this area of molecular biology and neurophysiochemistry has far-reaching implications for the

Christian concept of human nature, human personality, the "soul" and spirituality, and ultimately Christian wholism.

Researchers in biological sciences generally follow Darwinian evolutionary theories and proceed from materialistic, reductionistic assumptions. In other words, all manifestations of the mind, all psychological states, emotions, will, judgment, behaviors, are ultimately reducible to and explainable by neural activities, i.e. biochemicoelectrical events. I shall argue against the fallacy of such assumptions and projects.

Reductionism in science and its implications for Christian Wholism, body-soul and brain-mind interaction will be examined in Chapter 7.

Now returning to the research on psychoneuroimmunology and its implications, the anxiety on the part of some Christians is understandable, especially for those who believe in the duality of human nature consisting of the physical body and a spiritual soul which assumes a conscious, independent existence after physical death. The apprehension is the more troubling if all mental activities peculiar to humans can be traced to biochemicoelectric events of neurons in the brain, threatening the concept of an immortal soul residing in a person's body. Such perception of unease within the Christian community exists even though at present the question remains unanswered as to exactly how and when electrical firings of neurons as observed in the sodium-potassium exchange across the cellular membrane correlate with thoughts, emotions, will, freedom of choice, the totality of human cognitive and emotive experience we call mind. For those who are interested in a fuller discussion on this subject, I recommend reading in my "Toward a New Definition of Soul."[183] My understanding of human nature and composition is included in the discussions in Chapter 4, beginning on page 89.

With such a concept of "soul" and human nature described in Chapter 4, there should be no anxiety about the research findings from science. On the contrary, every new discovery that unlocks the complex, coordinated, interdependent functions of the mind and body can only accrue to our Creator's genius and glory. So let us examine how the science of psychoneuroendocrinoimmunology can further buttress the wholistic linkage of the multidimensional person.

A brief background of the interactions of brain and the human immune system sets the stage for our discussion. Virologist Fred Rasmussen, Jr. and psychiatrist Norma Brill since the 1950s have studied the impact of stressful life experiences on susceptibility to infection which was experimentally induced. Later John Hadden discovered the presence of *B*-adrenergic receptors on lymphocytes establishing the link between the sympathetic nervous system, which is closely associated with emotions (fear, fight, flight, elation, excitement, stressfulness and their counterparts) and the immune system of which lymphocytes play crucial roles. About the same time, Robert Ader and Nicholas Cohen demonstrated suppression of the immune system through behavioral conditioning.

Roger Bartrop and his research associates in clinical studies established changes in the immune system associated with grief and bereavement following spousal death. Hugo Besedovsky first mapped out a neuroendocrinoimmunologic network with his research on the effects of immunity on neuroendocrine function.

David and Suzanne Felten documented the sympathetic innervation of lymphoid tissues and Karen Bullock established sympathetic neural connection to the thymus. Furthermore, Edwin Blalock and Eric Smith proved that lymphocytes themselves could produce neuropeptides.

Thus a new era of exploding research began on lymphocytes and on finding their receptors for hormones and neurotransmitters. Concurrent research has also been directed to sympathetic nervous system on immunity, conditioned immune responses, correlation between depression and immunity, the effects of stressful life experiences on the immune system and resistance to disease, progression of AIDS and psychosocial factors, immunologic effects on behavior. Increasingly, brain-immunity research has included psychological and behavioral components. [184]

So what is this relatively new scientific discipline and what does it have to do with Christian wholism under discussion? In the following pages, I shall attempt sketching the contours of a big picture that would situate psychoneuroimmunology in the overall inquiry about wholism.

Psychoneuroendocrinoimmunology is an interdisciplinary study of the interactions among psychological, behavioral, neural, endocrine function, and immune system processes. Human adaptation is the product of a single, integrated network of defenses. "Each component of this defensive network serves specialized functions and, at the same time, monitors and responds to information derived from the others. Psychonueroimmunology studies the relationship among these systems. This integrative strategy…is necessary because …it is not possible to obtain a full understanding of immunoregulatory processes without considering the organism and the internal and external environment in which immune responses take place. Two pathways bridge the brain and the immune system: autonomic nervous system activity and neuroendocrine outflow from the pituitary. Primary and secondary lymphoid organs are sympathetically innervated, and these nerve fibers form neuroeffector junctions with lymphocytes, monocytes, macrophages, and granulocytes that possess receptors for these neurotransmitters.

Of interest are studies that show the neural and neuroendocrine effects on immune processes, the role of sleep and fever in immunity and health,[185] the central and peripheral action of cytokines on neural, neuroendocrine, and immunologic processes and on behavior,[186] the effects of behavior and stressful life experiences on immune function, immunologic effects of acute and chronic physical and psychosocial stressors,[187] immune changes associated with aging,[188] depression,[189] autoimmune and infectious disease, possible implication of the immune system in cardio-vascular disease and schizophrenia.

David Felten et al. claim that psychological stressors are transduced into modifications of neurotransmitters and neuro- and immunopeptides. The limbic-hypothalamo-pituitary axes and the hypothalamo-sympathetic axes are the two main efferent pathways affecting neuroendocrine, autonomic, and immune functions under stress.[190] There is interindividual variability of stress-induced endocrine and immune modifications. Immune impairment is associated with higher levels of perceived stress, ineffective coping, depression, and low social support.

Denise Bellinger have shown that "Noradrenergic sympathetic. Cholinergic, and peptidergic nerves fibers distribute to both primary and secondary lymphoid organs among cells of the immune system.... Immune cell products, such as cytokines, lymphokines, lymphotoxins, and chemokines, can be released from lymphoid cells and modulate nerve terminal activity, viability, and neurotransmitter release."[191]

The central nervous system (CNS) modulates immune functions through its regulation of autonomic and neuroendocrine outflow pathways that connect to organs and cells of the immune system. Recent research has also shown that "products of immune cells can communicate to the central nervous system, potently altering neural activity such as behavior, hormone release, and autonomic function. In this capacity the immune cells function as a diffuse sense organ, informing the CNS about events occurring in the periphery regarding infection and injury. Thus, the brain and immune system form a bidirectional communication network, with immune products signaling the brain, and the brain regulating immune function and coordinating host defense." Cytokine Interleukin-1 is a messenger from the immune system signaling to the brain. How the message is delivered is not quite settled. Perhaps it i initiates the cascade that leads to the release of those hormones to produce energy in preparation for its defense work. Interleukin-2 and interferon also participate in the mechanisms of host defense and immune response. They are produced by T-helper cells on antigenic challenges of the immune system.[192]

Experimental and clinical trials have shown interactions of exogenous and immune cell-derived endogenous opiods (*B*-endorphin, enkephlin, dynorphin) with nociceptors, resulting in the inhibition of inflammatory pain.[193]

It appears that we are witnessing a paradigm shift in the research under discussion. It is that "immunoregulatory processes can no longer be studied as the independent activity of an autonomous immune system."[194] I argue that such a paradigm shift is also occurring in the study of health. It is that health can no longer be studied as the independent aspect of human experience of an autonomous physicality. There needs to be a wholistic approach encompassing all the various dimensions including the spiritual, physical, psychological, mental, intellectual, emotional, social, relational, cultural, environmental components that inter- dependently affect the state of a person's health.

It is not the purpose of this book to delve into the very technical and complex data in psychoneuroendocrinoimmunology. As Sir Isaac Newton reflected upon his own life in his last days on earth, he remarked, "I do not know what I may appear to the world; but to myself...I have been...like a boy playing on the seashore, and diverting myself... finding a smoother pebble, or a prettier shell... whilst the great ocean of truth lay all undiscovered before me."[195] From our finite knowledge of what is revealed to us by God through the sciences, we can glimpse the infinite wisdom and grandeur of the Eternal One who shall some day recreate our resurrected body.

The big picture that I want to construct begins to take shape as we follow the contours of our discussions on psychoneuro- endocrinoimmunology: Beginning from the spiritual composition of our being with its cognitive and emotional aspects of religious life, through the mental-intellectual dimension and psychological components, to the physical dynamics of health and immunity defense which is influenced by psychosocial factors and one's environment, the loop of wholistic relatedness finally closes. That interrelatedness is secure in God's making, enhancement and preservation. To put it in practical terms, the spiritual experience which begins in the highest faculty of the mind at zenith signals an emotional response. It is then translated into actions and behavior, which through the pathways and neurotransmitters signal the body's cellular and immune response that science now is able to locate and map out. But this is only part of the story. There is a bidirectional pathway by which the immunal, hormonal, neural events at the nadiral pole of the loop also effect what transpires at the spiritual/mental zenith, as borne out by research studies enumerated above.

Such a construct, though intimated and intuited, clearly now rests on biblical as well as scientific foundation. Christian Wholism, I therefore argue, can be examined by scientists and non- scientists, theologians and non-theologians alike.

## Christian Wholism and Sexuality

That human sexuality is a significant dimension of the person requires little argument. God created us male and female. He is the Creator who designs the anatomy and physiology of sex and programs the sexual desire and stimulus. His purpose is to give us wholeness in the sexual union, whose byproduct is transcendent joy. Much wisdom and care have constituted His provisions for satisfying the human sexual need and intimacy.

To structure a definition of sex or sexuality in the Biblical and Christian context, even against the background of scientific knowledge, one needs to return to Genesis 2:7 where it reads, "God formed the man (fashioning and arranging all the cells, tissues, organs and systems) from the dust of the ground and breathed into his nostrils the breath of life, and the man became a living being." "So God created man in His own image, in the image of God He created him; male and female He created them" (Gen. 1:27). "God saw all that He had made and it was very good" (Gen. 1:31). What was very good included maleness and femaleness—sexuality.

Humans are created as relational beings, to reflect the image of the Godhead. Intertrinitarian relationship is reflective of the Godhead, as Jesus and God the Father spoke of each other in intimate terms At Jesus' baptism, the father said, "This is my beloved Son, whom I love...the Spirit of God descending...." Matt. 3:16-17. Thus all three persons of the Godhead were participating. At Gethsemane, Jesus cried out, "My God, my God, why hast Thou forsaken me?" Mk. 15:34. This prophetic, loving relationship model exemplified by the Godhead is to be part of the image of God to be reproduced in Adam and Eve. So it can be deduced and not unreasonable to assume that aside from its procreational function, sex is intended to have a relational significance. Clifford Penner, a Christian clinical psychologist with theology training and his wife Joyce Penner concur on this point.[196]

But is the relational dimension confined only to the physical and emotional? Both the Old and New Testaments provide many illustrations symbolizing the relationship of God with His people or Christ with His church in the intimate language as found in the relationship between husband and wife (the Book of Hosea and

Ezekiel 16). The Hebrew word *yada* "to know" referring to sexual intercourse is the same word used for man's "knowing God" (Gen. 4:1,17,25; Jer. 16:21).[197] I shall argue that sexual union, in its most ideal setting, is the artful, total integration of the spiritual, mental, emotional, physical being between husband and wife. However, in the fallen nature of humans, this ideal is infrequently attained and often perverted.

In Ephesians 5:25-33, the Apostle Paul uses the sexual symbolism to describe the relationship between the church (the body of Christian believers) and Christ and calls it a profound mystery. [198]

The Psalmist exclaims, "...No *good* thing does He withhold from those who walk uprightly." Psa. 84:11. "In thy presence there is fullness of joy; at thy right hand are *pleasures* forever more." Psa.16:11. Is sexuality something good, something pleasurable? If not, why did God create it in the first place? But if so, why would He remove it from Heaven and deny it to the resurrected body? [199]

I shall maintain that every truly good experience in this life is a micro-preview and foretaste of what is in store for the believers in the life to come. And as a corollary, every dastard encounter and heart-breaking event can only drive the man and woman of faith to that hope of a resurrected body—the ultimate antithesis of human tragedy and cosmic evil.

If God's original intent was for man and woman to become one flesh as the culmination of their physical, mental emotional, social and spiritual union in quintessential wholeness, might it not be that this is what is portended for the new Earth with our resurrected bodies? We dare ask such question, based on what we know and on the premise that male sexuality and female sexuality are complementary to each other—neither is perfect without the other. On this earth, it may be safely assumed that a man will never completely understand a woman's sexuality and psyche and vice versa, simply because the counterpart has a different biologic and anatomic makeup. It may be in Heaven God will combine these two complementary entities into one glorious resurrected body— the ultimate realization of the *telos* of Christian Wholism. With some imagination, it is not difficult to even postulate the anatomic realities. [200] Further discussions on sexuality and sexual ethics will be taken up in other and later chapters.

**Chapter Summary:** I have argued in this chapter that to be psychologically whole in the context of Christian wholism is for a person to have a realistic view of oneself and others; to learn acceptance of others as well as self; to live in the present, while aiming at long-term goals informed by past experience; to abide by values and one's belief-system; to have goals; to experience a feeling of belonging, worthiness, and to be sustained by a sense of competence, purpose, direction, and wanting to make a difference in life. In addition, a wholistic person continues to learn how to manage some of the destructive or unpleasant emotions such as anger, jealousy, envy, fear, anxiety, sorrow, pain, and suffering. We have also examined psychology and religion, psychoneuro-endocrinoimmunolgy, and discussed how their contributions could be helpful in achieving wholeness, healing, peace and joy. Toward the end of this chapter, we have also begun the conversation on human sexuality in the context of Christian Wholism, reserving a fuller examination under Christian ethics in the next chapter.

Having traversed the psychological terrain of our human existence, we can now construct a Christian wholeness model beginning at the central core of self which has been made whole through God's grace and by His power. From this center, the ever-expanding concentric circle of wholeness and interrelatedness first touches one's husband or wife, children, family and relatives. Then it widens to reach to friends, church, community, society, nation, then the world, the environment, the universe. Finally it ends where it has started in God from whose Being ultimate wholeness originates. As the circle of Christian wholism broadens, it bestows healing on marriage and friendship. It promotes genuine, caring church fellowship. It champions responsible citizenship and lives out the notion of universal brotherhood and sisterhood. It supports stewardship of the environment as essential to ecological wholeness in God's creation. And all along Christian Wholism seeks to grasp the hand of God—to exchange sin and brokenness for healing. There, near the heart of God, wholism replaces pressure and pain for peace, fear and jitters for joy, lostness for salvation, and fragmentary life for wholistic living.

# CHAPTER 6

---

## CHRISTIAN WHOLISM IN LIGHT OF
## CHRISTIAN ETHICS, CULTURE, ECOLOGY

### Christian Ethics and Christian Wholism

To inquire how Christian Wholism is in anyway related to Christian ethics, we must first examine what constitutes the discipline or the conceptual framework of Christian ethics.

In a postmodern, post-*shoah* world, morality, ethical norm, certainty, and secure borders for religion, philosophy and sovereign states are things of the past. Still for those with religious faith and ethical grounding, life's tragedies are challenges to be confronted with and to learn from. Peace, joy, healing, wholeness are forever beckoning. And justice remains an ethical quest.

As I defined earlier, Christian Wholism as a belief and practice that is grounded in God's creation of the human as a unitary whole person with physical, mental-intellectual, emotional, relational, socio-cultural, and spiritual dimensions in a dynamic interaction with the environment, the ecosystem. It involves a progressive integration of the spiritual attributes of love, justice, faith, hope, freedom, creativity, humility, and forgiveness along with the other dimensions of personhood in an ongoing process of peace and joy toward a perfectly harmonious development intended by God. This ideal will not be realizable in our lifetime. Its quest is a lifelong ongoing process with the ultimate expression only in our resurrected life at the Parousia.

I have argued all along that Christian Wholism is the path to peace, joy, and healing here and now as well as there and then for eternity.

In this chapter I shall only focus on the ethical relevance of Christian wholism. I submit that ethics is a lifelong discipline learning how to be the moral person in wholeness by the grace of God. It involves one's seeking to analyze and internalize the criteria of good and bad, right and wrong. It calls for the systematic study of reflective choices and attainable goals in its horizontal encounter with humanity.

I submit that Christian wholism can better inform an ethicist in the postmodern world. It will help in the decision-making deliberations on many biomedical and crucial ethical issues confronting us today—euthanasia, beginning and end of life issues, stem cell research, cloning, war and peace, justice and environmental ethical issues, as one reflects on and internalizes the essence of humanity whose *telos* (goal, end, purpose, rest, destiny) is wholeness.

The concept of Christian Wholism which encompasses one's personhood in various expressions including the ethical dimension, is an answer to human lostness as well as humanity's flourishing.

First a brief review. In the traditional academic setting, ethics is one of the three main branches of theology or philosophy. The other two are (1) ontology—the study of the nature of existence or being; investigating among other things origin, cause, order, relation, truth, perfection, ultimate purpose, reality; sometimes a synonym for metaphysics; and (2) epistemology—probing into the origin, nature, methods, theories and limits of human knowledge. How do we know what we know?

*Ethics,* [201] viewed in the context of scholarly philosophical or theological pursuit in the classical mode, commonly follows *the study of goodness (decision about good and evil) and the study of right action (decision about right and wrong),* [202] with other subbranches variously named applied ethics (normative ethics with direct bearing on practice and systems for decision-making guidance, such as biomedical ethics, business ethics, legal ethics, environmental ethics, and so forth); metaethics (semantics of ethical language and logic of its usage); casuistry (emphasis on particular cases and situations); moral psychology; and metaphysics of moral responsibility.

Normative ethics is concerned about identifying norms and standards for good and right behavior, decision-making, and outcome. "How we ought to behave. What should one do under the circumstance? What kind of person should I be? What relevant norms or standards or prior case study should we appeal to? Why certain standards and not others in a particular situation? Are the norms reasonable or appropriate in the present circumstance even if they worked well in prior situations? What are the ethical implications of our decision-making and what might the outcome be? These and other questions seeking a right course of action toward a life of goodness and justice with personal and social concerns constitute the ethical discourse in normative ethics.

The divisions of different branches of ethics are not distinct and the categorical descriptions are relative. The fundamental question in ethics which repeatedly demands our attention is: *What man or woman ought to be and to do in light of the truth as perceived?*

For the study of goodness, the term *teleological* (emphasizing orientation to ends or final goals) is often attached because it is the pursuit of goodness and happiness as the goal and end for one's life and that of others (*telos*, Greek for end, goal, fulfillment). When the value aspect of the goodness is stressed, such theory is axiological. The discipline in pursuing 'the good' is formalized as:

(1) Egoism (feeling good and pleasure, hedonism, Epicurism, with Ayn Rand and others as its modern exponents).

(2) Perfectionism (doing well and excelling at worthwhile things, championed by Plato, Aristotle, the Stoics, Thomas Hobbes, Friedrich Nietzsche). Aristotle argues that human good and happiness (*eudaimonia)* largely consists in being actively virtuous (and therefore the study of virtue ethics, preceded some 150 years by Confucius in China who also stressed the virtuous person being the goal of ethics and morality)[203] tying what is desirable to what is admirable in life in a rather distinctive way.[204] Contemporary proponents of virtue ethics include Alasdair MacIntyre, Stanley Hauerwas, and others.

(3) Consequentialism and Utilitarianism (Jeremy Bentham 1748-1832, English jurist and philosopher), John Stuart Mill (1806-73), and Henry Sidgwick (1838-1900)—*the greatest happiness and*

*utility for the greatest number of people with the presumption of a knowledge as to what constitutes the greatest happiness.* [205]

The ethical inquiry into what constitutes *right action* triggers one's concerns about the principles of right and wrong that govern our ethical decision-making and moral choices.[206] The task aims at defining what these ethical norms are and their justification. The norms vary from the Christian's commands of God, Biblical teaching of axiomatic principles (whose truth is self-evident upon reflection, thus intuitionism), to formalism *(Kantian categorical imperative*—"act only according to those maxims that can be consistently willed as a universal law," and rationality), and contractarianism (The Rawlsian ethic—a mixture of Kantian ethics and Lockean and Rousseauian social contracts—social cooperation among equals based on agreement reached after open debate and rational deliberation). All these norms, whether divine commands and biblical derivatives; self-evident truths or universal law; social contracts and mutual agreement, generally *invoke the presumed moral nature of humans a binding, obligatory duty (thus deontological ethics;* Greek *deont,* that which is binding and due).

By specifying the norms and ethical principles, one in essence asserts that a right action (doing what is right) is determined not just by the ends or the goal of achieving the "good" or happiness, but more importantly by an independent set of criteria of moral obligations, such as the Ten commandments and other Biblical teaching, justice, fairness, human rights, the Kantian imperatives, other axiomatic truths.[207] To illustrate, lying is against morality and ethics, not just because it leads to bad consequences in inter-personal relationship and social mistrust (against the good for all concerned), but is morally inexcusable in that it violates the higher ethical norm as described above. For Kant, truth-telling is a categorical imperative (a set of fundamental ideas in terms of which all other ideas can be expressed).[208] This categorical imperative or the ethical norm of universal application is arrived at from the observation that if every one lied constantly, there would be total disruption of the social fabric. Human social intercourse would grind to a stop.

The justification for the *ethical norms* finds its sources in the Bible (for the Christians); sovereignty of reason (for Kant and his followers); intuitive apprehension of truth that is self-evident (for the intuitionists); fairness of procedure and hypothetical consent of the governed (for the Rawlsian advocates); the wisdom of the prescription for promoting certain goals (for those who believe in their fundamental duty to promote certain ends of morality); the Hippocratic, the Geneva and other medical oaths (for physicians); and the U.S. Constitution (for American public servants). The list is long and changing with the times.

**Christian Ethics As Distinctly Wholistic**
Having acquainted ourselves with the general domain of ethics, we shall now turn our attention to Christian ethics. By definition, Christian ethics is ethics with a Christian orientation and biblical perspectives. Its distinctives which address the whole person, I shall argue, can become evident as we analyze the following characteristics:

A. Christian-Biblical ethics is distinctive in that it is grounded in a set of referential norms expressed in commands, Biblical imperatives, The Ten Commandments, principles, narratives, Sermon on the Mount, the life and teachings of Jesus as recorded in the New testament. Richard J. Mouw, armed with a safety-net of the need for philosophical tentativeness, nevertheless asserts, "For the Christian, the awareness of God's revealed moral directives should play a similar role (meaning a reference point in offering a theory of moral justification and appeal to reflective moral agency ) in moral philosophical theorizing. "If there is a God who has publicly announced moral preferences, then those moral publications should function as basic reference points for testing our accounts of moral meaning and value."[209] I argue that God's revealed moral directives and publicly announced moral preferences are embodied in His commandments and in the biblical teachings, which address the <u>needs of the whole person.</u> If so, they ought to serve uniquely and distinctly as the reference points and guides for our ethical deliberation and quest for wholeness.[210]

B. Christian ethics distinguishes itself not so much as drawing upon the norms, principles, rules, teachings from a Book called the Bible, because Hebraic ethics also bases its validation on a book called Tanach (Hebrew *Torah* law, *Nebehiim* the prophets,

*Kethubhim other writings*) and Muslim morality is based on the book of Koran. The distinction is found rather in the recurrent all-encompassing themes of love [211]; justice, [212] concern for the neighbor,[213] the disadvantaged [214]; grace and forgiveness (forgiving and even loving the enemy)[215]; the sinfulness of human nature[216]; the naked powerlessness to do the ethical task [217]; the problem of salvation from, healing and making whole of, not just immoral and unethical choices, but ultimately sin, evil and death.[218] I submit that that the believer's resurrected body is the ultimate wholistic answer to these existential problems presented in the Bible.[219]

C. The unique characteristic of Christian-Biblical ethics is implicit in its affirmation of a Creator-God who is the source of morality, who sets the requirements for ethical compliance for His created humankind, and who is also the Enabler and Forgiver of our human striving for obedient conformity to His commands. In mystery and wonder beyond our comprehension, the moral God who knows no sin will gift the sinner with wholeness and perfect restoration in a resurrected body which knows no corruption but reflects only God's ultimate moral nature. This Christian assertion sets it apart from all the relativistic, secular, and other theological ethics which assign no or little significance to the ultimate moral Being.

Christian ethics underscores the reality of a Creator of this moral universe in which are found certain absolute laws of morality and ethics that make the total human and wholistic fulfillment possible, not simply in this earthly life, but even more so, primarily in the life to come. Waldo Beach and H. Richard Niebuhr have similar thoughts when they write, "Biblical ethics begins with God and ends with Him. In this it is distinguished from those types of ethical thought which begin with the requirements of human nature or define human happiness or perfection as the final goal...."[220] Mouw sums up well when he concludes toward the end of his book, "Like all of the other expressions of our human restlessness, our moral quest can only find a satisfying resting-place when we arrive at the Divine Source." [221]

D. Christian-Biblical ethics is distinctively, wholistically unique in another very important aspect. The one who embraces it, speaking ideally, is a Christian who has been or in the process of being made whole, who in profound gratitude realizes his or her ethical obligation and moral mandate. The realization is underscored by one's overpowering sense of having been the recipient of God's grace and forgiveness, which are undeserved and unmerited. From this stance, the Christian ethicist desires to emulate Christ the supreme ethical Being who treats every human being with justice, dignity, and moral transparency. It is my observation that out of an "ethical" heart which has been made whole and which seeks to imitate the wholistic, ideal ethical norm, flows naturally his or her ethical conduct.

The virtue ethicist emphasizes the development of one's character and virtuous passions as central to moral decision-making. Richard Mouw notes that "Obedience to God's commands can also be seen as intimately connected to a concern for developing moral character in the human commandee.... Similarly, the development of character need not be treated as an alternative to an emphasis on decision making; it can itself be an important part of the preparation *for* decision making....It is important simply to be a friendly, patient, and good-hearted person, and it is in the 'little' situations of life where we often show very clearly 'what we are made of' morally."[222] With God's empowerment and instruction by His Spirit, the ethical ideals in the Sermon on the Mount, which at times seems to be humanly impossible, can be made do-able here and now in our Christian walk. [223]

That there is a vital nexus between the kind of ethical judgment one makes and what kind of person he or she is as reflected in one's character, experience, worldview, beliefs, lifestyle, is not a difficult conclusion to draw after some reflection. Since none of us is a detached, neutral observer or a *tabula rasa,* we bring with us to every ethical discourse and confrontation our particular set of presuppositions, perceptions, and core convictions. One's presupposition sets the framework of interpretation. The eye follows where the heart leads and what the mind conceives. Thus, *Christian ethics* which is person-centered and character-based is not just a set of standards to follow, important as standards are; it is much more than that.[224] It is not simply deciding what is good or evil, or which is the right or wrong action, critical as such deliberation is for any ethical task. It is all that and even more. It is ways of seeing, basic beliefs, and loyalties of the heart.

Lewis Smedes writes, "The commandments (as reference points for Christian ethics) tell us to do what we (everyone in this world) already know we should do," one can see that Smedes is arguing that every human being on this earth has in varying degree some residual moral knowledge of right and wrong as a result of his or her being created in the image of God. I agree. But life experience informs us that in some, this "spark of divinity" and moral residue are so attenuated, that by all appearance the embers are certainly not aglowing. Even those whose moral sense has been less corrupted by sin are still found far off from the ideal ethical norm and moral quintessence. What I am suggesting here is that mere moral knowledge is insufficient to meet the challenge as set by the kind of Christian ethical ideals embodied in the life and teaching of Jesus, the personification of God's moral being. It takes, I submit, a total transformation of the person through a spiritual rebirth, yes, a new creation as spoken by Paul (2 Cor. 5:17), to be the ethical person from whom shall flow the ethical judgment and concerns.

To sum up, I have argued that the *ethical person* as he/she has been transformed by the power of God and made whole by His Spirit, is central to the task in ethical decision-making. It is more than simply "doing" Christian ethics by anyone; *it is being the Christian moral person by the grace of God.* This stance leads me to redefine Christian ethics in the context of Christian Wholism:

**Thus in my view, Christian ethics is more appropriately thought of as a lifelong discipline in which one seeks not only to analyze and internalize the criteria of good and evil, right and wrong in the systematic study of reflective choices and attainable goals, but also in the midst of such pursuit learns** *to be* **and** *to do* **that which glorifies God.[225] To glorify God,** *inter alia,* **is to conform to His revealed will and purpose in Scripture, nature, history, one's own life, society, community, the Church, and more importantly to reflect Christ's character.[226] Reflecting Christ's character includes imitating His attributes of love and forgiveness; His truth and justice; His wisdom and purpose; His humility and obedience, His faith**

and hope, His goodness, ethicity, concern for the neighbor and the disadvantaged; as well as freedom, power and creativity.[227] In the context of Christian Wholism, to glorify God most certainly includes one's being made whole as well as committing oneself to making others whole through education, mentorship, modeling, and service.

So what do the theory and practice of ethics mean in the context of Christian wholism? Let me propose the following analytical schema for ethical decisions:

The schema consists of a triangle. At the apex of the triangle are the **Christian norms** (love, justice, freedom, creativity, human value, stewardship, humility, eschatological vision) **and biblical principles** for ethical discourse (teleological—goodness and happiness as the goal/end for oneself and others–formalized as perfectionism, utilitarianism; and deontological—right action independent of the pursuit of goodness, happiness and pleasure which must be subordinate to some binding obligation such as divine command or honesty, justice, beneficence, non-maleficence, equality, fairness, human right, Kantian categorical imperative).

At the bottom right of the triangle are located the **person in need** of caring, healing, and being made whole; or the ethical issue related to the Person, awaiting for resolution; or the threat to the integrity or rights of the Person and his/her property, clamoring for relief.

To the left of the bottom of the triangle are clustered a whole array of **situational factors**—the needy person's family, relatives and friends; his or her community, church and denomination; the person's employment, finance, insurance; his and her mission and vocation, loyalties to and interests in persons, groups, social causes and spiritual aspirations, national and global involvement; legal implications, Federal, State and regional laws and regulations; consent and confidentiality issues, conflict of interest; research protocol and human experimentation; human reproductive technology; emergency and life-death dilemmas. The list goes on.

In the center of the triangle stands the so called "Ethicist"—the minister, the professor, the philosopher, the medical doctor, the nurse, the psychologist, the counselor, the lawyer, the scientist, the next-door neighbor and whoever he or she may be "doing ethics" in that situation and at that time.

The Ethicist, here particularly the **Christian Ethicist**, is called upon to use discerningly the **Norms and Principles** described above, and to **apply them to the Person** in need or the **Issue related to the Person,** against the backdrop and **taking into consideration of** the entire constellation of **Situational Concerns**.

In describing the Christian Ethicist in the center of the triangle, emphasis is laid on the fact that none of us is a detached and neutral observer or a *tabula rasa*. The Ethicist brings with him/her a particular set of presuppositions, perceptions, belief-system, and faith-loyalties dimension. The core beliefs of the heart predicate the analysis by the mind, which often frames what our eyes see and what our ears hear.

The ethicist in this schema is one who has been made whole by God in multiple dimensions of his/her personhood, especially in the spiritual, moral and ethical realms. He comes to the ethical decision scene fully realizing his own brokenness and ethical limitations. Such intellectual humility delivers one from the trap of ethical arrogance in believing that one's deliberative conclusion is beyond questioning and as such it is worthy of intrusive paternalizing. For a Christian wholist, there should always be that self-acknowledgment of tentativeness in her ethical deliberation, realizing full well she herself is in the process of being made ethically whole.

At the apex of the triangle regarding the ethical norms, wholism mandates that such norms include principles, rules, trajectories reflecting the various dimensions of human living in which ethics plays a crucial role. Love, compassion, freedom, autonomy in personal life; justice, equality, respect, truth, human value, freedom in society; forbearance, tolerance, reciprocity in social relations; stewardship, entrustment, balance in ecology. And the list goes on.

To the right at the bottom of the triangle, the ethicist made whole is to apply the above-described norms to the person who is lost, broken, in need of healing, peace and joy, and burdened with problems awaiting a wholistic solution.

To the left of the triangle is the cluster of situational factors including spiritual, family-personal, psychological, ethical, sociocultural, economic, legal, political influences that impact on that person needing ethical advice and direction. Christian wholism emphasizes being sensitive to these situational factors in order to set the ethical deliberation against a whole background of elements that have bearing on the ethical issue under discussion. Such wholistic approach does justice to the ethicist as well as the one needing ethical assistance and most of all brings to the deliberative and decision process a richness and comprehensiveness which otherwise might be missing.

In sum, wholistic ethics advances the integrated and wholistic concept and practice of facilitating the transfer of wholeness from the ethicist made whole to the ethically fragmented individual and his/her problems, against a whole panoply of situational factors bearing on the subject. The outcome test for the success of such wholistic ethics may be the generating of peace and joy for the person in need, the satisfactory resolution of his/her problems as well as ethical proficiency in future decision making.

**Sexual Ethics and Christian Wholism**

Since this book's main focus is not sexual ethics with all the social and political implications that follow in tandem, I shall only comment briefly on God's purpose in gifting us sexuality as well as abortion and homosexuality and leave other subjects for another venue. Issues on sexuality are among the most contentious in political and sociocultural debates. The reasons are not hard to locate, since sex, gender, personhood, autonomy, freedom, rights, are some of the fundamental core values that shape our lives and make us into the kind of persons we are. For a fuller discussion on a variety of ethical issues, please refer to my other writings.[228]

In Genesis 1:27, 28, God created humans as male and female, and intended them to be fruitful and multiply. Genital sexuality with pleasure is implied and made essential for procreation. For what He had made, including the anatomy, physiology, sexual drive and orgasmic response, total union of all dimensions of a person, He pronounced, "very good." In Genesis 2:24, husband and wife are supposed to be united in one flesh. Does the 'one flesh' imagery connote more than mere genital complementarity and union? Some theologians and psychologists argue that an erotic sexuality is implied. Such eros addresses the whole person in all dimensions of passion, emotion, intellect, spiritual, and physical interaction. It teaches creative completion of one's personhood and integration with another human being. It opens up the person to the experiences of greater levels of self-acceptance and growth.[229] Human sexuality also has a symbolic function. It mirrors the Trinitarian relations of unity and differentiation—one essence with three distinct Persons. Sexual union in marriage also symbolizes the relationship between Christ and the Church, God and His people. For additional discussion, please refer to Chapter 5.

The word abortion is not mentioned in the Bible and with rare exception is there any specific Biblical text that speaks directly to this subject (abortion in our modern context). Most scholars concur on this point. However, our God is One who is eager to share with us about who He is and what He has, including wisdom (here gifted to us as wisdom for Christian discernment). I am confident that in the Word of God, under the guidance of the Holy Spirit, and aided by our sanctified intellect, moral guidance on the question of abortion can be discovered.

I shall begin from Creation. We derive life and power from the Creator. Life is a gift from God, precious and unique, and is not to be trivialized. Abortion, therefore, requires prayerful thought and serious deliberation. Human life, however, valuable as it is and important enough for the Son of God to sacrifice Himself for its ultimate redemption, does not possess the highest value in the totality of experience and our Divine-human interactions on earth. At times, a higher value perceived as one's heart conviction and measured against Biblical standards, that calls for the termination of a certain life, is legitimate and should be honored.

In the Protestant grand tradition, freedom of individual conscience is a veritable attribute based on the limited freedom and autonomy God has gifted us. This Biblical concept of human freedom can be inferred from Gen. 2:16; Josh. 24:15; Isa. 1:19,20; Isa. 55; Mt. 23:37; Lk. 15; Jn. 7:17; 1 Pet. 5:2; Rev. 22:17 and others. The fact that we have been created in the image of God (Gen. 1:27) means, among other things, that we have been gifted with whatever God possesses, though in a less degree and limited scope. What we have been gifted includes our limited freedom endowed by our Creator. It follows then that a woman must have the final say, using this limited freedom, in deciding whether or not to abort. To coerce someone to make this decision or deny her of this choice is antithetical to our Christian understanding. A further point that can be made is that the exercise of freedom by the mother <u>ought to be balanced against</u> her accountability to God, her commitment to the faith community, to the larger society, and obedience to the laws of the land.

The task of Christian ethics is both this-worldly and proleptic. The ethical orientation to this world requires us to see **justice** modeled in our theory and practice on the question of abortion. Our eschatological vision helps us to see that all our human striving is approximation of that heavenly ideal. Our task is always in the midst of a creation "that has been groaning"... "as we wait eagerly...for our redemption" (Rom. 8:22-23). In the interim, our Christian commitment must stretch us beyond the immediate reflection on abortion to tangible ways to educate others on the principles of Christian sexuality and family planning. This includes the prevention of unwanted pregnancy as well as the consequences of irresponsibility. How to strengthen family relationship obviating situations that may lead to the need for abortions or perpetuate teenage pregnancies should also be on the agenda. We ought to teach Christian principles expressed through moral behavior that tells the world that Christians stand for something—value of life, compassion for the mother, belief in individual conscience and responsible freedom. **The Christian message must include the condemnation of dehumanizing life, triviality of recreational sex, irresponsible parenthood, sex-gender injustice, and religious bias towards women who make the final, responsible choices on issues surrounding pregnancy**. And this message is most effective, and I argue, only effective, when it is instantiated by our redemptive caring.

On the subject of homosexuality in the context of Christian wholism, some suggestions for practical solutions are hereby offered:

1) For individual Christians who are born with or postnatally acquired "homosexual orientation" in a milieu of complex

developmental, psychological, relational history, they should be encouraged toward the direction of abstinence from homosexual activity when attempts to converting from homosexual to heterosexual sexual expressions have failed.

The Christian value system places one's relationship with God and other humans as paramount according to God's original creational intent (man and woman uniting to form a family and bonding community for rearing children). Humans are to love God and their neighbors as themselves. Sexual drives and desires, either heterosexual or homoerotic, ultimately must be surrendered to the control of His Spirit. Humans are to glorify God in whatever they do, including sexual expression, with proper boundaries. When expression runs counter to the Biblical model, sublimation of desire and self-denial may be the best course. Many celibate, consecrated Christians down through the ages have testified to the reality of such self-denying lifestyle. Christian communities have successfully modeled a bonding and loving support system, which is emotionally highly satisfying and sexually comparable to the ideal heterosexual context without actual sexual genital relations.

2) For Christian churches wrestling with homosexuals outside and within the church, it is of no purpose or good theology to label AIDS (acquired immunodeficiency syndrome), the "gay disease" as God's punishment for the gay community. Many AIDS patients have contracted the disease through no fault of their own or their lifestyle. Some have been infected through life-saving blood transfusions during surgery or in emergency or because of their hemophilia. Some were born of AIDS parents, while others are victims of heterosexual marital relations with their HIV positive husbands due to ignorance. Many other situations could be cited for such unfortunate patients who certainly are not God's targets for vengeance.

3) Christians must always give the clear message of the Biblical value system which emphasizes the sanctity of marriage and family and God's original design for the humans. In word and deed, Christians ought to speak up against gay activism and the bold gay agenda in schools and politics, especially advertisement to depict the homosexual lifestyle as an equally valid alternative. This is not done at the expense of gays' civil rights against discrimination in

the job and housing market. Christian love and tolerance do not equate with Christian cowardice and blind acceptance. The lives of generations of Christian youth and the foundations of Christian sexual ethics are at stake in view of the far-reaching implications of homoeroticism.

4) Since ministers, school teachers, pathfinders, boy-scout and girl-scout leaders have important modeling roles for traditional Christian values, they must not be individuals who live or advocate a homosexual lifestyle. For congregational members who openly flout the rules against their homoeroticism to the detriment of youth and the morale of the church community, they should be approached with love, dialogue, persuasion and prayers. When such measures fail to effect changes, definitive church policy measure must be instituted to prevent the continuation of such negative influence by these individuals. In order not to confuse the Christian message, same-sex marriage or adoption of children by same-sex couples ought not to be condoned within or outside the church by Christian ministers. Christians, clergy and lay, nonetheless, should always be ready to counsel and help in the spirit of Christian love while defending the Biblical truth.

5) For members who are born with homosexual "orientation," who desire by the grace of God to overcome the inclination, they must receive the full support of the church. There have been, contrary to the opinions by some pessimists, successful rehabilitation of homosexual oriented individuals resulting in a changed lifestyle, involvement with the opposite sex, and even ending in heterosexual marriage. For those who find it difficult or "impossible" to change to heterosexuality, it is suggested that the church ask the particular member to abstain homosexual genital acts if he or she wants to remain as members. For a redemptive church who wants to reach out to sinners as Christ did while on earth, the decision to ban church fellowship must ever be a heart-wrenching last resort after much prayer, counseling and consultation. One only has to recall that Jesus reserved the harshest condemnation, not for the sexual offenders, but for the Pharisees with pride, arrogance, and self-righteousness.

6) Individuals who have confirmed "homosexual orientation," who truly and openly live a disciplined life of abstinence, it seems

to me, ought not be barred from church activities and membership. From a practical point of view, there is no way of knowing about one's homosexual orientation unless the persons confesses it or through his or her set of likes and dislikes, social preference or demeanor, the latter of which understandingly are imprecise and always subject to interpretation. Only overt and publicly confessed homoeroticism can be used as a basis for church disapproval and constitute the grounds for discipline.

7) Whether homosexually oriented individuals who live a disciplined celibate life and shun any homosexual physical acts ought to be ordained is a question many churches are still wrestling with. Perhaps during the ordination interview, a "don't ask, don't tell" policy might be an option.

8) Education, prevention, and modeling of a healthy family dynamic must be the church's priorities in its total program of healing and ministry. The message to save the sick and the lost must ever be grounded in love, compassion, and forgiveness. The Church's mission, among others, is to proclaim that Christian wholeness and the fruit of the Spirit of love, joy, peace are within the reach of every sincere Christian. Jesus says, "And whoever comes to me, I will never drive away" Jn. 6:37. God is eager to restore to wholeness everyone who puts his/her trust in Him according to His perfect design for humanity.

### Music, Arts, Literature, and Christian Wholism

The importance of music in the Christian life and culture needs little refutation. In the cosmic drama of earth's creation, Jesus' incarnation, Christ's second coming, the grand resurrection, and the believers' final gathering in Heaven as portrayed in God's word, all these singular events were celebrated by music and singing. The Lord asked Job, "Where were you when I laid the earth's foundation...or who laid its cornerstone—while the morning stars sang together and all the angels shouted for joy? Job 38:4,7. One could imagine the glorious music resounding in Heaven and earth at the birth of the God-man Jesus when "Suddenly a great company of the heavenly host appeared with the angel, praising God and saying, "Glory to God in the highest, and on earth peace to men (and women) on whom His favor rests." Lk. 2:13,14. The Apostle Paul calls to our attention, "Listen, I tell you a mystery: We will not all sleep, but we will all be changed—in a flash, in the twinkling of an eye, at the last trumpet. For the trumpet will sound, and the dead will be raised imperishable, and we will be changed...."1Cor.15:51-52. And in Revelation 19:1,6,7, the Apostle John sees and hears in vision, "After this I heard what sounded like the roar of a great multitude in Heaven shouting: Hallelujah! Salvation and glory and power belong to our God...Then I heard what sounded like a great multitude, like the roar of rushing waters and like loud peals of thunder, shouting: Hallelujah! For our Lord God Almighty reigns. Let us rejoice and be glad and give Him glory!"

One may ask: What do all these passages have to do with wholism? I shall argue that when the good earth was created (some 5.5 billion years ago) and fashioned and made habitable for Adam and Eve and humanity some 6-10,000 years ago, God's creation was "very good," perfect and whole, without brokenness of sin and disruption by evil. This epochal event was celebrated with music by the angels as recorded in Job as quoted in the preceding paragraph. Then came the Fall which made necessary God's intrusion into human history through the God-man Jesus whose mission it was to make whole what was lost. There was nothing more appropriate than an angelic praise choir for such a redemptive provision. Lk.2. Then music and trumpet will usher in the triumphant resurrection of those who have been in the process of being made whole and restored to God's original wholistic design for the human person. And finally, what better medium there is than the combined voices of praise and gratitude from the redeemed thundering through space and time and eternity in celebration of the completion of God's task in making and remaking whole men and women, the crowning work of His creation! Rev. 19.

It was no coincidence that from the earliest history that God has gifted humans with musical talents—Jubal playing with strings and pipes (*kinnor* and *ugab*), Gen. 4:21. Throughout the Old Testament and the New Testament, we have stories of music and God's commanding us to sing and play instruments in praises to Him.

How David's harp music was used as a form of therapy to restore Saul' spiritual and psychological wholeness is found in 1Sam16: 14-23. "Whenever the spirit from God came upon Saul, David would take his harp and play. Then relief would come to Saul; he would feel better, and the evil spirit would leave him." [230] For the miraculous deliverance through the Red Sea on dry ground following the pursuit by the Egyptian armies, Moses and his people lifted up their souls in praise and gratitude with the song of Moses and Miriam, "I will sing to the Lord, for He is highly exalted…The Lord is my strength and my song; He has become my salvation… (Exo. 14 and 15).

In my view, the metaphor employed here by Moses saying, "The Lord is my song" is highly significant in the context of Christian whiolism. The God who is interested in making us whole in peace and joy is like a song which lifts our spirit and floods our soul with hope, courage, new energy, and rapturous delight. Franz Schubert (1797-1828), the prolific Austrian composer of *Ave Maria* fame,[231] captures music's heavenly dimension in his composition *An die Music*, when the lyrics by Franz von Schober read, *"Du holde Kunst in wieviel grauen Stunden, wo mich des Lebens wilder Kreis umstrickt, Has du mein Herz, zu warmer Lieb' entzunden, Has mich in eine bess're Welt entruckt, in eine bess're Welt entruckt. Oft hat ein Seufzer, dein er Harf entflossen, Ein susser heiliger Akkord von dir, Den Himmel bes'rer Zeiten mirer schlossen, Du holde Kunst, ich danke dir dafur, du holde Kunst, ich danke dir.* Translated the song in paraphrase tells us, "You lovely art, in how many grey, dreary hours, when life's circle of wildness entrapped me, have you fired my heart with warm love and lifted me to a better world! Often a sigh, escaped from your harp, a sweet, holy chord of yours, has opened a heaven of better times for me. You sweet, lovely, wondrous, wholesome, life-enhancing art, for that I thank you!

Shakespeare's line in Twelfth-Night, "If music be the food of love, play on; give me excess of it …" was set to music by the great English composer Henry Purcell (pronounced Pursel) to lyrics, "If music be the food of love, sing on, sing on, sing on, till I am fill'd, am fill'd with joy…" These instances give us insight into the universal human perception of music as the harbinger of joy, the hallmark of wholeness.

In the book of Psalms, there are many passages exhorting us to sing to the Lord and praise His name for what He has done for us and the created order. Psa.9,13,18,21,30,33,47,51,57,59,61,66,67, 68,71,96, 98, 100, 105,138, 144, 147, 149. The last book in Psalms ends with, "Praise Him with...trumpets...the harp and lyre...tambourine...the strings and flute...cymbals...resounding cymbals. Let everything that has breath praise the Lord." Psa. 150: 3-6.

Jesus no doubt was comforted as he participated singing a hymn with the disciples in the upper room before His crucifixion. Mt. 26:30. After disappointment, persecution, the death of the other Apostles, in his own lonely exile, the Apostle John took courage as he in vision heard the grand chorale encircling the throne of God, including "every creature in Heaven and on earth and under the earth and on the sea, and all that is in them, singing, 'To Him who sits on the throne and to the Lamb be praise and honor and glory and power, for ever and ever.'" "Hallelujah! For our Lord God Almighty reigns." Rev. 3:13-14; 19:6.

Does God sing? In Zephaniah 3:17 we read, "The Lord your God is with you, He is mighty to save. He will take great delight in you, He will quiet you with His love, He will rejoice over you with singing." Expressing Himself through the subsidiary mode of humanity in Jesus, God partakes of joyous occasions with singing.[232] And why not? In the range of soprano, alto, tenor and bass, and other ranges we have not even heard or thought about, the Redeemer shall join in in the Heavenly Choir as the Master conductor and sometimes as soloist, so I suspect.

In his own trials and sufferings while death was never far away, the Apostle Paul admonished the Ephesians and all of us, "Speak to one another with psalms, hymns and spiritual songs. Sing and make music in your heart to the Lord, always giving thanks to God the Father for everything, in the name of our Lord Jesus Christ." Eph. 5:19. To make music in our heart, there must be some musical inventory in our head and memory to make music from.

I shall argue that Christians wholistically bent should store in their memory at least 40 to 100 hymnal tunes, which at moments of low moods and unexpected trials can automatically spring forth in our heart, diffusing faith, hope and assurance of God's love, power, and intimacy. These internalized hymns are a strong deterrent to depression and restlessness.

Throughout the centuries, music has always been a central part of worship, liturgy, Christian movement, evangelistic outreach, at birth, in weddings, during baptisms, beside the sick beds, in farewells and at funerals. Christmas and Easter would be unthinkable without music. Wolfgang Mozart, a Catholic, has enriched the Christian world with his heavenly melodies *Ave verum, Regina coeli, Laudate Dominum,* and numerous other compositions. Johann Bach, a Protestant, has left a legacy of inspirational music of *Wachet Auf, Ruft uns die Stimme (Sleepers Awake), Jesu, Joy of Men's Desiring, Sheep May Safely Graze, Bist Du Bei Mir (Thou art with me), A Mighty Fortress is Our God, O Sacred Head Now Wounded from the Passion Chorale with lyrics by Bernard of Clairvaux, and many others.* Ludwig Beethoven's *Creation Hymn (Die Ehre Gottes aus der Natur);* Joseph Haydn's *The Heavens Are Telling;* Georges Bizet's *Agnes Dei,* Franz Lizst's *Un Sospiro,* and Charles Gounod's *Sanctus.* And who can forget George Frideric Handel's *Ombra Mai Fu, Largo, The Messiah's Hallelujah Chorus, I know That My Redeemer Liveth and scores of others.*

In the Catholic and Protestant traditions, untold oceans of peace and joy have flowed from the hymns by Ambrose, Zwingli, Isaac Watts, Charles and John Wesleys, John Newton, William Cowper, Henry Lyte, William Monk, Fanny Crosby, J. H. Gilmore, Sarah Adams, Lowell Mason, E. A. Hoffman, Maltbie Babcock, Horatio spafford, Thomas Ken, Louis Bourgeois. The list goes on.

In the context of Christian Wholism, what can music contribute? Aristotle and Plato believed that "music...directly imitates the passions or states of the soul—gentleness, anger, courage, temperance, and their opposites and other qualities; hence when one listens to music that kindles a certain passion, he becomes imbued with the same passion; and if over a long time he habitually listens to the kind of music that arouses ignoble passions his whole character will be shaped to an ignoble form. In short, if one listens to the wrong kind of music he will become the wrong kind of person; but conversely if he listens to the right kind of music he will tend to become the right kind of person.[233]

The Chinese philosopher Lin Yutang quoted Confucius as saying that if one should desire to know whether a kingdom is well-governed, if its morals are good or bad, the quality of its music will furnish the answer....Character is the backbone of our human culture, and music is the flowering of character." [234] Frank Gaebelein warned that "those areas of thought and activity that are closest to our humanness and our relation to God are most severely twisted by the bentness in us."[235] Manfred Clynes, a pianist, neurophysiologist, inventor and researcher observed, "Music in fact is an organization created to dictate feeling to the listener. The composer is an unrelenting dictator and we choose to subject ourselves to him, when we listen to his music."[236]

There is a widespread belief even among Christians and Christian leaders and musicians that music is per se neutral, without moral qualities either for good or evil, that morality has to do with human actions and relations, and nothing to do with notes, rhythm, harmony, tone color, tempo or melody of a musical composition. Or there is that corollary that as long as the lyrics include Christian terminology or religious words, it matters not what style of music (hard rock, heavy metal, techno rap, hip-hop, reggae, punk, ska, retro, and what not) is adopted. This is a mistaken position, in my view, since the impact of undesirable music is the music itself in that the words are either not clearly articulated or they do not matter at all.

No argument, however, is made here that there are different criteria for moral and ethical discourse and aesthetic and musical evaluation. The latter emphasizes content, unity, variety, creativity, balance, integrity, climax, logic, harmony, rhythm, phrasing, accentuation, and a feeling of inevitability.

Laying aside the morality issue, I shall argue that since we are made in the image of God we have been programmed with a particular bodily and mental rhythms reflecting peace and order of a wholistic person in which all the different spheres are working harmoniously. A crude example would be the quiet humming of a complicated piece of machinery in operation. One can easily detect the malfunction when extraneous noise is heard signaling that the machinery is breaking down. Music which can powerfully affect one's emotions, is in fact a form of emotion communication. "the tonal structures we call "music" bear a close logical similarity to the forms of human feeling....The patterns of music is that ...form worked out in pure, measured sound and silence. Music is a tonal analog of emotive life." [237]

Manfred Clynes tells how musicians can manipulate the pitch and loudness of individual tones to embody essentic forms in a melody line (how the expression of emotion occurs through certain predictable forms). This is achieved much the same way as tone of voice is modulated to make a sentence meaningful. A melody has direct access to engender the emotional quality in the listener without the need of auxiliary symbolism (words for example). It can touch the heart as directly as can a physical touch. A caress or an exclamation of joy in music needs not to be consciously translated into a touch caress or a physical 'jump for joy' to be perceived as of such a quality. It does so directly through perception of essentic form.[238] Thus music can communicate emotions and messages without words.

So how does music convey emotions? It does so through the melody—the horizontal arrangement of musical notes, which is the most prominent and identifying part of the musical piece. A good melody should incorporate rise and fall with pitches going up and down within an acceptable range; must include satisfying proportions with beginning, middle and ending giving a sense of completeness; must at some point come to a climax, usually at the end with a resolution (a sense of peace and a feeling of rest); must be such that evokes an emotional response by the listener. A beautiful melody leaves an indelible, recurrent impression in our mind, an aesthetic experience we want to return time and again. [239]

Music also conveys emotions through harmony, the vertical structure of the musical piece with chord structures. It provides personality to the piece with consonance and dissonance. It has been said that melody mainly responds to the Spirit, harmony to the mind, and rhythm to the body, with obvious overlapping.

Then there is the rhythm which is the driving force of music. It is defined as the orderly movement of music through time. Just as the heartbeat is the life of the body, rhythm is the life of the music and provides its essential energy. Without rhythm, music is dead. Melody and harmony must unfold together, and rhythm makes the simultaneous unfolding possible.[240]

In the discussion of wholism, I argue that music impacts our emotions powerfully, could alter our mind and affect the body. And emotions in turn are interrelated to other dimensions of our person. Good music then is what contributes to our wholeness resulting in peace and joy and bad music is what results in the dampening of our cognitive functions, in the loss of our affinity for the spiritual, and the diminution of inner peace and genuine joy. Cultural conditioning, repeated exposure, association with pleasant or unpleasant life experiences are factors among others that add to the variables. One may ask, "Does Handel's Messiah hold as much meaning and emotional power for a Buddhist monk than a devout Christian musician?"

Using a balanced set of criteria however construed, there should be a great deal of concern regarding listening to music. Admittedly there is much good music conducive to our Christian walk in the category of contemporary Christian music. Certain kinds of contemporary music, however, specifically the hard rock variety in its various genre, must compel our strict scrutiny. The deleterious effects of the loud, relentless beat which is one defining quality of rock, have been explored by both Christian and non-Christian leaders, theologians and scientists. I ask, "When could the "still, small voice of God" speak to our brokenness and our fallen state amidst the cacophony of discordant noises and shouts and wails?" The potential of rock for altering consciousness, its effect on the mind, spirit, Christian life style, with its association with overt aggression, violence, and lessening resistance to illicit sex and drug culture must be critically examined if one is seriously thinking about the concept and practice of Christian wholism. [241]

Under the Science Section of *Time* was the headline—Music on the Brain, the writer reports a conference "The Biological Foundations of Music" sponsored by the New York Academy of Sciences," which experts in neuroscience and neurology, brain imaging and psychology met to exchange ideas and research projects. What seems clear to the scientists is that the ability to experience and react to music is deeply embedded in the biology of the nervous system. While music tends to be processed mostly in the right hemisphere of the brain, no singe set of cells is devoted to the task. Different networks of neurons are activated, depending on whether a person is listening to music or playing an instrument, and whether or not the music involves lyrics.

Some German scientists using faint magnetic fields emitted by the brains of professional musicians, showed that intensive practice of an instrument leads to discernible enlargement of parts of he cerebral cortex, which is most closely associated with higher brain function. And there is also indication that music can affect levels of various hormones—including cortisol (has to do with arousal and stress), testosterone (male sex hormone involved with aggression and arousal), oxytocin (nurturing behavior), and endogenous opioids (endorphins). In addition, using PET scan (positron emission tomography), Dr. Zatorre has shown that the parts of the brain involving processing emotion seem to light up with activity when a subject hears music. Such studies further validate what Christian Wholism has asserted about the interrelatedness of all the dimensions of a person. [242]

Like music, other art forms, and literature can also impact our total person in various dimensions. The lights and shadows, shades and tones in painting complementarily produce the wholistic artistic impression, whose beauty speaks to our soul. Artistic excellence energizes our mind; its beauty lifts our spirit. Its chromatic harmony eases our tensed muscles, its vivid imagery puts a spring to our steps.

The negative space together with the mass of a sculpture invites our circumferential inspection to obtain a wholistic impression of its art with balance, rhythm, proportion, dynamism, perhaps asymmetrical symmetry of a geometric or biomorphic form. The lofty architecture lifts our visual focus far and high to remind us we are only part of the whole ecocomplex. And who can be unmoved as poetry and other literary form evoke that transcendent reality engulfed by cosmic wholeness, peace, joy and mystery?

Involvement in projects of outreach and Christian mission endeavor reconfirms the brokenness in us and others everywhere in the world. God's gift of wholeness is never given for our own private consumption. It is meant to be shared, and in sharing this gift of wholeness, we ourselves are made whole again and again.

## Christian Wholism in the Area of Finance

Jesus while on earth spoke more about wealth and poverty than He did on doctrines and church. For Christians, the attitudes towards financial matters, money, and wealth spread through a wide spectrum. In our present day culture, there are the health and wealth gospel and a theology which argues for promised material blessings as authenticating God's approval. In previous eras, self-denial, the vow of poverty, unfeigned rejection of anything monetary, and spirituality's disdain for wealth were common. Modern liberation theology condemns wealth concentrated in a minority even if the wealth is ethically acquired. Most Christians stand somewhere in between with qualified or unspoken approval for wealth acquisition as not being contrary to the will of God. That riches could have the imprimatur of the most high comes from a citation of 1 Kings 3:13, when God promised Solomon what He would give him in his lifetime. God said to Solomon, "Since this is your heart's desire and you have not asked for wealth, riches and honor...I will also give you wealth, riches and honor, such as no king who was before you ever had and none after you will ever have." 2 Chr. 1:11,12.

Centuries before, God spoke through Moses, "But remember the Lord your God, for it is He who gives you the ability to produce wealth...." Deut. 8:18. Some of the patriarchs and God's stalwarts like Abraham, Lot, Job, David were given great wealth in their lifetime and riches were often a sign of God's blessings on His covenanted children.

In Jesus' first announcement of His mission on earth, He called attention to, "The Spirit of the Lord is on me, because He has anointed me to preach good news to the poor." Lk. 4:18. Jesus himself was a man without earthly wealth even though He possesses everything made that was made. "Foxes have holes and birds of the air have nests, but the Son of Man has no place to lay His head." Lk. 9:58.

And to the young rich ruler who asked, "What must I do to inherit eternal life?" Jesus answered, "...Sell everything you have and give to the poor, and you will have treasure in heaven. Then come, follow me." Lk. 18:22. Some Christians interpret this passage to mean that Jesus was condemning the rich ruler for his wealth. I like to think that what Jesus was concerned is not the illegitimacy of wealth but the sole reliance and idolatry of wealth that stood between the ruler and eternal life. Thus the idolization of riches must be removed and the riches transposed from his heart to hi spirit in preparation for a life of service in following the master's footsteps. After the rich ruler apparently declined a paradigm shift, Jesus commented, "How hard it is for the rich to enter the Kingdom of God! Indeed it is easier for a camel to go through the eye of a needle than for a rich man to enter the kingdom of God." Lk. 18: 24-25. The camel is the largest animal in the surroundings and the needle hole is symbolically the smallest. Jesus' hyperbole is effectively employed to call attention to the fact how impossible it is to gain eternal life by relying on one's effort, wealth, and human work, but without God's grace. This is so, not just for the rich, but for everyone who has other idols like the idol of wealth for the rich young man. "Who then can be saved?" asked the disciples. "With man this is impossible, but not with God; All things are possible with God," Jesus answered. Mk. 10:27. With God's empowering, the camel beast is transformed into a needle threader (also called a camel in some regions of the world). Such a camel slips through the needle hole with facile agility!

The earlier Protestant ethos in financial matters was energized by John Wesley's advice, "Make as much (money) as you can; save as much as you can; give as much as you can."

All wealth ultimately can be traced to God the Creator. The abundance of resources provided by God for humanity's use and enjoyment are incalculable. They include land crops, harvests of all varieties of fruits and nuts, forestry and lumber, minerals, oil deposits, fish and treasures from the sea, cattle on a thousand hills, human ingenuity, physical labor, commerce, inventions, scientific discoveries, genetic engineering in agriculture and animal industry, and the list is by no means exhaustive. These earthly material gifts and provisions by God and goods and human services are converted into different forms of purchasing power, such as paper cash, silver and gold, securities (bills, notes, bonds from government and commercial banks), equities (common and preferred stocks.), land and other property ownership, human capital of labor and intellect. The precious metal gold and silver in the Bible are symbols of wealth and blessings. It was one of the birthday gifts for Jesus by the Magi. Precious as it is, gold is worth next to nothing for a starving person when there is no food available for purchase. Riches, symbols of wealth, money and other medium of exchange, all are relative based on demand and supply, financial and political stability. During the World Wars, people used wheelbarrows to transport German marks which were so depreciated so to be worth almost nothing. A Christian's treasure is not of this world; it is safeguarded in Heaven.

How then is finance important in Christian Wholism if indeed it is? It is not money but the lust for money that is the root of evil. Money idolatry destabilizes the equilibrium so essential in achieving wholeness, peace and joy in one's life. The all-absorbing pursuit of material wealth inevitably results in neglect in other spheres of one's personhood and wholeness. Spiritual growth, intellectual development, physical and emotional nurture, relational structures of family and community, and social concerns are all pushed aside by the obscene ambition to be rich for riches' sake.

Money in the hands of dedicated Christians can be means for the extension of God's kingdom on earth. It is food for the hungry, shelter for the poor, education for the disadvantaged, health and healing for the sick. It can even promote peace, harmony and wholeness in the family and among friends. According to many researches, money or lack of it is at the top of factors contributing to marital dispute and breakup, and probably church dissolution.

"Give me neither poverty nor riches, but give me only my daily bread. Otherwise, I may have too much and disown you and say, 'Who is the Lord?' or I may become poor and steal, and so dishonor the name of my God." Prov. 30: 8, 9. Is it possible that many Christians are not wealthy because they cannot be trusted with wealth and riches without risking their eternal destiny? God in His mercy withholds certain material goods from His people as He foresees what the possible consequence would be. It is not an uncommon experience to witness what seems a godly person at the beginning ending up to be irreligious and even an enemy to God's cause once he or she has become materially wealthy and "self-sufficient." Wealth can dilute one's interest in the spiritual realm faster than most other life's possessions. It is often a prelude to inordinate pride and a fall in grace, a luring path to self destruction and moral insolvency. "For where your treasure is, there your heart will be also" Mt. 6:21; Lk. 12:34.

On the other hand, poverty per se is no virtue; it only increases the burden for someone and society. In a free and affluent society with plenty of resources and opportunities, with exceptions such as one's hereditary poor health and mental impairment or life's unpredictable, unavoidable misfortunes, poverty is often the result of indolence, sloth, addiction, repetitive foolish choices, and wrong attitudes. "A little sleep, a little slumber, a little folding of the hands to rest—and poverty will come on you like a bandit and scarcity like an armed man" Prov. 6:10. Material deprivation may force a person to look to God for help, thus nurturing his/her dependence upon God. But that dependence and situational turning to God is no guarantee that such will continue once the need is met. The poor could curse God as loudly as the ungodly rich jest about His impertinence.

In the context of Christian Wholism, how should one manage one's finance? This book is not about financial management and planning, but a few brief suggestions may be in order:

1) Resist greed which probably traps more naïve people than many other moral lapses in the area of finance. The amount of investment return in terms of interest or dividends is inversely proportional to the safety of the investment. Individual and churches have been lured into pyramid-type of schemes which promise 25 % or more annual return, only to end up losing all the principal in the investment. Greed is the unseen actor behind all forms of gambling, including lottery. Winning a lottery oftentimes is the worst that can happen to a person. Follow-up history of winners reveals many of them have become alcoholics, drugs addicts, severely depressed and dysfunctional, with broken marriage, ruined careers, and a high incidence of suicide.

2) Diversification should be considered in the apportionment of investment vehicles. Large percentage should be in Treasury notes and bonds because of their safety and backing by the full force and resource and taxing power of the U. S. Government. Emphasize savings and avoid indebtedness.

3) Nothing can substitute for hard work. Work, diligence, judicial planning and management and careful investment over the long term will yield result.

4) Opt for a simple life style—go for the second level of simplicity beyond complexity. Avoid entanglement in complicated financial deals and fanciful investments. Almost all of them are landmines of one form or the other. Tax saving and interest deduction should only be a secondary consideration to the basic value of the investment or purchase, or the rationale and need for loans. Avoid debts, loans, large credit card purchases as much as possible.

5) If one is faced with a lack of financial expertise and wisdom, first acknowledge the lack and ask God for knowledge and resolve to improve upon it. If the problem is temptation of being lured into questionable ventures, be aware of this area of weakness as well as the time and person that facilitates such tempting occasions.

6) Visualize through the Holy Spirit's empowerment one's success in overcoming such temptation and pitfalls.

7) In the area of finance where your weakness is, always consult a trusted relative or friend before committing yourself to any large purchase or investment. Find someone in the family, friends' or church circle that you make yourself accountable to.

8) Read God's word and seek His guidance and trust in His wisdom and power.

9) Finally, ask this question: "Is the whole financial venture worth my peace of mind and joy in the Lord?" The hallmark of a right financial decision that considers the wholeness dimension as well as the perceived will of God, after careful deliberation and prayers, is often a profound peace. If there is turmoil and mental unrest, beware! The unrest is often the conflict between God's pleading and your masked self-will and rationalization.

## Christian Wholism and Ecology

In this section, let us extend our inquiry into another domain and turn our attention to the relevance and importance of environmental ethics in relation to our contemporary world and its future in the context of pandimensional wholeness.[243]

The radical school, the so-called deep ecology, which among other things recognizes the equal intrinsic value of all beings, generally takes an anti-hierarchical position (essential parity of species). In other words, all beings and natural entities have the equal "right" to live or remain unmolested. Pushed to the extreme, one may argue that because the oxygen molecules have the right not to be imprisoned in a human lung, one should not breathe.

The views from the ecofeminist—nature and environment as the Body of God—that planets and cosmos are where God is embodied—a touch of pantheism and panentheism. (the blurring of God as the Creator and the created). The main critique of ecofeminist is placing the ecological blame on the patriarchal, dualistic, hierarchical system of thought, and the technocratic and consumerist social order. Another metaphor used by ecofeminist is the earth as *Gaia* (the earth goddess of the Greeks).[244] They call attention to the shunning of domination and a retrieval of a "sacramental" sense of the universe. The ecofeminist concerns include marginalized people and the treatment of animals, the persistence of sexism, classism, and racism.

Let us survey the dominant views of advocates of animal rights, animal liberation, speciesism, nonanthropocentrism, their criticisms, as well as Charles Pinches' "theological speciesism"—which affirms a unique human roll, that of caretaker of diversity on God's good earth while respecting animals, nonanimal life, ecosystems; concern not just for the well-being of whole species but also the individual members of species; attention not only to sentience and suffering but also animals social needs, as well as plants' endangered species, and the grave moral implications of genetic manipulation to create new species.

What are the various viewpoints of the so-called "naturalists"—the generic for all the holistic, ecocentric environmental philosophers and ethicists derivative of the Aldo Leopold's school of 'land ethic'. The adherents by and large emphasize conservation, preservation of species, prudential use of natural resources, the land being a community to which humans have the duty and obligation to preserve its integrity, stability and beauty. An uneasy balance is struck between the rights of non-humans and the primacy of moral consideration for fellow human beings. Environmental holists who argue that the good of the whole has priority over the good of individual parts regards the earth itself as a living organism, and that it is the bio-center whose interests must take precedence over any other interests. To them, nonhuman organisms, species and ecosystems are all moral entities and should be endowed with "interest" and "moral significance Peter Wentz' environmental justice is based on a deontological position, in which direct moral concern is owed to living individuals, species, and ecosystems—a mix of "Biocentric Individualism" and "Ecocentric Holism."[245] The principle pf "closeness," which attaches hierarchically  the strongest moral obligations to those who are "close" to humans, lesser moral obligations to nondependent nonhuman animals, and even lesser ones to "nonsentient constituents of the environment." Most naturalists resist absolutizing (such as meat-eating, animal-keeping, zero-population growth). They all seem to agree on the oughtness that what is should be to the extent possible preserved in such manner as to promote healthy survival of species and ecosystems. Dr. Smith points out the one consideration largely missing from these naturalists' discussion—that being the relationship between ecological degradation and the plight of the world's poor. [246]

Let us examine the reflection of the liberation ecotheologians who link the ruination of ecosystems with oppression of the poor, the powerless, the voiceless. The chief concern from this group is how enforced poverty and the subjugation of peoples are bound up with assault on the natural environment. The new paradigm of Boff's ecology and liberation is radically ecocentric—that human interests do not automatically take precedence over other interests, that "rights" belong to nonhuman beings, to animals, other living species, to landforms, to air and sky, to the environment at large, and to the cosmos.[247] My question, if air molecules have as much as right that I have, what right do I have to breathe and entrap those molecules in my lungs and then later blow them out as carbon dioxide? McDonagh finds problematic the concept that humans created by God are charged with stewardship of the environment in that humans are given proprietary (ownership) rights over the rest of creation, that a creature is somehow incomplete unless improved by human hands, that the stewardship notion underscores the disjunctions between God and creation, between human and the rest of the natural world, that stewardship signifies management of a reified earth, stripped of any divine presence.[248] Ecojustice-the cry of the earth parallels the urgency of human justice towards the cry of the poor. The liberation visional ethics calls for a "pastoral ministry of sustainability" focusing on environmental responsibility and reverence for all beings, human and non-human. It wants to call to attention the linkage between the exploitation of peoples and the obliteration and exhaustion of Earth's other creatures and features. There is a need for a reconceptualization of power and human relatedness as a pressing task as we attempt to find solutions in this area.

The essence of Global Ethic as formulated by the Parliament of the world's Religions, and the Trinitarian theology of creation as subscribed by the World Council of Churches is the commitment to a culture of non-violence, respect, justice and peace, and the affirmation of the "whole" of life and respect for the community of living beings and preservation of Earth, the air, water, and soil. The PWR's declaration of global ethic is human-centered, but more so biocentric, as it argues for the intrinsic value of living things—and notably of non-human living things. Smith also includes some discussion on the "Oriental" approach to ecological issues and brings out the fact (quoting Tu Wei-Ming) that the religions of the East in general tend to de-center the role of the human, that a less adversarial, less individualistic, and less self-interested approach to civilization than Western traditions, with harmonious living, humility, sustainability the recurrent theme.

Lynn White argues that the Judaeo-Christian tradition bears much blame for environmental devastation and degradation because of its emphasis of God's transcendence, the other-worldly destiny of the human, the biblical notion of human "dominion" over the earth, and the orientation toward progress. Though there is no unanimity among the members of WCC to the ecological challenge, the general direction is toward a just, participatory and sustainable society with careful attention to the situation of all living things, and especially to animals, but also to the larger questions of ecosystems and planetary survival. The heart of the world religions' ecotheology is focused on a good life which is non-violent, nonexploitive, nonabusive, biota-reverent, life-restorative, and ecosystemic.

Professor Donald MacKay asserts that "unlike the rest of the natural world known to us, however, human beings have powers of foresight, planning and action that make us specially responsible in the eyes of our Creator. With these powers, according to the Bible, goes a special obligation toward the Creator. Men are commanded, not merely permitted, to 'subdue the earth' (Gen.1:23). This is not to be done, indeed, in a spirit of arrogant independence, but as the stewards of God's creation." [249]

In the discussion of wholism and ecology, reference must be made to the eco-ethical reflections by contemporary Catholic magisterium, including US Catholic bishops, Pope John Paul II, and the Catechism. The Pope upholds a hierarchical anthropology and the catechism presents a christocentric and trinitarian vision of creation which conceives of human dominion" as a ministry on behalf of creaturely "harmony" and as a role of stewardship. But the "dominion" is limited. The hierarchical order of the human as *imago Dei* and the animal as a creature is intended for the service of the human. The stewardship role is a call to cooperate in and with creation rather than a license to exploit and waste. A recurrent thorny issue in Catholic environmental ethic is the problem of population. How this tension can be creatively held between conflicting points of views is a subject for continuing dialogue.

It would be well for us to summarize some of the convergence as well as divergence in the ethical thought representing different schools. There is virtual unanimity in the concept of "sustainability" of our ecosystem and environment—not merely maintaining the status quo, but rather deliberately promoting and working toward a natural environment that is in keeping with its optimal functioning and "integrity." Emphasis is generally shared on human responsibility and moral considerability is extended to beings beyond *homo sapiens*. Much disagreement remains on the subject of "rights" and how widely it should be extended to and who should make the decision as to who and what has the rights. Despite this divergence, there is a growing ethic of respect and the acknowledgment of "intrinsic value" in all lifeforms and their support systems, from the religious, intuitional, and philosophical perspectives. Other points of contention among environmental ethicists include, as mentioned before, the granting of hierarchical value based on species, sentience, moral capacity, reason, the image of God, place on the food chain, living versus non-living; and also species preservation and technology intervention.

Then of course the question: How to make people change their views and habits? I suggest the answers may include persuasion, incentives, attitudinal change, education, and religious rebirth or by environmental legislation with sanctions and penalties following strict enforcement. Daunting challenges include human greed and proneness to take the path of least resistance. Politics, national, cultural, religious and non-religious bias, just to name a few, at times all loom as giant obstacles. Safeguarding God's creation based on our honored stewardship and entrustment mandates a visionary environmental ethic and praxis of ecojustice virtues. But our passion for wholeness in all dimensions including the ecological could not help but move us to better confront the challenge.

# CHAPTER 7

---

## CHRISTIAN WHOLISM—AN ANSWER TO
## HUMAN BROKENNESS

I have argued in the preceding chapters that Christian Wholism touches every sphere of one's life. I have also argued that a man or a woman is a unitary, integrated whole person expressing himself or herself in spiritual, physical, mento-intellectual, psychological, emotional, relational, and socio-cultural dimensions. Our life experience informs us that there is brokenness and lostness in each of these dimensions.

Before we make a summary statement in this chapter, I want to discuss the mind-brain relationship in the context of Christian Wholism. I submit that the multiple dimensions of our personhood cohere and integrate in the sphere of the spiritual, which for lack of a better term resides in the mind or "soul". But where is the mind without the brain? And what is mind? And where is the "soul"?

In the interest of time and space, I shall refer the discussion of "soul" to my other writing.[250] Here, we shall focus our inquiry on the mind and brain.

Historically, mind-body and mental-physical studies have occupied the attention of philosophers, theologians, ethicists, psychologists, psychiatrists, biochemists, pharmacologists, neurologists, and currently neuroscientists of different subspecialties. I shall attempt to paint a big picture in order to make sense of the different theories in mind-brain controversies. Hopefully I could arrive at a position that is helpful to a discussion of wholism from a Christian perspective.

That the brain is a substance requires no debate. Whether the mind is material, non-material or supramaterial needs elaboration. 1) If the mind is nothing but material, in what way does it relate to the brain? Is it the same material, nothing more or less than the brain itself, or is it some material other than the brain? Discussion under A.
2) If the mind is immaterial or insubstantial, in what way does it interact with the brain? Can a non-substance interact with a substance? By substance I mean a material thing consisting of matter, a physical entity with definite chemical composition and physical dimensions; observable, measurable, quantifiable, reproducible theoretically at least. Discussion under B.
3) If the mind is something other than material or non-material, what is it? Does it belong to some ultradimensional reality beyond our time-space-energy-matter physical universe? Discussion  C.

A) As early as 2600 years ago, Greek Milesian philosophers postulated a single material substratum for the universe, namely water.[251] If mind is also included under the category of material substance, then mental perceptions—thoughts, beliefs, free choice, volition, emotions are non-existent. Proponents of this school range from the eliminative materialists who flatly deny the reality of what is called mental phenomena, to reductive materialists who reduce mental experience to physical and behavioral events. Thomas Hobbes, Rudolf Carnap of Vienna, B. F. Skinner of Harvard, especially Gilbert Ryle of Oxford, espoused that the mental must be understood entirely in terms of the observable, that which can be witnessed, either action or behavior.[252] Central-state theorists in this camp attribute all mental states to neurophysiological brain states like the hardware of a computer. A subcategory emphasizes the functional aspect of mental event (like the software of the computer) and behavioral outcome. It also credits non-human animals and artificial intelligence with mentality.

Many neuroscientists today are taking this reductionistic approach. For them, our joy, sorrow, hope, fear, faith, doubt, intention, belief,  desire, will, imagination, memory, love, peace, inspiration, volition, free choice, creativity are nothing but interacting patterns of subcortical and cortical activities consisting of biochemical and electrochemical neural events, and that we are only physiochemical machines. Against the background of my Christian worldview and personal experience, this reductionistic conclusion is not satisfactory to me. Something is missing in the total equation. I shall cite the following. [253]

Recent exponential growth in the field of neurological sciences, psychobiology, psycho-neuroimaging, "neurotheology," computer analogs and medical research has pointed to close linkage between brain, mind and behavior. Francis Crick, who helped develop the radar during World War II and later as the co-discoverer of DNA (deoxyribo-nucleic acid, the main constituent of the chromosome in genetic transmission), has stated, "You are *nothing but* a pack of neurones and you are ... *no more than* the behavior of a vast assembly of nerve cells and their associated molecules." Afterwards, however, he had self-doubt about the statement. "While writing it down, my mind was constantly assailed by reservations and qualifications. If anyone else produced it, I would unhesitatingly condemn it as a house of cards. Touch it, and it collapses..." [254]

I shall argue that we are not just a pack of neurones as Crick claims and that all which transpires in the realm of human experience is not just stimuli and neural responses. To subscribe to such a materialist-reductionist philosophy is tantamount to saying that when I am moved by Handel's "I Know that My Redeemer Liveth" or Mozart's "Laudate Dominum" from the *Vesperae Solennes De Confessore K339,* it is nothing but sound waves bombarding the tympanic membranes of my ears causing a successive relay of molecular disturbance, through the ossicular system and the cochlear-vestibuli and excitation of the hair cells of the organ of Corti, via the auditory neuropathway to the supratemporal plane of the superior temporal gyrus and lateral temporal lobe and insular cortex and lateral parietal operculum, and through other nuclei and different pathways to a group of my brain cells which can discern the meanings of two experiences of more than ten billion fold in difference and through the reticular formation to other areas of the brain which mediate the response with secretion of nor-epinephrine, serotonin, corticosteroids and endorphin-like substances!

Granted, this may all be true physiologically and biochemically. But there is another dimension of reality for me that is transcendent which very few non-Christians can understand or appreciate. This aspect of reality, however, is not just unique for me but is commonly shared within a Christian community. Similar spiritual experiences such as reading scriptures, prayers, communion service, hymn singing, hearing sermons, other worship activities, and witnessing through testimony and service all add up to conflate into a shared communal discernment by an enormous number of Christians. And this combined Christian discernment lends validity and objectivity to the transcendent reality that I spoke of .

Objectivity, so crucial in scientific research in line with reliability and reproducibility, simply means that most phenomena in life can be understood and perceived without undue influence of prejudice by most people with comparable training and experience under similar circumstances. If such spiritual reality is a verifiable experience for large groups of people in different cultures throughout the centuries, is it not reasonable to at least include it as reliable information, no less than the raw data for sociological, psychological, anthropological investigations in theological and scientific disciplines?

There are other scientists of international stature such as Professor Roger Sperry, a Nobel Laureate in Medicine and Physiology, who repeatedly challenges the mechanistic, deterministic and reductionist materialism. For example, on the subject of consciousness, he asserts, "Consciousness is conceived to be a dynamic emergent property of brain activity, neither identical with nor reducible to, the neural events of which it is mainly composed.... We do not look for conscious awareness in the nerve cells of the brain, nor in the molecules or the atoms in brain processing." [255] In other words, Sperry is admitting to another level of reality apart from the merely physicalistic.

Donald MacKay reinforces my argument when he writes, "Nothing could be more fraudulent than the pretense that science requires or justifies a materialist ontology in which ultimate reality goes to what can be weighed and measured, and human consciousness is reduced to a mere epiphenomenon." [256] Epiphenomenon has been defined as an additional, vague byproduct of the sequence of the physical events in our brain. More discussion on epiphenomenalism will come under (B).

And John Polkinghorne, Professor Emeritus of Mathematical Physics at Cambridge University, who became an Anglican priest some years ago, points out that the reductionist programme in the end subverts itself. It destroys rationality and replaces thought with electrochemical neural events. Such events cannot confront one another in rational discourse, they are neither right nor wrong, but just happen. On this view, the world of rational thought discourse dissolves into the absurd chatter of firing synapses and that cannot be right, none of us believes it to so.[257] Materialist-reductionist would put our thoughts, feelings of compassion, the saints' longing for the *visio Dei* (the beatific vision of God), our gratitude and praise to Him, all under the category of epiphenomenon or worse yet, in the category of neuronal events of electrocircuitry and biochemistry. Furthermore, there are serious implications for theology and ethics if one is to accept the materialistic reductionist views of reality.

Nonreductive physicalism posits the mental and brain events as logically complementary (according to Dr. MacKay) and that the irreducible duality of human nature as duality of aspects rather than duality of substance. Malcolm Jeeves, the foremost experimental psychologist and President of National Academy of Science and Letters of Scotland thinks " the mind 'determines' brain activity as analogous to the relation between the software and the hardware of our computers. In this sense in complimentary fashion mental activity and behavior depend on the physically determinant operations of the brain, itself a physiochemical system. When the system goes wrong or is disordered, there are changes in its capacity for running the system, that we describe as the mind or as mental activities. And likewise, if the mind or the mental activity results in behavior of particular kinds, this in turn may result in temporary or chronic changes in the physiochemical makeup and activity of the brain, its physical substrate." [258]

Nonreductive materialism, nonreductive physicalism, emergent materialism appeal to the view that a well-functioning brain is the material seat of mental capabilities and properties which emerge from but do not reduce to physical capabilities, properties, etc. The word underlinesupervenience, which is often used in such discussions, is defined as a dependence relation between properties or facts of one type, and properties or facts of another type.[259] Donald Davidson writes: "Mental characteristics are in some sense dependent, or supervenient on physical characteristics. Such supervenience might be taken to mean that there cannot be two events alike in all physical respects but differing in some mental respects, or that an object cannot alter in some mental respects without altering in some physical respects Dependence or supervenience of this kind does not entail reductibility through law or definition." [260]

Philosopher S. Blackburn, Fellow Emeritus of Oxford's Pembroke College, calls attention to the limitation of the concept of supervenience. He cites an example of supervenience in reference to perception: the face in the picture supervenes upon an array of dots. "It is certainly true that to create the face no more is necessary than to create the array of dots. But that seems to be because the world contains perceivers such as ourselves; relative to different perceptual powers there would no longer be a face in the picture. So, strictly, God had to generate the perceptual sensitivities capable of responding to just that array in just that way. Similarly, to create secondary qualities, such as those of colour, it is not only necessary to create a world in which surfaces reflect light in various ways, but also to create the kinds of perceptual systems that detect the variations in just that way...We do not have, in cases like this, reassuring examples of the necessity that supervenience claims require...In the case of ethics, it is quite unsatisfactory simply to cite the supervenience of values on natural facts, and then to hope that this makes the intelligible bridge required. The problem is obviously to explain the necessity in question...." [261]

B) If the mind is non-material, what then is it? Rene Descartes, a dualist, believed that the mind was composed of an immaterial substance and the brain with a material substance causally influencing each other in the pineal gland. Sir John Eccles, a Nobel Laureate, locates the mind and brain interaction in the language-controlling, processing modules of the left hemisphere's cerebral cortex. He believes that mind is able to influence neuronal processing and can read the ever-changing pattern of cortical activation. On the subject of consciousness, Eccles writes, "It is dependent on the existence of a sufficient number of such critically poised neurons, and, consequently, only in such conditions are willing and perceiving possible. However, it is not necessary for the whole cortex to be in this special dynamic state...Interaction of brain and conscious mind, brain receiving from conscious mind in a willed action and in turn transmitted to mind in conscious experiences...Let us be quite clear that for each of us the primary reality is our <u>consciousness</u>—everything else is derivative and has a second order reality. We have tremendous intellectual tasks in our efforts to understand baffling problems that lie <u>right at the center of our being</u>...." [262]

<u>Epiphenomenalism</u> as a philosophical doctrine asserts that "physical states cause mental states, but mental states do not cause anything. Epiphenomenalism implies that there is only one-way psychophysical action—from the physical to the mental.[263] Dr. McLaughlin raises the question as to how an extended substance—substance that occupies space—in Cartesian concept of dualism can affect states of an unextended, thinking substance (*res cogitans,* substance that is not extended in space). He goes on to question "how epiphenomenalism can allow that we are ever intentional agents. For intentional agency requires acting on reason, which, according to the causal theory of action, requires a causal connection between reason and actions. Since epiphenomenalism denies that such causal connections are possible, it must either maintain that our sense of agency is illusory—or offer an alternative to the causal theory of action."[264]

Since philosophy of mind is not the main focus of our discussion on Christian wholism, I shall take leave at this point from further inquires in this direction. Readers may want to study Daniel Dennett's instrumentalism (denying propositional attitudes such as belief and desire as real inner causal states of people, other than mere calculational-predictive devices); consciousness and *quale* (the quale of a mental state or event is that state or event's feel, its introspectible 'phenomenal character', its nature as it presents itself to consciousness); homuncular functionalism, machine functionalism, behaviorism, cognitivism, monism, idealism, phenomenalism, interactionalism, artificial intelligence and computer model of the mind, and the list goes on.[265]

C) If mind is neither a material substance nor an immaterial entity such as an epiphenomenon, what is it that we could narrow down for philosophical and theological discourse, especially in the context of Christian wholism under discussion?

In the following paragraphs, let me submit my brain-mind model as a tentative approach to this conundrum. I shall label it as **nonreductionistic transphysicalism**.

In my view, the human mind is a gift from our Creator who is the greatest Mind in this Universe. Our mind is causally the image of His Mind. The qualities, characteristics, capacities, capabilities, aspects, events, expressions of the human mind are dependent (supervenient) on the created, material brain with its billions of neurons. However, such dependence does not catapult to the conclusion that all the manifestations and capabilities of the mind are nothing but the physical, biochemical, electroneural manifest-tations of the brain. There is a bidirectional interaction between the mind and the brain, but not on one to one, numerically identical, causally equivalent basis. In other words, the whole of brain-mind in integrated function, is greater than the sum of all the brain's component parts, that the whole brain-mind has properties that the parts of the material brain lacks. The properties of this transphysical mind cannot be solely defined by the properties, aspects, biochemical, neuroelectrophysical events of the organic brain. The laws and the language to describe this transphysical brain-mind complex are not deductible from nor reducible to any laws of composition or coexistence or behaviorism. This transphysical mind is closely another aspect of life and consciousness,

Then some may ask: Is this nonreductionistic transphysicalism a mystery? The answer is a qualified yes, but it is no more mysterious than life, consciousness, self-awareness, "soul," faith, hope, love, freedom, creativity, time, will, intentionality, prayer, sin, evil, death, eternal life, or God. I submit that the one who truly understands the human mind is God. Science being confined to a closed system and not admitting to other than the time-space-matter-energy reality will find it difficult to understand this supra-dimension of reality, where the transphysical mind and thoughts dwell.

When God formed the man from the dust of the ground, I could picture Him fashioning the intricate and complex brain with great care, arranging billions of neuronal junctions and trillions of synaptic switches, tracts, relay systems, the specialized nervous tissue, and placement of each neuron.[266] That He took such great care in the physical substratum of the body in constructing the brain can be appreciated from the assumption that He intended it to be His "computer" for communication with humanity. The hardware must be perfect with almost infinite gigabytes for storage of the person's salvation history (especially after the Fall for the positive and negative or neutral responses to His grace), the modems for relaying prayers, the megamega Hertz for speed in processing information, the built-in self correction and antivirus protection (lost during the Fall). The hardware must be versatile enough to accept His own softwares, many versions in progression including desire for spiritual transcendence, sexual desire, affinity for arts, music, literature, software for reasoning, judgment, altruism, moral deliberations, ethical reflection, aspiration for excellence, creativity, freedom, independence, sociality, intimacy, purposiveness, unfettered imagination, adventure, beauty, play, communicative proficiency, and hundreds of other programs.

After the hardware is in place, He breathed into the physical structure before him the breath of life, and the human became a living "soul" with the humming, as it were, like that of a well-run machinery-like entity with screens of activity in multiple colors and resplendent sound. Gen. 2:7. The nerve center, the brain, has downloaded the software of "consciousness," "locomotion," "speech," "personality," and Adam is alive!

In this scenario, the mind is God's breath, His spirit-life. It is neither material like the brain from the dust of the ground, nor like the shadow of the brain, the epiphenomenon, but a transphysical "entity" known only to God. I shall argue that there are at least several levels of mind, hierarchically ordered: the lowest level being shared by animals, underdeveloped as well as well-functioning humans. The middle levels operate in ordinary circumstances, common learning, daily living, computer-like functions. The highest level or dimension touches the indistinct boundary of the eternal, the tangential plane of faith and prayer and union with God.

A crude analogy may explain what I mean. We know water is composed of oxygen and hydrogen. Water as liquid gives us a sense of wetness (a property of sense-data, a *quale*). But wetness is not characteristic of oxygen and hydrogen. In the form of ice, water is dry and "burning." In the form of hot steam, it really burns. Water in the form of steam is so powerful as to be able to cut steel. As wetness is to water, so is "mind" to brain. Wetness is not reducible to oxygen and hydrogen, nor mind to brain. Water as ice is analogous to middle level of brain capacity and quality, greater in volume, harder, "stronger." Water as steam as a metaphor of higher level brain function is stronger still and more incisive, powerful enough to break through physical and metaphysical barriers.

According to Peter Strawson and Dr. MacKay of Oxford, there are many underlying substances in the universe. Some substances are physical, material, while others like persons have both physical and mental qualities. "One may describe the events surrounding human action in two ways. (I would say perhaps more than two). When reporting my own experience, I tell my I-story. This is my personal view, and rightly includes my intentions, wishes, and beliefs. A neuroscientist might at the same time tell the brain-story of that same experience, which includes reference to changing levels of electrical activity and cerebral blood flow in various parts of my brain but not my mental states. These are two ways of describing the same underlying reality. They complement each other. It is people, not brains, who think. Yet thinking is not possible without a properly functioning brain.[267]

I argue that my model of brain-mind as nonreductionistic transphysicalism seems to flow with the most basic life experience within the context of Christian worldview and Christian wholism. The mind being the spirit-life of God energizes the brain. It accords the brain with multiple capacities and functional expressions. It makes it the master "brain" in our being—in a top-down manner, screening, triaging, directing, coordinating, integrating, storing, updating, purging what transpires in life. The mind enables data retrieval from the brain and replays such in dreams. It magnifies another set of data in imagination. It censors one segment in creative memory. It articulates another set of data in speech and action, and reaches forth to link with the eternal through the domain of prayers, hope and faith. The mind dances in the rhythm of desire, intimacy, and love. It touches every dimension of our personhood—spiritual, intellectual, physical, psychological, social, and relational.

My model of nonreductionistic transphysicalism would seem to remedy the dearth of life's most noble emotions and treasured beliefs in reductive materialism. It would free nonreductive physicalism from the "nothing buttery" of the physical material strata from which "emergence" occurs or "supervenience" depends. Emergence here refers to the phenomenon in which mental capacities, properties, etc. emerge from, and thus do not reduce to physical capacities, properties, etc., even though token mental states (events, processes, etc.) are token neurophysiological states (events, processes, etc.).[268]

Nonreductionistic transphysicalism could resolve the problematic Cartesian ontological dualism by linking the functioning of our mind to a higher Being, who is our Creator. It explains the novel, creative manifestations of the mind beyond the computer model. It answers to the "necessity" requirement of a unified person with a master command. In my construct, the mind preserves the profound mystery, the utter privacy of that inner life known only to ourselves and God. No stimulation of any center of our brain or the recording of any neuroelectric, biochemical events could ever give the scientists the access to the privity of our thoughts. The Heisenberg uncertainty principle of quantum physics might be invoked to prove or disprove such a scenario.[269]

Nonreductionistic transphysicalism while standing to argue against reductive materialism does not fear scientific reductionistic tendencies. Will scientists and philosophers succeed to reduce theology, ethics, philosophy, psychology, anthropology, sociology to molecular biology, chemistry, then physics, then quarks and antiparticles with their intrinsic angular momentum measured in units of Planck's constant divided by $2\pi$? The probability of success in such undertaking could possibly be measured on a scale comparable to that of creating life from non-life. Even so, transphysicalism finds reasons to rejoice in the enormity of God's creative genius.

Nothing would give me a better occasion for thanksgiving and celebration on a day than when scientists are able to isolate a biochemical endorphin-like substance produced in my brain that accounts for the feeling of wholeness, peace and joy. Few things could excite me more than to know what is this biochemical substance that circulates in my system when I am overwhelmed by beauty and transcendence in music, art, poetry, the human form, nature, inspiration, thought, human relation, and encounter with God?

If atoms and molecules are the substrate of this biochemical entity, should I not rejoice in the work of the Creator who created these subatomic particles? Should I not give Him praise for the stimulus, the signaling for the production of these endorphin-like substance? Reductionistic explanation would not detract one whit from crediting my joy and peace to His creative genius and infinite provisions. Reductive materialism may be a formidable threat to those whose theology includes a self-existent, self-conscious soul that is liberated at death. But such is not the case with my construct of "soul" as discussed earlier.

My concept of nonreductionistic transphysicalism is only the initial unveiling of a new approach to the brain-mind discussion. Further refinement and argumentation await additional research and reflections. Christian wholism presupposes integration and the coming together of all the dimensions of our personhood in a unitary being. The mind is too important a subject to be mired in confusion and abandoned because of neglect. After this long detour, let us now return to the focused discussion of Christian Wholism.

Our sin nature and the evil confronting our world evidence that we have lost the clarity of God's image in us, lost our rightful position before God, our ability to directly communicate with Him. We have lost our inheritance and abode in His Kingdom, our fellowship with Him and almost the possibility for eternal life. Physically we have lost our perpetual renewal and healing gene; psychologically our capacity for intimacy with God and others because of our estrangement. Mentally, we are deprived of the ability to comprehend the universe and God, and spiritually our *shalom.*

Let me cite an example here. In a full orchestra, you have the strings section (violins on the left, violas, cello on the right, woodwind in the front center, behind it the brass section, and at the back the percussion drums. Sometimes you also have a choir. So it is with our person. There are many dimensions that make up our person, the spiritual sphere, the mento-intellectual attributes, the physical dimension, the psychologico-emotional component, the relational aspect, the socio-cultural extension. A good orchestra is made up of colorful string sections, bright brasses, clear woodwinds, stirring percussion support, and a magnificent choir, all working harmoniously to reflect the conductor's vision and his master directorship. **For the Christian, God through His Spirit, is the conductor to integrate all the different dimensions of our being into the state of wholeness to which we aspire.**

In other words, like a superb orchestra, there ought to be relative wholeness in each of the dimensions of our person. Of course, there is usually more wholeness in one sphere than that of another. But ultimately for a beautiful life through Christ's transforming power and grace, there must be a harmonious development of different aspects of our person.

I have discussed in the context of Christian wholism what it means to be spiritually whole, what it means to be psychologically well-adjusted, mento-intellectually vibrant, physically fit, relationally healthy, financially sound, ecologically responsible.

I submit that Christian Wholism is an answer to the lostness and brokenness as it seeks to heal and make whole organically and functionally these dimensions of life. There will be different combinations and degrees of wholeness in these spheres as one progresses in the journey and seeks by the grace of God to internalize this concept and put it in practice.

You may ask how we can present the idea of wholeness to someone, for example, with an amputated leg? Or to a woman with post-mastectomy scars, which constantly remind her of her organic and aesthetic disunity, or to someone with chronic debilitating or terminal illness? As discussed earlier, the different spheres of our personhood, like the different sections of an orchestra, are interrelated and interdependent. There is a symbiotic mutuality in the totality of the relationship. Since there is usually more wholeness in one sphere than that of another, one dimension can to a certain extent compensate for another.

Christian Wholism presupposes the spiritual sphere being dominant in that it is the master liaison between God and other spheres of personhood. A person with an amputated leg, physically speaking, is not whole in an organic sense, but she can still be whole and functional in another sense. Using a religious metaphor or synecdoche, the leg or foot is used to propel one's motion to a particular destination to bring good tidings, Isa. 52:7. The person, even though she is bedridden or with her lower limbs amputated, could still reach that particular destination through her letters, email, phone calls, thoughts, prayers in order to make contact with another person and to bring comfort, peace and joy.

I am also thinking of a Cathedral as a symbol of wholeness in this instance. You may find a broken window here, a fallen roof tile there, a creaky door, a stained wall, a cracked floor, but the tower bell continues to ring out sacred music, its altar though in disrepair to minister the Sacrament, and the choir to sing heavenly melodies. The Cathedral stands whole in image, in symbolism, in its coherent statement of spiritual emphasis and its call to a higher reality. I recall a bombed-out German Cathedral in Cologne (Köln) which did just that.

Analogies could also be made between the Cathedral and human organ-tissues breaking down in aging, in chronic degenerative diseases, terminal illnesses, as well as mental impairment. Such dire existential realities threaten to tear away our concept of wholeness. The Apostle Paul must have been thinking along this vein when he said, "Though outwardly we are wasting away, yet inwardly we are being renewed day by day" toward that ultimate wholeness, I might say, in 2 Cor. 4:16.

Gerald Winslow, Ph.D., Dean of Faculty of Religion at Loma Linda University, California, tells the following story:

> My father taught me about the grace of wholeness at life's end…We knew that his heart was failing and there was little to do medically.

When I took him to the airplane for the return flight, he said, "This is my last trip." We both knew what he meant. I kissed his forehead for what I knew would be the last time on this earth…Two weeks later…my father had died at home in the loving care of my mother, sister and brother-in-law. He (nearing his 89th birthday) had wanted nothing more than to rest in the arms of Jesus until He comes again. My last, best memory of Dad is of him walking through our home, nearly blind but cheerful, whistling "Amazing Grace." This son of the Alberta prairie had become an Adventist as a young man, and he never lost the blessed hope of a restored universe. Dad died whole.

After we have examined wholism in the various spheres of our personhood and being, I conclude that the concept of wholeness in the Christian context embodies the ideas of completion, perfection, oneness, integration, soundness, integrity, harmony, regained health, restored relations with God, peace with ourselves and our fellow human beings, and respect for the environment. On this earth, the reward of wholeness in progress is peace; the hallmark of wholeness in action is joy.

Our progressive journey and unceasing quest for wholism, however, must be guided by a vision of eternal life in our resurrected bodies—the ultimate fulfillment of wholism. Realism and integrity prompt our admission of failure and perhaps many trials, disappointments and unsuspected landmines. Nonetheless, Christian Wholism is buoyed up by Christian faith and hope that are grounded in an all-knowing, almighty Creator whose passion is to make humanity whole. The terminus of wholism leads to the One who is truth, love, grace, justice, and omnipotence personified, the Grantor of our promised resurrected body. Hallelujah must be the fitting epilogue for Christian Wholism.

[1] Walter Bauer, William Arndt, Wilbur Gingrich, Frederick Danker, *A Greek-English Lexicon of the New Testament and Other Early Christian Literature* (Chicago: University of Chicago Press, 1979), 403, 893, 187.

[2] *Remember the Sabbath day by keeping it holy. Six days you shall labor and do all your work, but the seventh day is a Sabbath to the Lord your God. On it you shall not do any work.... For in six days the Lord made the heavens and the earth, the sea and all that is in them, but He rested on the seventh day. Therefore the Lord blessed the Sabbath day and made it holy.* (Exo.20:8-11).

There are at least three major emphases in this fourth commandment—rest; creation and the implied re-creation-redemption; and celebrative remembrance of delivery from bondage* (from Egypt then and now from sin, oppression, injustice, poverty in contemporary Christian life). My observation is that the rest motif is only preparatory to the more important truth that it is God who created the Heavens and the earth, and especially the moral human being after His image, who will be redeemed and sanctified through a re-creative process to be gifted with wholeness in our resurrected bodies to enter into the eschatological eternal rest as the final consummative event.

God rested after the events of creation, surely not because of fatigue or frustration. He rested, to reflect as it were, that the creation project was indeed "very good," the latter especially in reference to the finished product of humanity. He celebrated with other members of the Trinity on this rest day and set an example for humanity to do the same. Human beings are forever, on this day, to remind themselves and others that God is the Creator, and that humans are the creatures, and that they are forever and in totality dependent on Him. Karl Barth keenly observes, "thus it (the Sabbath Commandment, my emphasis) points him away from everything that he himself can, will achieve and back to what God is for him and will do for him. It reminds man of God's plan for him, of the fact that He has already carried it out, and that in His revelation He will execute His will with him and His work for and toward him." **

The purpose of the Sabbath is to memorialize the first creation as we know it, including the human being with a moral and ethical sense; His second creation—the redemptive intrusion into history of the Incarnate Jesus; the spiritual re-creation of man and woman whenever he/she accepts His gracious offer of salvation; and the final consummation yet to come when humanity shall enter the eternal rest–arm in arm, heart to heart with the Creator.

The deeper meaning of the Sabbath also embraces an ethical dimension beyond its merely pointing to festivity and rejoicing (Sabbath--festival, holy day, holiday, Saturday or Sunday, the Lord's day, the day of rest and renewal, the blessed day "The Lord blessed the Sabbath day"). Not only are we to rejoice in and with God for His creation, our re-creation, and our creatureliness with the imprint of the image of God. We are also called to celebrate the *moral and ethical universe* within our heart wherein dwells righteousness and justice, moral and ethical decision-making--a moral universe created in us by God, in which His attributes of love, justice, freedom, creativity, truth, beauty, and relational and communal wholeness may find their expression.

The preparatory "rest" mode is a call to the physical, spatiotemporal, spiritual and mental insulation (not isolation) against what one on the six days ordinarily thinks, acts and reacts. The purpose of the Sabbath, as I see it, is for the human to have a periodic time, an insulated mental and physical space, the appropriate emotions and mood, the psychic and physical energies, and the relational calm— to reflect, ponder, appreciate, give thanks, rejoice for God's gift for our ultimate restoration and all that it implies, and in sum to practice Christian wholeness of body, mind and spirit and to respect the multiple dimensions of personhood and their needs in ourselves and others.

* Besides other meanings, by this fourth commandment, Israel is commanded to observe the Sabbath in order to remember its slavery and deliverance, and also the nature of the Sabbath in Egypt at the time of the exodus. Memory alone does not serve to arouse sympathy for the slaves. Brevard Childs in "The Decalogue," *Exodus, A Commentary* (London SCM Press, 1974), 417. Also Deut 5:12.
** Karl Barth, *Church Dogmatics, vol. III part 4* (Edinburgh: T.& T. Clark, 1961), 53.
3    *Sozo* from the Greek root *sos* meaning to save, heal, preserve, be whole, make whole (Jesus says in John 12:47 , "For I did not come to judge the world, but to save [*sozo*] it...."; "Believe in the Lord Jesus, and you will be saved...." passive voice of *sozo—sothese* is used here in Acts 16:31; "Thy faith has healed thee [made thee whole, *sesoken*, perfect tense of *sozo*] Lk.18:42. *Hugies* in Greek meaning healthy, sound, whole; "Will thou be made whole? (*hugies*) Jn.5:6; *hugiaino* meaning be well in body, to have sound health, be whole or wholesome; *iaomai* meaning to cure, to heal, to make whole. Walter Bauer, William Arndt, Wilbur Gingrich, Frederick Danker, *A Greek-English Lexicon of the New Testament and Other Early Christian Literature* (Chicago: University of Chicago Press, 1979), 798, 832. Also James Strong, *The New Strong's Exhaustive Concordance of the Bible*, 1198, Greek Dictionary, pp.70,73.

Not only is healing, salvation, wholeness conceptually linked, but there may also be some etymological crossover between the notion of wholeness, wholism, holism, and holy and holiness. Wholism, holism comes from the Greek root *holos* meaning whole. Holy, holiness comes from Heb. *Hasid, chacyid, qodesh, qadowsh* (sacred, holy, set apart, separated from human infirmity, impurity, and sin—the idea of ultimate, perfect wholeness), and the Greek *hosios*. The English word "holy" derives from *halig, haleg, hal* meaning whole. *Hasid* is used to describe someone who readily accepts the obligations which arise from the people's relationship with God"—the loyal, the pious, the faithful, and trusting one. Ephesians 4:24 pictures holiness (*hosiotes*) as one of the qualities of the new man ("be made new in the attitude of your minds and to put on the new self, created to be like God in true righteousness and holiness"). I shall argue as stated in my definition of Christian wholism that our ultimate wholeness is to be consummated in our resurrected body in which righteousness and holiness shall find their full expression. Horst Seebass in *The New International Dictionary of*

Notes 193

*New Testament Theology* NIDNTT gen.ed. Colin Brown, vol.2 (Grand Rapids, Michigan: Zondervan Publishing House, Harper Collins, 1986), 236-238.
⁴ *The Oxford Bible Commentary*, ed. John Barton, John Muddiman (Oxford: Oxford University Press, 2001), 855.
⁵ Brown, Francis, et al., "BDB" *A Hebrew and English Lexicon of the Old Testament* (Oxford: Clarendon Press, 1951), 872-873, 338-339
⁶ According to a recent, personal correspondence with Professor J. Goldingay, PhD, DD, formerly of University of Nottingham, and Archbishop of Canterbury at Lambeth, England, now David Allan Hubbard professor of Old Testament at Fuller Theological Seminary, the Hebrew word for "whole" is *tamem* or *tam*. "Wholeness/integrity" is *tom*. "Be whole/complete" is *tamam*. The adjective most often refers to animals for sacrifice, which have to be whole and without defect. It is often applied to human beings, who are also called to be whole in a moral sense: e.g. Noah, Gen 6:9; Abraham, 17:1; especially Job, e.g. Job 1:1; puzzlingly Jacob, Gen. 25:27 (perhaps because the word occasionally suggests "simple"—he lived a simple life at home?). Lovers think their beloveds are *tamem* (Song of Songs 5:2; 6:9). Occasionally one or other of the words applies to God, but mostly indirectly. Unfortunately the Greek Bible translated *tamem* with a word meaning "flawless/blameless", as if it were a negative rather than a positive word, and this persists in English translations.
Psalm 18:23-32 is noteworthy: V. 23: 1 was *tamem* (NRSV "blameless", KJV "upright"; // "I kept myself from wrongdoing");V. 25: With the person who is *tamem* you show yourself *tamem* (the verb) (// "faithful");V. 30: This God—his way is *tamem* (NRSV, KJV "perfect"; // "smelted/proved true");V. 32: The God who makes my way *tamim* (NRSV "safe", KJV "perfect"; // "strengthens me"). For the noun, see Ps 7:8 (// righteousness); 25:21 (// uprightness); 26:1, 11; 41:12; Prov 19:1; 20:7 (NRSV "integrity").The "whole" person is an "integrated" person? Here integrity is something you do/live. Elsewhere it characterizes your inner being: see esp. the gentile Abimelech in Gen. 20:5-6, who is much more integrated than Abraham.
*The New Interpreters' Bible*, vol.8 (Nashville: Abingdon Press, 1995),195-196 reads: What is the meaning of the troublesome *be perfect* in verse 48? In the Gospels, these words are used only by Matthew, who has changed Q's "merciful." preserved in the Lukan version in 6:36, just as he has inserted it into the Markan text in 19:21. It is thus not a problematic word he seeks to dilute, but a word he chose to sum up Jesus' demand in 5:21-48. Neither here nor in 19:21 does it express a two-level ethic, with "perfection" only for the elite, but is the command of Jesus to every disciple. While *perfect* should not be diluted for the comfort of the disciples, neither should it be understood in the Greek sense of absolute moral perfection, an impossible ideal for human beings to attain. Contrary to the Greek abstract ideal of perfection, of being untarnished by concrete involvement in the material world, for Matthew it is precisely amid the relativities and ambiguities of concrete action in this world, which is God's creation despite its fallenness, that the disciple is called to be perfect. Nor does

Matthew understand perfection in the Qumran legalistic sense of keeping all the laws of the community, an externally attainable goal that still leaves operating room for one's own selfish will. Matthew takes the word from the Bible (the LXX uses it often) particularly from texts such as Deut. 18:13: "You shall be perfect before the Lord your God." The biblical word is *tamim*, which means "wholeness." To be perfect is to serve God wholeheartedly, to be single-minded in devotion to the one God, just as God is One, the ethical stance appropriate to a monotheistic faith (cf. Deut 6:4-6). It is the kind of living called for in all the antitheses, and it is their appropriate summary, corresponding to the "pure in heart" of 5:8.

"Perfect" in the OT means "without moral blemish." Critical and Exegetical Commentary on the Gospel according to Matthew, p.56. in *The International Critical Commentary on the Old and New Testaments* (Edinburgh: T &T Clark, 1975).

[7] According to Prof. J.I. Durham, *salom*—Heb. for peace, wholeness embodies the additional meaning denoted by *teleios* (toward the end, reaching the goal, perfect, complete), that is not apparent in *eirene* (Greek word for peace). *The New International Dictionary of New Testament Theology* (NIDNTT), gen. ed. Colin Brown, vol.2 (Grand Rapids, Michigan: Zondervan Publishing House, Harper Collins, 1986), 778.

[8] Eugene H. Peterson, *The Message—the New Testament in Contemporary English* (Colorado Springs, CO.: Navpress, 1993), 417-418 (italics mine). Dr. Peterson is Professor of Spiritual Theology at Regent College, Vancouver, BC.

[9] James I. Packer, *Concise Theology—A Guide to Historic Christian Beliefs* (Wheaton, Ill.: Tyndale House Publishers, Inc., 1993), 146. This is how Regent College's Professor Packer, D. Phil. From Oxford University, and a senior editor of *Christianity Today*, interprets "it" in this biblical passage.

[10] Alister McGrath, *Christian Theology*, 2nd ed. (Oxford: Blackwell Publishers Ltd, 1998), 165-167.

[11] Brown, Francis, et al., "BDB" *A Hebrew and English Lexicon of the Old Testament* (Oxford: Clarendon Press, 1951), 1022-1023.

[12] Hartmut Beck, Colin Brown in *The New International Dictionary of New Testament Theology* (NIDNTT), gen. ed. Colin Brown, vol.2 (Grand Rapids, Michigan: Zondervan Publishing House, Harper Collins, 1986), 777.

[13] Ibid., 778.

[14] F. Foulkes in *New Bible Dictionary*, 3rd ed. (Leicester, England: Inter-Varsity Press, Downers Gove, Ill.: IVP, 1996), 891.

[15] Walter Bauer, William Arndt, Wilbur Gingrich, Frederick Danker, *A Greek-English Lexicon of the New Testament and Other Early Christian Literature* (Chicago: University of Chicago Press, 1979), 227.

[16] J.H.Thayer, *Greek-English Lexicon of the New Testament* as quoted by C. L. Feinberg in *Evangelical Dictionary of Theology*, 2nd ed., ed. by Walter Elwell (Grand Rapids, MI: Baker Academic, 2001), 896-897.

[17] Millard Erickson, *Christian Theology*, 2nd ed.(Grand Rapids: BakerAcademic, 1998), 968.

[18] John B.Wong, *The Resurrected Body--Y2K and Beyond* (Lanham, New York, Oxford: University Press of America, 2000), 5-8. Here the readers can find a more thorough discussion of my Christian presuppositions.

[19] Packer, op. cit., 3.

[20] Wong, op. cit., 6.

[21] Norman Geisler, *Baker Encyclopedia of Christian Apologetics*, "New Testament Manuscripts," (Grand Rapids: Baker Books, 1999), 531-537.

[22] Philip Schaff, ed., *The Creeds of Christendom*, 6th ed., vol.2 (Grand Rapids: Baker, 1983), 27-30.

[23] Elwell, op. cit., 243-244.

[24] Erickson, op. cit., 715-719.

[25] Alister McGrath, *Intellectuals Don't Need God & Other Modern Myths* (Grand Rapids: Zondervan Publishing House, 1993), 128-133.

[26] Geisler, op. cit., 131-134.

[27] Wong, op. cit., 2.

[28] Necessary (a condition in the absence of which no effect occurs) in the sense that both the breath of life (God's Spirit) and the dust of the ground are necessary in creating a living being. The transformed state is the essential condition, without which neither of the two necessary choices can exist. For example, being a number is essential to numerical 4, whereas being four seasons is not essential to the numerical 4, it is only accidental.

[29] Wong, op.cit. 218-219. For a full discussion, read chapters 7 and 8 of this book.

[30] Lewis M. Hopfe, *Religions of the World*, 7th ed., ed. M.R. Woodward (New Jersey: Prentice Hall, 1998), 202.

[31] Charles Manske, Daniel Harmelink, *World Religions Today* (Irvine, CA: Institute for World Religions, 1996.

[32] Huston Smith, *The World's Religion, Revised ed.*(San Francisco: Harper Collins, 1991), 154-193. Also see Wing T. Chan, *A Source Book in Chinese Philosophy* (New Haven: Princeton University Press, 1963); also by the same author, *Outline and Bibliography of Chinese Philosophy* (Far Eastern Publications, Yale University, 1969). James Legge, *The Four Books:Confucian Analects, The Great Learning, the Doctrine of the Mean, and the Works of Mencius* (New York: Paragon Book Reprint Co., 1966). Arthur Waley, *The Analects of Confucius* (London: George Allen & Unwin, Ltd., 1938).

[33] Ian Markham, *A World Religions Reader* (Cambridge, MA: Blackwell Publishers, 1996), 155-184.

[34] Ch'u Chai, Winberg Chai, *Confucianism* (New York: Barron's Educational series, Inc., 1973), 156-172.

[35] Lao Tzu, *Tao Te Ching*, translated by John Wu (New York: Barnes and Nobles, 1997), 3-165.

[36] Hopfe, op. cit., 189-197.

[37] Manske, op. cit., 18.

[38] Diana Eck, *On Common Ground—World Religions in America* (New York: Columbia University Press, Harvard University Pluralism Project, 1997).

[39] Manske, op. cit., 81.

[40] Hopfe, op. cit., 356-387.

[41] Wong, op. cit., 110. For a fuller discussion, read the chapter "The New Body and Christian Anthropology."

[42] Robert S. Ellwood, *Many Peoples, Many Faiths*, 5th ed.(New Jersey: Prentice Hall, 1996), 237-260.

[43] Markham, op. ccit., 223-224.

[44] *The Cambridge Dictionary of Philosophy*, Robert Audi, general editor (Cambridge: Cambridge University Press, 1996).

[45] William Reese, *Dictionary of Philosophy and Religion—Eastern and Western Thought* (New Jersey: Humanities Press, 1995).

[46] Richard Popkin, Avrum Stroll, *Philosophy Made Simple*, 2nd ed. (New York: Doubleday, 1993), 82-92.

[47] St. Augustine, *The Confessions of St. Augustine*, translated by Rex Warner (New York: New American Library, Mentor Book, 1963), 17.

[48] Norman Geisler, *Baker Encyclopedia of Christian Apologetics* (Grand Rapids: Baker Books, 1999),338.

[49] Ibid., 338-342.

[50] Ibid., 339.

[51] David Clark, Norman Geisler, *Apologetics in the New Age—A Christian Critique of Pantheism* (Grand Rapids: Baker, 1991), 117-208.

[52] Lawrence Cahoone, ed., *From Modernism to Postmodernism—An Anthology* (Cambridge, Mass.:Blackwell, 1996), ix.

[53] Bradley Holt in "Spiritualities of the Twentieth Century," *The Story of Christian Spirituality* (Minneapolis: Fortress Press, 2001), 308-310.

[54] *Christianity Today*, "What Exactly is Postmodernism?"( November 13,2000), 75-80

[55] See Post-modernism in *An Oxford Companion to Philosophy,* eds. T. Honderich (Oxford, New York: Oxford Univ. Press, 1995), 708. "In its broad usage, post-modernism is a 'family resemblance' term deployed in a variety of contexts for things which seem to be related—if at all—by a laid-back pluralism of styles and a vague desire to have done with the pretensions of high-modernist culture. In philosophical terms post-modernism shares something with the critique of Enlightenment values and truth-claims mounted by thinkers of a liberal-communitarian persuasion; also with neo-pragmatists like Richard Rorty who welcome the end of philosophy's presumptive role as a privileged, truth-telling discourse. There is another…current preoccupation…with themes of 'self-reflexivity' or the puzzles induced by allowing language to become the object of its own scrutiny in a kind of dizzying rhetorical regress. To this extent post-modernism might be seen as a lidic development of the so-called 'linguistic turn' that has characterized much philosophical thinking of late."

See also the discussions in Jean-Francois Lyotard's "Answering the Question: What Is Post-Modernism?"*The Continental Philosophy Reader*, eds.R. Kearney, M. Rainwater (London, New York: Routledge, 1996), 425-437.
[56] Frederic Burnham, ed., *Postmodern Theology—Christian Faith in a Pluralist World:* The Emerging Postmodern World by J. B. Miller (San Francisco: Harper & Row, 1990), 8-11. Stephen Toulmin, *Cosmopolis* (Chicago: Univ. of Chicago Press, 1990).
[57] R. H. Popkin and A. Stroll, *Philosophy Made Simple,* 2nd ed. (N. Y.: Doubleday, 1993), 307.
[58] J. B. Miller, *Postmodern Theology—Christian Faith in a Pluralist World,* ed. F. B. Burnham (San Francisco: Harper & Row, 1989), 18. Contributors of this volume include Robert Bellah, UC Berkeley; Diogenes Allen, Princeton Theological; George Lindbeck, Yale; James Miller, Carnegie-Mellon University; Sandra Schneiders, Jesuit school of Theology, CA; and Rowan Williams, Oxford University.
[59] Robert Audi, gen. ed. *The Cambridge Dictionary of Philosophy* ( Cambridge: Cambridge University Press , 1996), 634.
[60] David Dockery, *The Challenge of Postmodernism* (Grand Rapids: Baker Academic, 2001), 11-18.Dr. Dockery specifically mentions the poststructuralism of Jean-Francois Lyotard, the deconstructionism of Jacques Derrida, the radical subjectivism of Michael Faucault, and the reader-focused hermeneutic of S. Fish.
[61] David Ray Griffin, W.A. Bearslee, J. Holland, *Varieties of Postmodern Theology* (Albany, NY: State University of New York Press, 1989), 1-7. Griffin lists eight types of post-modern theology or four basic types with two versions to each type: (1) the constructive or revisionary post-modern theology, with both the Protestant (A. N. Whitehead) and Catholic (Teilhardianism and Heidegger-ianism) versions; (2) the deconstructive or eliminative variety (J. Derrida, M. Heideggar, R. Rorty); (3) the post-modern liberationist theology (G. Gutierrez, C. West, H. Cox); and (4) the restorationist or conservative variety (a return to Aquinas' medieval theology—union of theology and politics).
[62] Alvin Plantinga in *Forum on Reason and Religion,* Dialogue with Peter Fosl (Philosophers' Journal, Spring, 2000), 48.
[63] John Polkinghorne, *The Faith of a Physicist* (Minneapolis:Fortress Press, 1996)1.Dr. Polkinghorne, FRS, a mathematical physicist, is President of Queen's College, Cambridge University, and also an ordained priest in the Church of England. He says in this book, "My concern is to explore to what extent we can use the search for motivated understanding, so congenial to the scientific mind, as a route to being able to make the substance of Christian orthodoxy our own...I do not find that a trinitarian and incarnational theology needs to be abandoned in favour of a toned-down theology of a Cosmic Mind and an inspired teacher, alleged to be more accessible to the modern mind. A scientist expects a fundamental theory to be tough, surprising and exciting.
[63a] N. Tom Wright (Oxford), *For All God's Worth* (Grand Rapids: Eerdmans, 1997), quoted in John B.Wong's *The Resurrected Body-Y2K and Beyond...127.*

[64] Such description of what constitutes a scientific method as regularly found in some textbooks has been challenged by critics including P. Medawar, a Nobel Laureate and former director of Britain's National Institute for Medical Research, "...what passes for scientific methodology is a misrepresentation of what scientists do or ought to do..."; by I. Lakatos in *The Methodology of Scientific Research Programmes,* J. Worrall and G. Currie  eds. 1978, "...One can today easily demonstrate that there can be no valid derivation of a law of nature from any finite number of facts; but we still  keep reading about scientific theories being proved from facts.Why this stubborn resistance to elementary logic?"; by Sir Karl Popper and others including philosopher of science C. Hempel in *Philosophy of Natural Science* as quoted by  W.R. Bird in *The Origin of Species Revisited, vol.II*  (Nashville: Regency/Thomas Nelson, 1991), 20, "...The transition from data to theory requires creative imagination. Scientific hypotheses and theories are not *derived*  from observed facts, but *invented* in order to account for them...."

*My view on this controversy* is that the problem may lie in whether one includes in the scientific method the very initial stage of launching of this method. By that I mean whether one's intellectual or spiritual inquisitiveness (prompted by one's worldview or prior experience or "inspiration") launches one into an interactive engagement of observations, reflections, hypotheses-generating, theory-forming thought process. If it is true as the story goes that Newton formulated the theory of gravity after observing apples always fall to the ground, one should note that Newton's fertile mind had been at work and asking questions on the universe with hypothetical frame-of-mind, albeit informally and perhaps non-differentially, long before sitting on the park bench and seeing apples dropping. And on the other hand, it is doubtful that Newton had had a well-laid out hypothesis on "gravitation-like subjects" and then specifically went out to observe critically certain facts.

[65] *Forum on Reason and Religion,* Alvin Plantinga, Peter Fosl (Philosophers' Journal, Spring, 2000), 48-50. Dr. Plantinga, foremost contemporary Christian philosopher states, "When the Christian adds to the scientific epistemic base what she thinks she knows by faith—that God has created us human beings in His image...what we get is a base that doesn't support sociobiological science at all. Hence Christians are not subject to any problem or cognitive dissonance here...."

[66]  Ian Barbour, *Religion and Science* (San Francisco: Harper, 1997), 77-105. Dr. Barbour uses conflict, independence, dialogue, and integration as the four ways relating science and religion.

[67]  John Haught, *Science and Religion, From Conflict to Conversation* (New York: Paulist Press, 1995),9-26. Dr. Haught posits four ways in which science and religion can be related: conflict, contrast, contact, confirmation.

[68]  John Brooke, *Science and Religion—Some Historical Perspectives* (Cambridge: Cambridge University Press, 1996), 42-51.

[69] Evolution is a general term which includes in the scientific arena (1) Biological/organic—evolution (evolution of *organisms* all from one or more common ancestors, so that single celled organisms evolved into invertebrate animals and plants, then vertebrate fish, then amphibians, then reptiles, then birds and lower mammals, then primates, then man **(Macroevolution)**; the mechanisms acting in **microevolution** (inherited variability within a population can alter the probability of survival of individuals; mutations selected by natural forces result in diversification of varieties [many kinds of dogs] in a biological species) together with environmental changes, give rise to **macroevolution (trans-species evolution [from reptile to bird, etc.])**;(2) Biochemical/chemical evolution—evolution of the *first life* from nonlife; (3) Cosmic/stellar evolution— evolution of the *universe,* including galactic clusters, galaxies, stars, and solar systems. See *The Origin of Species Revisited* by W.R. Bird, 2 vols. (New York: Philosophical Library and Nashville: Regency, 1991), vol. I, p.17 & 140.

Darwinism—the theory (1855-60) which posits that species originate by descent with slight variation from parent forms through the natural selection of individuals best adapted for survival and reproduction. Neo-Darwinism—the theory (1900-05) that modifies Darwin's original theory of evolution holding that species evolve gradually by natural selection acting on genetic variation over long time spans.

Theistic Evolutionism—accepts the processes of organic evolution as guided by God's innumerable acts employed to create humans. Adherents typically allegorize the Genesis account as poetic representation of the spiritual truths of man's dependence on God his Creator and the symbolic acts of man's disobedience in the fall from God's grace. Despite their denial of the historicity of the Fall and Adam and Eve, most theistic evolutionists still subscribe to the doctrines of original sin and the human need for redemption. Critics of this school see the untenable position of denying the historical of Adam and the analogy between Christ and Adam in Romans 5:12-21.
See *The Battle of Beginnings—Why Neither Side Is Winning the Creation-Evolution Debate* by Del Ratzsch, Ph.D., Professor of Philosophy of Science at Calvin college (Downers Grove, Ill.: Intervarsity Press, 1996), 66, 180-195. Also see Richard Dawkins's *The Blind Watchmaker* (N.Y., London: W.W. Norton, 1987,1996), 140-41; P.P.T. Pun in "Evolution" *Evangelical Dictionary of Theology,* W. A. Elwell, ed. (Grand Rapids:Baker, 2001), 416-421.

Progressive Creationism—one variety is called day-age theory (the day-age theory can be further divided into the traditional interpretation, the modified intermittent day interpretation and the over-lapping day model. Advocates reject a literal six-day, 24-hour day creation and interpret the 24-hour day as geological ages. They accept the antiquity of the earth and of humans but acknowledge the direct creation of man and general species as recorded in Genesis 1 and 2. Most of the progressive creationists accept Noah's flood as a local, confined phenomenon in the Mesopotamian areas. They allow intrakind development (micro-evolution: variations within a kind [species] such as wolflike animals—

foxes, jackals, hundreds of varieties of domestic dogs, dingoes, coyotes and others); but reject <u>interkind</u> development (macroevolution: fundamental changes from reptile to bird, bird to mammal, ape to man).

<u>Fiat Creationism</u>—rejects all forms of evolution. Proponents of fiat creationism (with two foci: Biblical creationism and scientific creationism) believe in the literal 24-hour day six day Creation, a relatively young universe, including the earth (up to about 9,000 years), universal cataclysm as a result of the Noahic flood (which in part explains the fossils findings) and meteorological catastrophes. They oppose the principle of uniformitarianism (the present is the key to the past) and question the accuracy of Carbon-14, radiometric different age-dating techniques), subscribed by traditional geologists and biologists. The Biblical creationists believe that the basic kinds of life forms created by God's fiat during the Creation week were preserved in the Ark and subsequently dispersed throughout our world as we find them today rather than having evolved, as the evolutionists claim, from organic matter to simple life, from lower to higher forms.

<u>Gap theories</u>—(1) Big gap—here proponents posit an indefinite long period of time between Genesis 1:1 and 1:2, 3 or prior to verse 1. (2) Medium gap – perhaps millions of years between each of the eight creative acts in Genesis 1; the word "day" (Hebrew *yom*) refers to a geological age (hence day-age theory). (3) Multiple small gaps—perhaps thousands of years between the lives of the people mentioned in the genealogies of Genesis 5, 10 and 11 (hence generation gap theory). For this theory, Adam remains historically the first human who lived in the far distant past.

One version is that there had been "pre-Adamites" in an original creation prior to the Biblical creation week, which was destroyed by God as a result of Lucifer's rebellion, leaving the earth formless and void as described in Gen. 1:2. Thus the antiquity of planet earth (some 4.5 billion years as projected by scientists) is made compatible with Scripture.

For comments on different theories, their arguments and counterarguments, please consult *Evangelical Dictionary of Theology, 2001 op. cit. 415-422; The Moody Handbook of Theology*, Paul Enns (Chicago: Moody Press, 1989), 301-304; *Genesis, Creation, and Creationism*, Lloyd Bailey (Duke Univ.) (New Jersey; Paulist Press, 1993), 7-41; *What Is Creation Science* Henry Morris and Gary Parker, Rev. ed. (El Cajon, Ca: Master, 1987); *Science. Scripture and the Young Earth by Henry Morris and John Morris* (Institute for Creation Research, El Cajon, Ca, 1989); *In The Beginning: Compelling Evidence for Creation and the Flood, 6th ed.* by Walt Brown (Ph.D. from MIT) (Center for Scientific Creation, Texas). Leonard Brand, Ph.D, *Faith, Reason, and Earth History (Berrien Springs, MI.: Andrews Univ. Press, 1997).*

Ariel Roth, Ph.D., after researching the fossils, writes, "Instead of being a final court for the evolution of life, the fossils might be more a final court of appeal for creation. Scientists often suggest that new ideas should be put to what is called the falsification test (search for any idea which will show that the concept is false. One way to falsify the evolutionary hypothesis would be to see if the fossils do not show a continuous sequence through the geologic column, especially between major groups. We should find all major groups connected with each other in lower fossil layers, instead of appearing abruptly. As is well known, the record is abysmally lacking in intermediates. The problem extends beyond the phyla and division level to the sudden appearance of hundreds of smaller isolated groups throughout the column. To this must be added the question of highly erratic rates of evolution that have little time for evolutionary changes. Very complex, improbable major developments such as the Cambrian Explosion are restricted to a few dozens of million years. The data suggests that the general model of evolution has been essentially falsified." Ariel A. Roth, "What Fossils Say about Evolution" in *Origins: Linking Science and Scripture* (Hagerstown, MD: Review and Herald Publishing Asso.,1998), 190.

Other synthetic theories—old universe (8-15 billion years) and old earth (4-5 billion years) but with a short chronology of human life (6-10,000 years), beginning with the historical Adam as depicted in Genesis. A chronological gap is present prior to Genesis 1:1 or between Gen. 1:1 and 1:2, during which God had created the universe and the earth billions of years ago with subsequent creation of life forms which left their fossil remains.

[70] Wolfhart Pannenberg "Human Life: Creation versus Evolution" in *Science and Theology, the New Consonance* (Boulder, CO: Westview Press, 1998), 137-149. Dr. Pannenberg speaks about the creative, spontaneous self-organization in the process of evolution from inorganic matter to the first organisms corresponding to the blowing of the divine wind, the Spirit of God that breathes life into ever new creatures and thus blows through the evolution of life until it overcomes all perishableness in the resurrection of Jesus Christ. To me, this sounds like theological poetry couched in scientific vocabulary.

[71] "The Truth Behind Noah's Flood" *Scientific American Frontiers* 5-14-2002.

[72] Alvin Plantinga, *God, Freedom, and Evil* (Grand Rapids: Eerdmans, 1999).

[73] Michael Peterson, ed., *The Problem of Evil, Selected Readings* (Notre Dame: University of Notre Dame Press, 1992).

[74] Stephen W. Hawking, *A Brief History of Time* (New York: Bantam Books, 1990).

[75] Frank J. Tippler, *The Physics of Immortality* (New York: Anchor Books, 1995), 210. Scientific insights point to the conclusion that human existence on this planet earth depended upon a very delicate balance among the fundamental forces of nature and on very specific initial circumstances for the universe.

[76] From these verses the Christian doctrine of imago Dei has issued. This doctrine sets the Christian concept of humankind distinctly from all others. We shall analyze some the implications in the later discussions.

[77] I shall argue that man was formed from the extant created material—the dust of the ground—instead of *ex nihilo* as for the other created entities so as to serve as a reminder that we humans are ecologically bound in a special relationship to this earth and in our shared dependence on God's sustaining power. What affects

us affects the earth and conversely the sins of humankind have direct consequences on this globe. Paul says, "...For the creation was subjected to frustration, not by its own choice, but by the will of the one who subjected it, in hope that the creation itself will be liberated from its bondage to decay.... The whole creation (including our environment) has been groaning...." (Rom. 8:20-22, parenthesis mine). It is to be noted, however, though humans share many of the same kind of atoms and molecules with other animals and the plant kingdom, they are distinguished from the rest of the created order. Many secular philosophies and the New Age Movement have blurred the important distinction between man and the so-called "Mother Earth", between the woman and the whale (or any other animal for that matter). I shall elaborate on this point in the discussion of imago Dei which is to follow.

An additional point may be made in connection with the molding of the earthen raw material in the creation of the first human being and its significance for the believer's resurrected body. It is that the physical elements were used with great skill and care by God (as if He really enjoyed sculpting and shaping the human anatomical form prior to His infusion of His breath of life, the Spirit). My conclusion is that God bypassed speaking the Word "magically" in compressed time in the creating of humankind out of nothing (which He could have easily done but did not) so as to linger, as it were, in the enjoyment of His crowning work (not just the beauty and perfection of the external form but the intracorporeal intricate neurological network with billions of tracts and relay systems, every glistening tendon, every muscular fascicle, every DNA molecule, every physiological check and balance of the cell, down to the minuetest detail and complexity) and to attach significance to both the work and the materiality of His masterpiece. This was not unlike a "Michelangelo" sculpting away ever so carefully a choice piece of marble. Granted, some of the Biblical language is metaphorical. But I shall contend that even the metaphors are important in pointing and in comparison to the reality in the larger context.
[78] My interpretation of "work" in the pre-Fall existence carries none of the contemporary connotation of work as being drudgery, something to shun. In that idyllic setting, work must have been like "play," every moment an exquisite enjoyment. In our resurrected bodies, I could envision that Heaven is all for "play." And why not?
[79] Some theologians may want to contradict my statement by quoting Psa.22:6, when David cries out (or typologically and prophetically referring to Jesus), "But I am a worm and not a man, scorned by men and despised by the people..." or Job 25:6, "...how much less man, who is but a maggot—a son of man, who is only a worm." My answer would be: In the Psalms, David was in the pit of depression when everything looked dark and hopeless, as if he had been forsaken by God. This represented somewhat of an aberrational phase of his emotional profile and not the dominant and general trend. His low self-concept and view of man through the lens of depression and gloom are predictable and must not be taken as his norm. For in the very psalm to follow, David's confident hope

returns, when he affirms: "The Lord is my shepherd.... I will fear no evil, for You are with me.... You anoint my head with oil.... Goodness and love will follow me all the days of my life, and I will dwell in the house of the Lord forever" (not as a worm but as a child of God and joint-heir with His Son).

Regarding the passage in Job, it was Bildad, Job's critical friend speaking, whom Job countered: "I will teach you about the power of God....Why then this meaningless talk?" Even then, there is truth in what Bildad says when he reinforces what Eliphaz has said, "Can a mortal be more righteous than God? Can a man be more pure than his Maker? God places no trust...in those who live in houses of clay...crushed more readily than a moth!" (Job 4: 17-19). See my discussion of Job's frame of mind and his faith in the ultimate vindication of his integrity and personhood.

[80] H.D. McDonald, *The Christian View of Man* (London, Westchester, Ill: Crossway, 1981, 85), 27.

[81] R.S. Anderson, *On Being Human* (Grand Rapids: Eerdsmans, 1982), 215-226.

[82] Irenaeus (ca 130-200) located the imago mainly in the human reason and juxtaposed "likeness" (Latin *similitudo*), the original righteousness *(justitia originalis)* lost in the Fall as a seed and promise yet to be fully realized in Adam had he not sinned, and could now only be restored by Christ. (Emil Brunner, *Man in Revolt* (Philadelphia: Westminster, 1979), 504 ff.

[83] Augustine declares: "For not in the body but in the mind was man made in the image of God.... It is in the soul of man, that is, in his rational or intellectual soul, that we must find that image of the Creator which is immortally implanted in its immortality...." It should be pointed out that Augustine was influenced by neo-Platonism (Plotinus' synthesis of Plato's philosophy and Oriental mysticism to which later was added Christian thought, in the 3$^{rd}$ century), so his concept of the rational soul *(scientia)* and spiritual soul *(sapientia)* include the capacity for self-transcendence in the human spirit where the human person is centered. His mystical contemplation led him to imply that the power of transcendence placed him so much outside of everything else including perhaps his own memory that he could find what he wanted to find only in God ( *The Confessions of St. Augustine,* Book X, Chap. 17, p. 228, trans. R. Warner (N.Y. New American Library, 1963). By inference, it may be said that Augustine sees in the rational and spiritual soul constitutive of the imago Dei a capacity for transcendence to reach the transcendent God, a capacity here and now for relating to God, albeit in the form of hunger and longing much of the time without full comprehension of Him.

[84] See L. Berkhof, op. cit., 209, 210 for part of the discussion. Thomas Aquinas (1225-74 AD), the greatest medieval theologian, influenced by scholastic theology and Aristotle, represents the dominant voice in Catholic theology through his *Summa Theologica* and other writings. The Thomistic concept of the imago Dei is structured on three levels: knowledge of God and love for God as a natural endowment; actual conformity to the image in knowing and loving

God; and finally perfection in the knowledge of and love for God. Sin does not efface the ontic imprint of the imago on human nature which is capable of natural reason, of knowing order, ethics, arts, and nature, science, and metaphysics. Man in the image of God and after His likeness, is composed of form (the soul) and matter (the body) with potential and progressive actualization.( See R. S. Anderson, op. cit., p.218; Aquinas' Selected Philosophical Writings, Oxford Press, 1993 and W. A. Elwell, op. cit., p. 1091-92).

[85] John Calvin, *Institutes of the Christian Religion* I. 15:3 (Grand Rapids: Eerdsmans, 1949).

[86] H.D. MacDonald, *The Christian View of Man* (Westchester:Crossway, 1981, 1985).

[87] *Basic Writings of St. Augustine,* W. Oates ed., "On the Morals of the Catholic Church" (NY: Random House, 1948), I, 329, 330; II, 818.

[88] H.D. McDonald, op.cit., 679

[89] Soren Kierkegaard, *The Gospel of suffering and the Lilies of the Field* (Augsburg publishing House, 1948), 211-212.

[90] *The Divine Imperative* and *Nature and Grace* by Emil Brunner (NY: Macmillan, 1937, 1934) as quoted by P. Ramsey. Also E. Brunner, *Man in Revolt* (London: Lutterworth, 1962)

[91] Anderson, op. cit. 224.

[92] H.D. McDonald, "Doctrine of Man" in *Evangelical Dictionary of Theology,* W.A. Elwell, ed., (Grand rapids: Baker, 1991), 679.

[93] E. G. White, *Education* (Mtn. View, CA: Pacific Press Publ., 1952), 17.

[94] Paul Ramsey, *Basic Christian Ethics* (Chicago: the Univ. of Chicago Press, 1980), 255.

[95] Carl F. H. Henry in "Image of God", *Evangelical Dictionary of Theology* (Grand Rapids: Baker, 1991), 546.

[96] *Racovian Catechism* (London: Longman at al, 1818; Lexington: American Theological Library Association, 1962). Also S.O.P. Mowinckel, "the Psalms in Israel's Worship Vol.1 (N.Y.: Abingdon, 1962), 57.

[97] Ray Anderson, *On Being Human,* op. cit., 73-87. "Human freedom is not a freedom *from* that which binds the self, but a freedom *for* that which determines the self.... For all creatures but the human, creaturely nature determines destiny. The human creature, in dependence on the determination of the Creator's summons to be in relation, escapes the blind determination of creaturely nature itself. It escapes existence under the edict by which nature becomes fate. It is given a destiny which lies quite outside the determination of its own creaturely nature. This destiny is the determination of the creative divine Word. Biblically, it is expressed by the summons into the seventh day, the day of God's own perfection and rest. No other creature of God's making participates in the destiny of the seventh day. This is the biblical concept of freedom: not to be determined by the creature of the sixth day, but to be drawn into the seventh day by a determination which is experienced as a creaturely life of solidarity with

creation, but oriented toward fellowship and participation in the life of God" (p. 80 in his book).

[98] Richard Swinburne of Oxford, *The Evolution of the Soul* (New York: Oxford Univ. Press, 1986), 176-180. 148-153, 302-312. Professor Swinburne is of the opinion that the functioning of the soul depends on the proper functioning of the brain. Without the latter, one cannot have consciousness. However, he states that that does not mean the soul does not exist prior to evidence of consciousness during sleep or in a fetus. Souls and persons therefore continue to exist through sleep in that we can have mental activities of which we are not aware, but of which we can easily be made aware. For a fetus, he states that the soul begins to exist only shortly before it first begins its function. Swinburne leaves unanswered in what form post-mortem life is envisaged—embodied or disembodied. His anthropology is based on a substance dualism with the person composed of a body and a soul. He states that we should think of the soul in terms of a light bulb which needs to be placed in a functioning light socket in order to work. From this illustration, it may be concluded that Swinburne does not subscribe to the concept of natural immortality of the soul. He believes that at resurrection, it is the intervention of God when believers are given new bodies, that new life obtains. Unfortunately, there are gaps in Swinburne's construct, such as identity, uniqueness, personhood, transformation that need some kind of closure. I have attempted to address these difficult issues in the theological construct I have proposed.

[99] John Macquarrie, *Christian Hope* (New York: Seabury Press, 1978), 113. Macquarrie calls to our attention that if the soul is projected as an entity which is linked with a body, that would mean that the soul has a mode of being analogous to that of the body. Both would be "things" even though they are conceived as different types of "things." My concept of soul does not posit the "soul" to be a "thing" as disparaged by Macquarrie.

[100] See Anderson, "On Being Human: The Spiritual Saga of a Creaturely Soul," in *Whatever Happened to the Soul? Scientific and Theological Portraits of Human Nature*, eds. W.S. Brown, et al. (Minneapolis: Fortress Press, 1998), 175ff. "The life of the person [soul] emerges simultaneously with the bodily form of human existence. While humans experience their life as personal life, this life [soul] has no life independent of the body."

[101] Terence Penelhum, *Survival and Disembodied Existence* (New York: Humanities, 1970), 46 f. Penelhum does not believe that the soul is something contingently distinct from the body because identity is necessarily linked with a set of conceptual devices which are open to the public view. His thought lends to my concept of identity as discussed.

[102] Anthony G. N. Flew, *Philosophy of Religion* (Belmont, Wadsworth, 1987), 388. Flew is of the opinion that memory is dependent on bodily identity. If soul is linked to self-awareness and consciousness, any discussion of soul tends to end in a language about an object, which would become a thing. It is noted that many problems surface in the discussion of the nature of the soul and identity.

*My concept of soul and identity confront these issues and posit a reasoned response and solution to the alleged difficulties.*
[103] *This multidimensional identity* has at its core our individual redemptive history (vertical, "social" relatedness to God (Jesus calls us His friends [Jn.15:15]), enfolded by our genetic and "soulish" expressions, and enriched by our horizontal, objective, external, social identity (social here refers to relatedness in the human community, contrasting to the vertical relatedness to God).
[104] D. Cairns, *The Image of God in Man* (London: Collins, 1973), page 63. "...man's being, though linked with the divine, is itself essentially not divine, but created, and thus dependent on God, and of a different order from His own being though akin to it."
[105] In an attempt to extol the merits of evolution, when speaking on evolution in relation to Christian anthropology, H. W. Robinson states, "Our backward look to the dim beginnings of life provides a longer view, but the principle still holds that thanksgiving ought to be deepened by the vision of lowly origins." (H.W. Robinson, *The Christian Doctrine of Man p. 242, see below).* Would that Robinson might add that the creatures from the Hand of God ought to burst with joy and thankfulness to know that he/she was made perfect and beautiful from the beginning, not of lowly origins of slime and chemical broth, but from virgin dust of the ground, through the consummate skill of the Creator of this universe for a purpose and a destiny!
[106] H.W.Robinson, *The Christian Doctrine of Man* (Edinburgh: Clark, 1952), 165. The concept of Adam's fall through his disobedience is markedly and characteristically different in the Eastern and Western theologies. To the Greek Orthodox and other Orthodox churches, Adam's act is only the primary type of man's sin. For Western Christianity, Adam's disobedient act is the fountain-head of all the sins of humanity.
[107] R. S. Anderson in "On Being Human: The Spiritual Saga of a Creaturely Soul", in *Whatever Happened to the Soul? Scientific and Theological Portraits of Human Nature,* eds. W. S. Brown, et al. (Minneapolis: Fortress, 1998), 181.
[108] Most Roman Catholics, most Presbyterians and Baptists, and much evangelical scholarship believe in the tripartite or trichotomous tradition (spirit, soul and body as three distinct entities; thus an anthropological duality of soul and body being separate and distinct). In the *Westminster Confession of Faith* subscribed by most Presbyterians and other Christian Reformed churches, one finds "Of the State of Man after Death, and of the Resurrection of the Dead," paragraph one which states "The bodies of men, after death, return to dust, and see corruption; but their souls (which neither die nor sleep), having an immortal subsistence, immediately return to God who gave them. The souls of the righteous, being then made perfect in holiness, are received into the highest heavens, where they behold the face of God in light and glory, waiting for the full redemption of their bodies; and the souls of the wicked are cast into hell, where they remain in torments and utter darkness, reserved for the judgment of

the great day. Besides these two places for souls separated from their bodies, the Scripture acknowledgeth none." *The Book of Confessions*: The Westminster Confession of Faith, Chapter XXXII, 6.162., 1958.

This body-soul dualism is also widely prevalent in popular Christianity and secular culture. Joel Green of Graduate Theological Union of Berkeley notes that this popular dualistic view has been "propagated by the enormously influential Chinese Christian writer of the last half of the twentieth century, Watchman Nee in his 3 volumes of *The Spiritual Man*" (New York: Christian Fellowship, 1968).

[109] The trichotomic conception of human nature had been generally favored by the Greek or Alexandrian Church Fathers (Clement of Alexandria, Origen and Gregory of Nyssa endorsed it; Athanasius and Theodoret repudiated it). The dichotomic view has found acceptance in Roman Catholic theology with Augustine having given it prominence. This concept carried through the Middle ages (Anselm of Canterbury) and on through the Reformation (Luther and Calvin).The Protestants have generally adhered to the bipartite concept of human nature with exception of some challenges among German and English theologians in the 19th century, who reverted back to the trichotomic view. (L. Berkhof, *Systematic Theology* [Grand rapids: Eerdmans, 1959], 191-192). See also P. Enns, *The Moody Handbook of Theology* (Chicago: Moody Press, 1989), 306. This Protestant challenge was of course of a different nature than our contemporary theological and scientific interest in the monistic, physicalist, and material-reductionist concept of the human, in which the soul is either inseparable from the body or non-existent apart from the body or entirely a non-entity. See my later discussion under "Toward a New Definition of Soul".

Also see C. Tresmontant, *A Study of Hebrew Thought,* trans. M. Gibson (N.Y.:Desclee Co., 1960). Hebrew thought reminds us that man does not have a soul; he is a soul.

[110] J.B. Green in "Bodies—that is Human Lives, a Reexamination of Human Nature in the Bible" in *Whatever Happened to the Soul?—Scientific and Theological Portrait of Human Nature,* eds. W. S. Brown, et als. (Minneapolis: Fortress Press, 1998*), 149ff.*

[111] Those who argue for the concept of soul as having an independent existence often cite these passages. I would only like to draw their attention to the symbolic language in Revelation—the slain Lamb obviously referring to Jesus as He opens the seals; the rider of a pale horse in the preceding paragraph was named death, where death is admittedly not a person. Similarly, the souls of those martyrs could very well symbolize the life-blood (Lev.17:11 "For the life (*nephesh* or soul) of a creature is in the blood) that is being poured as sacrifices under the altar (Lev. 4:7).

[112] To the dualists, my brief response to these cited texts is hereby offered for consideration. Deut. 6:4-5 and Mark 12:30 describe the different dimensions of the whole person in his/her love for the Lord and are not a theological compartmentalization of the constituents of the human person. For Matt. 10:28,

see my "Toward a new definition of Soul"--identity-information-soul, which is determined, sustained and guarded by God alone, and which God alone can destroy (latter half of this verse 28), pp. 196-202.

In **Luke 1:46**, soul and spirit are used interchangeably, referring to the non-material aspect of the person. 1 Cor.5:3 is figurative speech. In Hebrews 6:19, the soul is the totality of the living person and eschatologically our resurrected life. The "your souls" in James 1:21 can be interpreted merely as emphatic pronouns for "you." "Spirits" in 1 Peter 3:19 refer, at least as an arguable interpretation, to the living persons in the prison house of sin in the days of pre-Flood years, whom Christ tried to save through the preaching by Noah. If these spirits were disembodied souls, one would have to subscribe to the doctrine or something similar to purgatory into which Christ descended between His crucifixion and resurrection in order to give a second chance to those who had not made their decision in this life. To open this Pandora's box would require much pro and con discussions. It is sufficient to note that there is in the Protestant tradition a strong sentiment against such unbiblical concepts of both purgatory and second chance for salvation after death.

**Luke 23:43** Jesus answered him (one of the two criminals hung on the cross), "I tell you the truth, today you will be with me in paradise." (Greek: *amen soi lego semeron met emou ese en to paradeiso*—truly to you I say today with me you will be in the paradise). Since in the original Greek, there is no punctuation, an alternative reading in our modern context could mean, "Truly to you I say today, you will be with me in the paradise [because of your faith in Me]" (parenthesis mine). Such reading is possible in view of the fact that after His resurrection Jesus told Mary (three days after He had promised the criminal that he would be with Him in Heaven) that He had not yet returned to His Father (John 20:17). Thus if Jesus would not be in paradise yet, the criminal could not have been with Him on the day of crucifixion. And since we have argued that the soul does not assume a conscious, independent existence apart from the body and since death is pictured as a sleep, a state of unconsciousness, Jesus refers to Jairus' dead daughter as being asleep [Mk. 5:39] ) and there are other instances in the NT where death is also described as sleeping (Acts 7:30; 1 Cor. 15:51-52; 1 Thess. 4:13-17; Mt. 27:52; Jn. 11:11-14 and others), the criminal's entrance to the paradise would have to await till the day of Resurrection, unless there is a reason to believe, which I find none, that there was a special resurrection just for the thief.

**2 Cor. 5:1-9**: J.A.T. Robinson concludes that this Pauline passage refers not to death but to the parousia, thus not to the distinction between soul or spirit and body, but between the future resurrection body and the present mortal body. ( B. O. Banwell in "Body", *New Bible Dictionary*, 3rd ed. (Leicester, Eng.; Downers Grove, Ill.:IVP, 1996), 144.

In **Phil. 1:20-24**, the dualists may want to argue that Paul is theologizing the doctrine of an intermediate state for his conscious soul to be immediately with Christ at the moment of his death--"I am torn between the two; I desire to depart and be with Christ, which is better by far; but it is more necessary for you that I remain in the body." But such interpretation may not be consistent with Pauline teaching that death is a sleep – a period of suspended consciousness for the believers, who are not aware of their surroundings or the lapse of time (1 Cor. 15:51, 52; 1Thess. 4:13-17). On the resurrection morning, given his transformed and glorious body, Paul will not experience say some two or more thousand years of waiting. To him resurrection will have come like the twinkling of an eye, as if right after his death. This is Paul's ardent desire—to be in union with Christ—in the totality of his resurrected body.

**Heb. 12:23** "But you have come to Mount Zion...to the spirits (*pneumasi*) of righteous men made perfect (*teteleiomenon*, having been made perfect), to Jesus the mediator of a new covenant...." The dualist will likely equate the spirits with souls and as such, they would represent the disembodied conscious souls of perfect, righteous men. *For my new definition of soul, which is the individual's identity sustained and preserved by God, there is no conflict even though one interprets this passage as referring to a heavenly scene with all the righteous dead.* Alternatively, the righteous men made perfect can refer to living sanctified Christians who have been made "perfect" or have become mature in spiritual development by the grace of God ("...that they may be made perfect [*teteleiomenoi*, having been perfected] in one...Jn.17:23, KJV and "Be perfect [*teleioi*], therefore, as your heavenly Father is perfect" Mt.5:48, NIV). In this case then, the spirits personify the highest level of the function of the human mind in its spiritual interaction with God (see my definition of spirit).

[113] It is important to point out here that this type of monism must be clearly distinguished from the New Age or other type of philosophical monism which affirms that there is no ontological differentiation between God and human in that all are in One and One in all. This New Age monism is contrary to the teaching of Scripture which repeatedly underscores the difference between the Creator and the created, and the unbridgeable yawning gulf between God and humankind. "All men are like grass and all their glory is like the flowers of the field. The grass withers and the flowers fall, because the breath of the Lord blows on them....(Isa. 40:6,7). "To whom will you compare Me? And who is my equal?" says the Holy One (Isa. 40:25). And Genesis chapters 1,2,3 amply describe the distinction between Creator and creature.

[114] R. S. Anderson, *On Being Human*, op. cit., p. 209.

[115] R. S. Anderson in "On Being Human: The Spiritual Saga of a Creaturely soul" *in Whatever Happened to the Soul? Scientific and Theological Portraits of Human Nature*, op. cit, 178, 179.

[116] In the discussion of soul, the subject of its origin often surfaces. There is the *creationist* doctrine which posits that God is the immediate creator of the human soul at the moment when He gave it a body (Lantantius, Jerome, Thomas Aquinas, John Calvin, other reformed theologians). The *traducianistic* view (*Latin: traducianus*, transmitter), subscribed to by Tertullian and Martin Luther and Lutheran theologians, argue that both soul and body are derived from one's

parents and propagated together. Augustine was reluctant to commit himself definitively to one view or the other. For the one who does not claim the soul as an independent entity, he/she is spared from such conceptual agony.
[117] J.A.T. Robinson, op. cit.
[118] S. Wibbing, in NIDNTT, ed. C. Brown, op. cit., p. 233.
[119] R. Gundry, *Soma in Biblical Theology,* op, cit., p. 23.
[120] R. S. Anderson, "On Being Human: The Spiritual Saga..."in *Whatever Happened to the Soul? Scientific and Theological...* op. cit.
[121] H.W. Robinson, *the Christian Doctrine of Man,* 3 rd ed. (Edinburgh: Clark, 1958), 27.
[122] One can make the argument that from this verse it is deduced that God's Spirit acting on the inert terrestrial matter (adama) to create Adam's whole person or bodily life with all the expressions of life qualities.
[123] Gunther Harder in "Soul", NIDNTT, C. Brown, ed., op. cit., 682-686.
[124] R. Bultmann, *Theology of the New Testament,* Vol. I, trans. K. Grobel (NY:Scribner's Sons, 1951), 192-193.
[125] R. Bultmann, op. cit., p.194-195.
[126] R. Bultmann, op. cit., p. 204-205.
[127] K. Barth, *Church Dogmatics*, III/2, p. 433.
[128] Wolfhart Pannenberg, *Anthropology in Theological Perspectives,* trans. M. O'Connell (Philadelphia: Westminster, 1985), 523.
[129] Anderson states, "Spirit, we conclude, might be considered the life of the soul (the person) as an orientation toward God, summoned forth by the divine Word and enabled by the divine Spirit." Such a definition of spirit would obviate an answer to the question. (Anderson, *On Being Human,* op.cit., p.212.)
[130] Many years ago, there was a front page news caption, *"How Much Does the Soul Weigh?"* When I was in surgical training in a hospital, I was told by a fellow resident that in the small town where he had come from, there was an elderly orderly who was very interested in matters of soul. When he officially retired, he volunteered his service to a nursing home where were housed some 120 very elderly lady patients. Almost not a day went by without a death in this nursing home. This orderly would often hold a moribund patient in his big arms (he was 6ft 5in, weighing 250 lbs) and weighed the two together (him and the patient) before the patient died, and again weighed the two after the patient had expired. By subtracting the two sets of numbers and averaging them for a whole series of patients over a two-year period, he came up with a figure for the weight of a "soul,"—approximately 4oz. The anecdote continued, as I listened to this resident surgeon. One day this retired orderly was screaming down the corridor and appeared utterly distraught when he found out that one patient weighed more after death than when she was alive. Impossible, impossible!! His theory of the weight of the exiting soul was about to be exploded.

After a thorough investigation over a period of several days, this orderly finally recaptured his composure. It was then discovered that a nurse had

Notes

211

replaced the denture in the patient's mouth after the latter's demise right between her brief ante- and postmortem period.

[131] See J. B. Green's article, "Bodies—That is, Human Lives: A Re-examination of Human Nature in the Bible" and also W. S. Brown's article "Cognitive Contributions to Soul" in *Whatever Happened to the Soul? Scientific and Theological Portrait of Human Nature,* eds. W.S. Brown, et al. (Minneapolis: Fortress Press, 1998).

Theologians opting for the wholistic human person as a unity of spirit, soul and body include H. W. Robinson, Oscar Cullmann, G.C. Berkouwer (Man--*The Image of God,* Grand Rapids: Eerdmans, 1962), 200; Stanley Grenz (*Theology for the Community of God,* Nashville: Broadman & Holman, 1994) 207-12.

[132] For readers who are interested in this subject, please consult *Cloning Human Beings* (President's Report and Recommendations by the National Bioethics Advisory Commission, Rockville, Maryland, 1997).

[133] Wong, op. cit. Refer to a fuller discussion and arguments for the new concept of soul.

[134] The waiting is in our earthly perspective only. The dead, based on our discussions, have no consciousness of the passage of time, so that one thousand years of waiting in the grave from the time of death to resurrection would be like the twinkling of an eye (1 Cor. 15:52).

[135] Some would argue that angels could have been created in God's image too, since in the original Hebrew "Let us make...in our image...in our likeness" are all in the plural. At one time, this was taken to refer to God's Trinitarian plurality. But recent scholarship interprets the "us" as referring to the heavenly court and possibly the angelic host surrounding the Creator-King (*The NIV Study Bible,* K. Barker, gen.ed. (Grand Rapids: Zondervan, 1995), p.7 footnotes. By inference then, I may interpret, the image of God could have also referred to the image of the angels who themselves bear the image of God. My answer would be: Even though the reading could be so interpreted, at least no other created entities (animals and vegetation) on earth were created in His image.

Another nuanced reading can be added to the "Let us" phraseology. Does the sentence construction give the idea that there was a consultative and deliberative session among the Trinitarian members before endowing the human with their very own image? All the preceding creative acts appeared rather mechanical and procedural "Let there be light ....Let the water teem with living creatures....Let the land produce living creatures...." Of course, this is only an anthropomorphic projection. Who can know the Mind of God!

[136] A thorough discussion of Trinity is beyond the scope of this treatise. Any standard text on systematic theology treats this subject as one of the cornerstones of Christian theology. Both in the OT and NT there are many intimations and indirect references to the validity of this assertion. Experientially, we, the human, may be analogized as a trinity (spirit, mind and body) or metaphysically the universe as a trinity (time,space, matter/energy[interconvertible]). Augustine approaches this mystery from a negative perspective by saying that absent the

Trinity, fellowship and love in God involving in interrelationship of divine perfections in their eternal exercise and expression independent of the creation of the world and man would be impossible (Geoffrey Bromiley on Trinity in W. Elwell, EDT op.cit., p.1112).

[137] R.S. Anderson, *On Being Human.* op.cit., p.224.

[138] Karl Barth, *Church Dogmatics,* III/2 (Edinburgh: Clark, 1958)1:184-185.

[139] I can hear the clamor of the psychologists and animal scientists claiming the findings of animal intelligence and many near-human or even suprahuman capacities. I do not dispute such discoveries. Yet I challenge any of those animal scientists to this fundamental reality: Who is doing the research on whom? Surely not the animals collecting data on humans and postulating hypotheses and theories to explain the phenomena. And who is contemplating the universe, vast as it may be compared to the puny human creature? And most recently, man is the one who succeeded cloning sheep and not gorilla cloning woman.

Augustine labels God's creation of the natural world as *vestigia Dei* versus man's image of God as *imago Dei.* Boer believes that *vestigia* is better translated as "footprints" to give the word the right meaning instead of "ruin" or "faint trace" or "residue". (Harry R. Boer, *An Ember Still Glowing* [Grand Rapids: Eerdmans, 1990],13). For many years, the human appendix has been considered a vestigial organ, but now we know it has a role in the general scheme of immunocompetence of our body.

[140] "Be fruitful and increase in number" Gen.1:28 might possibly have a nuanced meaning in revealing God's intention to have many human images of God to adequately reflect His character.

[141] E. G. White in *Education,* "True education...has to do with the *whole being,* and with the whole period of existence possible to man. It is the harmonious development of the *physical, the mental, and the spiritual* powers. It prepares the student for the joy of service in this world and for the higher joy of wider service in the world to come." P.13, (italics mine).

Also E. G. White in *The Ministry of Healing,* "In the ministry of healing the physician is to be a coworker with Christ. The Savior ministered to both the soul and the body. The gospel which He taught was a message of spiritual life and of physical restoration..." p. 111.

[142] Princeton Religious Research Center, Princeton, N.J. and G. Gallup, 1990 and 1994.

[143] Dale Matthews, *The Faith Factor* (New York: Penguin Books, 1998), 15, 16.

[144] Ibid., 19, 20. Also see Margaret Poloma and M. Pendleton, "The effects of prayer and prayer experiences on measures of general well-being." Journal of Psychology and Theology, 19 (1). 1991: 71-83.
Jeffrey Levin and H. Vanderpool. Religious factors in physical health and the prevention of illness. Prevention in Human Services 9(2). 1991: 41-64.

[145] Jeanie Davis, Dr. Tonja Hampton, Web MD Medical News, May 16, 2002.

[146] Proceedings of the Symposium were published by Intervarsity Press, Downers Grove, Illinois.

[147] Ibid., 32-35.
[148] Roderick Firth, "Ethical Absolutism and the Ideal Observer," *Philosophy and Phenomenological Research,* 12, No.3 (1952), 317-45.
[149] A comment must be made here, even though the models of ethical consultation and decision process are not the focus of this book. Obviously there are many advantages for a multidisciplinary committee as enumerated. But there are others who feel that at times such a committee can get mired in debates and personal preferences prolonging a critically needed decision to the detriment of the patient's wholistic care and well-being.
[150] Raymond Duff, A.G.M. Campbell, "Moral and Ethical Dilemmas in the Special-Care Nursery," in *Ethics in Medicine,* ed. S. Reiser, A. Dyck, W. Curran (Cambridge, Mass.: Massachusetts Institute of Technology Press, 1977), 539-43.
[151] Robert Herrmann in "The Tension between Scientific Objectivity and Values in Whole-Person Medicine." Proceedings of the International Symposium on Whole-Person Medicine (Downers Grove, Ill.: Intervarsity Press, 1980).
[152] Ibid., 60.
[153] C. Trevarthen, ed. *Essays in Honor of Roger W. Sperry* (Cambridge: Cambridge Univ. Press, 1990), 382-385.
[154] Herrmann, op. cit., 62,63.
[155] John Brobeck in "Whole-Person Medicine and Scientific Medicine," Proceedings of the International Symposium on Whole-Person Medicine (Downers Grove, Ill.: Intervarsity Press, 1980), 80. Dr. Brobeck, MD, PhD, a physiologist from Yale University and Univ.of Pennsylvania, is a professor of medical sciences.
[156] Edmund D. Pellegrino in "Educating the Christian Physician," Proceedings of the International Symposium on Whole-Person Medicine (Downers Grove, Ill.: Intervarsity Press, 1980), 101-103.
[157] Ibid., 106-107
[158] Sigmund Freud, *The ego and the id* (London: Hogarth, 1927).
[159] Abraham Maslow, *Motivation and Personality* (N.Y.: Harper & Row), 1954.
[160] G.Allport, *The Pattern of Growth and Personality* (N.Y.:Holt, R & W), 1961.
[161] David Benner, Peter Hill, editors, *Baker Encyclopedia of Psychology & Counseling* (Grand Rapids: Baker Academic, 1999), 547.
[162] Victor Frankl, *Man's search for meaning* (Boston: Beacon, 1963).
[163] Rollo May, *Man's search for himself* (New York, Norton, 1953). Existential psychotherapist and researcher.
[164] E. Gellhorn, G. Loofbourrow, *Emotions and Emotional Disorders: A Neurophysiological Study* (New York: Harper & Row, 1963).
[165] K. Lorenz, *On Aggression* (New York: Harcourt, 1966).
[166] Henry Cloud, John Townsend, *Boundaries*(Grand Rapids: Zondervan, 1992).
[167] *Harrison's Principles of Internal Medicine,* 13th ed. (New York:McGraw-Hill, 1994), 49-54.
[168] Siang-Yang Tan in *Baker Encyclopediaof Psychology and Counseling,* eds. D. Benner, Peter Hill (Grand Rapids: Baker Academic, 1999), 817-818.

[169] Ibid., 1905-1906.

[170] A. M. Rizzuto, *The Birth of the Living God* (Chicago: Chicago Univ. Press, 1979).

[171] Jean Piaget (1896-1980) was a Swiss psychologist known for his research on and contribution to the development of intelligence, psychology of intelligence

[172] G. William Barnard in "Psychology as a Religion." *Religion and Psychology: Mapping the Terrain* (London, New York: Routledge, 2001), 302.

[173] William James, *The Varieties of Religious Experience* (Cambridge, MA: Harvard University Press, 1985).

[174] Carl G. Jung, "Archetypes of the Collective Unconscious" in *The Basic Writings of C.G. Jung*, trans. By R. Hull, Ed. V. de Laszlo (Princeton University Press, 1990), 299-300. *The Collected Works of C. G. Jung (20 vols.)*, Read, Fordham and Adler, eds., R.C.Hull trans, (Princeton,N.J.: Princeton University Press., 1953-79).

[175] J. A. Sanford "Jungian Analysis," in *Baker Encyclopedia of Psychology and Counseling*, eds. D. Benner, Peter Hill (Grand Rapids: Baker, 1999), 658.

[176] Carl G. Jung, *The Basic Writings of C.G. Jung*, trans. by R. Hull; ed. V. de Laszlo (Princeton University Press, 1990), 187-241.

[177] The Basic Writings of C. G. Jung, xxiii.

[178] Ibid., 269, 270.

[179] The Basic Writings of C. G. Jung, xxii.

[180] D. J. Frenchak in Baker Encyclopedia, op. cit., 657.

[181] Diane Jonte-Pace, William Parsons, *Religion and Psychology: Mapping the Terrain* (London, New York: Routledge, 2001), 15-27.

[182] Barnard, op.cit., 297.

[183] Ibid., 116-121.

[184] Robert Ader, David L. Felten, Nicholas Cohen, *Psychoneuroimmunology*, third ed.(New York, London: Academic Press, 2001), xxi. Vol I and II. David Felten, MD, PhD was chairman of Department of Neurobiology and Anatomy at the University of Rochester School of Medicine before becoming the Director of the Center for Neuroimmunology at Loma Linda University School of medicine. He is presently at University of California, Irvine, College of Medicine.

[185] Ibid.,667-702.

[186] Ibid., vol. I, 1-17, 517-546, 547-562. Cytokine, by some usage, refers to any protein released by a cell that can in turn affect itself or other cells. Here it is restricted to include only those substances produced by immune cells which can affect immune mechanisms in an autocrine or paracrine fashion. Many cytokines can also elicit immunoregulatory neuroendocrine responses and may even play a role in brain physiology. A cytokine can behave as a neurotransmitter and a hormone as a cytokine.

[187] Ibid., 189-226.

[188] Ibid., 701-713. There is high interindividual variation in age-associated immunological changes, and physically healthy old people, including centenarians, show remarkable little difference in immunity from younger

persons. Moreover, such healthy old people are likely to be cognitively intact and to demonstrate psychological well-being suggesting that aging reflects parallel processes in immune and central nervous systems.
[189] Ibid. vol. II, 383-398.
[190] Ibid. vol.II, 217.
[191] Ibid., vol. I, 55-100.
[192] Ibid., vol. I, 563-579; 585-614.
[193] Ibid., vol. II, 111-118.
[194] Ibid., vol., xxii.
[195] David Brewster, *The Life of Sir Isaac Newton* (New York: Harper & Bros., 1842), 300-301.
[196] Clifford and Joyce Penner, *The Gift of Sex* (Dallas, London: Word Publishing, 1981), 35-44. Clifford Penner, Ph.D., is a clinical psychologist with seminarian background. Joyce Penner, M.N., is a nurse.
[197] See BDB, *A Hebrew and English Lexicon of the OT,* op.cit., 393-394. Also at common law and under statute, carnal knowledge is defined as sexual intercourse.
[198] Penner writes, "We *do* believe that it is in this mystical union of two bodies (husband's and wife's) that body and spirit come closest to a merger. Most of the time we let our minds control us. But in the moment of orgasm we are released from that control; climax is something that we experience as a totality. Everything about us enters into it. Perhaps this is how the sexual experience represents our relationship to God. In this total, intense fusion of the body, emotion, and spirit we are connecting with what it can be like to be totally one with God.This is, indeed, a mystery. One day we will understand it fully. Meanwhile, we can simply accept and enjoy the truth of it." Penner, op. cit., p. 40. I may add, one day in the world to come, with our resurrected body, we shall more fully understand this mystical union with other believers and with God.
[199] Some will argue that Jesus has already said that at resurrection, people will be like angels. But the rebuttal is: to be like does not mean to be identical. We say, a certain son is like his father—in many respects, yes, but surely not identical. Are angels of neuter gender? Even so, that does not preclude our continuing to be sexual beings in Heaven.Or is Jesus only referring to the angels' non-marital status? I have argued elsewhere that we have no existence except bodily existence.We can also extend this assertion to say that there are no human bodies other than sexual bodies, no body-selves except sexual body-selves.
[200] "A different mechanism of sex differentiation operates in humans and most other mammals.Rudimentary "indifferent gonads," which can become either testes or ovaries, form in the early embryo. Which way they develop depends on the sex chromosome present. The Y chromosome carries a gene that causes the gonads to express a cell-surface protein called H-Y antigen. When H-Y antigen is present, the gonads differentiate into testes. The testes, in turn, produce the hormone testosterone, which must be present to induce differentiation of the male reproductive tract. In human embryo, the testes begin differentiating in the

sixth week of development. If this does not occur, the gonads differentiate into ovaries in the following week. In this case, the rest of the female reproductive tract develop automatically, without hormonal signals from the ovaries.... Researchers have identified 19 different gene loci involved in human sexual development, most located on the autosomes....In some animals, sex is determined by environmental factors...temperature...chemicals...when two or three are gathered together, some will be male and some female." *Biology,* 3rd. ed., Arms, K. (New York: Saunders College Publishing, 1987), 310-311. See Neil Campbell, *Biology* (UC, Riverside. New York, L.A.: Cummings,1996), 226 ff. Also see Guy Murchie's *The Seven Mysteries of Life—an Exploration in Science and Philosophy* (Boston:Houghton and Mifflin, 1981), 128-129. "In the case of animals...changing sex is relatively easy even when the young one is grown, because such measure as increasing feeding may turn a male into a female... Fish...not only changing form male to female as they grow but a few, like groupers and guppies, developing the ability to switch sexually back and forth within seconds...."

From the science of embryology, we then learn that at the very beginning of life, at least the first 6 weeks, there is no differentiation of sex in humans. It is a unity in being. From observations, toward the end of life, the sexual different-iation between man and woman also begins to obliterate, as shown in their external characteristics. There is, so it seems, a sexual convergence. My observation is shared by medical specialists in geriatrics.

[201] Ethics—derived from the Greek *ethikos* (*ethos* meaning custom or usage). Aristotle used the term to imply character and disposition. Later Cicero employed the Latin word *moralis* as its Greek equivalent. Both words connote practical activity. In our discussion, I shall use the terms interchangeably, i.e. ethics=morality; ethical=moral. See W. L. Reese's *Dictionary of Philosophy and Religion* (New Jersey, London: Humanities Press, 1995), 156.

Ethics, as an academic discipline, is often subdivided into (1) philosophical ethics (which examines human moral responsibility by means of reason, logic and argumentation in the context of this present existential life; (2) theological or religious ethics (which studies the human ethical responsibility in the context of the insights and beliefs of a certain religious community or tradition, oriented not only to this life but also that of the future; (3) Christian ethics (which engages in all dimensions of ethical discourse as it draws upon biblical teachings and the traditions of the Christian Church, and analyzes ethical problems in contem-porary and eschatological perspectives; it is a distinctive species of theological ethics. And Biblical ethics is a subspecies of Christian ethics, drawing its norms, principles, rules, insights strictly from the Bible, and usually downplaying the contributions of ethical thought from Christian traditions and philosophy (my interpretation).

By stressing the particular sphere of ethical inquiry, ethics can also be classified as general personal ethics (dealing with interpersonal relations); social ethics (ethical deliberation on a larger scale involving society and all its entities, government policies, often with legal entanglement—abortion, euthanasia, homosexuality, gender and racial discrimination, poverty, globalization); biomedical ethics (which tackles the ethical challenges arising in clinical situations, in physician's treatment, in doctor-patient relationship, and in science and technology related to modern health care and delivery; medical ethics is a species of normative ethics because it appeals to certain norms and standards in decision-making and discourse and asks how one ought to do or give an ethical pronouncement on a certain ethical issue in a certain situation with concerns for personal, biomedical and societal outcome and consequence); legal ethics; business ethics; environmental ethics, etc.

202 *The Cambridge Dictionary of Philosophy*, Robert Audi, ed.(Cambridge: Cambridge Univ. Press, 1996), 244.

203 The cardinal virtues of justice, temperance, courage and wisdom. Later under the Christian influence, hope, faith and love (charity) were added to the classical virtues.

204 *Encyclopaedia of Bioethics,* revised ed., Warren Reich, ed. (New York: Simon and Schuster Macmillan. 1995), 723.

205 See Jeremy Bentham's *An Introduction to the Principles of Morals and Legislation* (New York: Methuen, 1982); Henry Sidgwick's *The Methods of Ethics*, 7th ed. (Indianapolis: Hackett Publishing, 1981).

The consequentialists claim that all moral and ethical obligations and virtues are to be interpreted in terms of good, well-being and desirable consequences. The good and desirable are equated with pleasure, happiness, satisfaction of human desires and aspirations, and avoidance of pain and the intrinsically human ill and evil. Whether a certain act is right or wrong hinges on whether its general and long-term effect is better than any other alternatives available in any given situation. Applying to society and to the whole world, this means whether there is a net balance of good, pleasure, happiness, freedom from pain for the greatest number of people. Theoretically, the consequentialist-utilitarian position leads to the principle that the end justifies the means. Opponents find in this position its most unsatisfactory feature. On reflection, to make this theory measure up to its ideal, one would have to be omniscient to know what is the "good," what constitutes good to each individual, what is the net balance of the "good." Sidgwick distinguishes egoistic hedonism (one's own experience of pleasure that is intrinsically good) from universal hedonism (the pleasure experienced by any other sentient being is what defines what is intrinsically good. In our contemporary society, should one fetus with genetically documented severe Down's syndrome be aborted in order to conserve limited medical and societal resources for the betterment of many children? Should the medical cost of a kidney transplant be denied to a 70-year-old pediatrician who has labored sacrificially all her life in the inner city for the welfare of children so that the funds can be used to inoculate 10,000 African children?

Notwithstanding the ethical issues inherent in consequentialism and utilitarianism, its greatest utility is found in social planning, government policies, and political agendas. Bentham and his adherents indeed used the theory to attack aristocratic entrenchment, royal privileges in an effort to reform the British legal and political systems.

It is not to be understood that the consequentialists/utilitarians lack a sophisticated system or a conceptual framework (compared to their counterparts, the deontologists) in order to implement their theories.They have a way to define what is the human good; a technique for measuring, "quantifying" and comparing the "good"; a justification for some practical guidelines in determining among several alternatives what is the best means to maximize the greatest good for the largest number of people. It is not the focus of our discussion for various arguments pro and con on this subject. Mention, however, must be made that there are the so-called act consequentialism and rule consequentialism, similar to act and rule deontologism. The act variety requires one to perform some particular action which in a particular situation would bring about the best consequence or the maximal good for the greatest number of people. The rule variety demands that some moral and ethical rule or principle be followed in order to maximize the best consequence. As can be seen, the rigorous enforcement of the rule variety of consequentialism/utilitarianism pushes one toward the deontological camp (to be discussed later), as well as blurs its differentiation from the act variety. For example, if one is to follow the principle of justice strictly in order to bring about the maximal consequence, one is siding with the deontologists in insisting that what is right does not depend only on the consequence but also on a set of obligatory criteria or universal principles (including justice). And to follow the rules of justice to its logical end leads one to do the just act (thereby falling into the act variety of consequentialism).

[206] While discussing principles and ethical rights and wrongs, it is recognized that there are those who subscribe to a form of ethical and cultural relativism which denies any objectivity and meaning of ethical terms. These non-cognitivists (A.J. Ayer, C.L. Stevenson) claim that all ethical terms and judgments only stand for emotions (the Emotivists), attitudes, proposals and recommendations. For example (my interpretation), when one states, "It's morally wrong or unethical to bribe a public official," the non-cognitivist does not consider the statement to mean that bribing is intrinsically wrong. To her, this only means that the person merely expresses his emotion or attitude toward bribing and perhaps suggests a proposal or recommendation that bribing not be done. The emotivist's analysis of moral judgment as the expression of the appraiser's attitudes instead of an assertion  has met criticisms that challenge their explanations for conditional moral judgment or the amoralist position. See David Brink's (UCSD) discussion under Emotivism in *The Cambridge Dictionary of Philosophy,* op. cit., 223-24.

[207] In addition to the Decalogue, there are biblical norms that can service our ethical discourse. The concept of justice, *mishpat* and *tsedaqah* (Micah 6:8; Deut. 32:4; Psa. 89:14; Isa.28:17), freedom, autonomy (Matt.23:37; Jn.7:17;

1Pet.5:2Isa.1:19,20; Isa.55; Rev.22:17; Lk.15),creativity (Gen. 1:26-28, 9:6, man made in the image of God, therefore endowed with the gifts of His attributes, albeit to a lesser and lower degree), and human value (quality of life, inalienable rights to life, liberty and the pursuit of happiness), Mt.10:30-31; Gen. 9:6; Psa. 139:13-16; 1 Pet.1:18-21; Jn.3:16).

A few remarks about freedom and autonomy, so essential and popular in the ethical domain, may prove useful. Our human freedom, in whatever way one defines it (the positive, active, creative form of freedom versus passive freedom, which is mere absence of duress, constraint, compulsion, external coercion of any form), is at best a limited freedom (distinguished from God's absolute freedom to be and to do what is logical and self-consistent with His character). Life experience confirms the reality of this limited freedom. I was never free to choose to be born, never was free to select my gene pool. Even now I cannot choose to live without air or water. However, to say that my freedom is limited does not negate the fact that this freedom I now possess is genuine and substantial. It is a gift from God, determined and sustained by Him (James 1:17). It is not the erratic, irrational or illusory variety. In close connection with this concept of freedom, the principle of autonomy (self rule) in the Christian context does not mean that man or woman has the absolute ability and rights for self-rule over the body, the mind, property, the earth, its resources, wealth independent of any support or obligatory duty to others other than himself or herself.

[208] Reese, op. cit., 83. (Greek: *kategoria ; kata*, against; *agoreuein,* to assert; the word takes on the meaning of assertion, prediction).

[209] R.J. Mouw, *The God Who Commands* (Notre Dame, Ind.: Univ. Notre Dame Press, 1990), 41. See especially his Introduction and chapters 1, 2 and 9 of this very thoughtful and balanced book which argues for points of contact between the divine command ethicists and other ethical persuasions in the moral quest for the ultimate nature of moral and ethical reality in our existential pilgrimage.

[210] I concur with Mouw's broader concept of fearing God and obeying His commandments as the whole duty of man (Eccl.12:13) as to include not only the divine utterances with a specific grammatical form (imperative mood or perhaps optative—my interpretation), but also "whatever God requires of us....all that the Creator instructs us to do—whether that guidance is transmitted through parables, accounts of divine dealings with nations and individuals, or sentences which embody commands."

[211]The Biblical overarching principle of love is embodied in the Ten Commandments and their derivatives.In Matthe22:37-40, quoting Deuteronomy 6:5-6, Jesus says, "You shall love the Lord your God with all your heart, with all your soul, and with all your mind. This is the first and great commandment. And the second is like it: 'You shall love your neighbor as yourself'...." The Christian foundation of all morals and ethics rests on this bi-directional love—to love God in response to His grace and love others in active service and relational integrity. This bidirectionality is clearly delineated in the first four command-

ments in our vertical relationship to God and the last six commandments in our horizontal relationship with our fellow human beings.

Lest one thinks that the love commandments have abrogated the Ten Commandments, he or she only has to construe a kind of love devoid of content and totally subjective to anyone's standards and whims. Jesus says, "Do not think that I have come to abolish the Law or the Prophets; I have not come to abolish them but to fulfill them. I tell you the truth, until Heaven and earth disappear, not the smallest letter, not the least stroke of a pen, will by any means disappear from the Law until everything is accomplished. Anyone who breaks one of the least of these commandments and teaches others to do the same will be called least in the kingdom of heaven, but whoever practices and teaches these commands will be called great in the kingdom of Heaven. For I tell you that *unless your righteousness surpasses that of the Pharisees and the teachers of the Law, you will certainly not enter the kingdom of Heaven"* Mt. 5: 17-20 (emphasis mine). Inasmuch as Jesus is the most complete personification and embodiment of the love principle, His emphasis on the commandments, the Law, is significant. His calling to our attention that our righteousness (*dikaiosyne,* alternative translation as justice) must exceed that of the Pharisees and teachers of the Law (analogous to moral philosophers and perhaps secular ethicists) gives one a handle to understand the distinctives of Christian ethics. It is a case then that the love commandments do not replace the Decalogue, but only capsulize it. Comparing the two love commandments enunciated by Jesus, one writer has observed that one commandment has priority over the other. One is the "first and great" love commandment and the other is "second." God is to be loved with one's heart; the neighbor is to be loved only as one loves himself/herself... God is to be loved supremely and man/woman only finitely. Other biblical support for the preeminence of the love ethic can be garnered from the writings of the Apostles. Paul hails love as the supreme virtue. He declares, "....faith, hope and love. But the greatest of these is love." (1 Cor. 13:13). The Apostle John has this to say, "...Anyone who does not love his brother, whom he has seen, cannot love God, whom he has not seen" (1 Jn.4:6). "Above all, love each other deeply...," exhorts Peter in 1 Peter 4:8.

[212] The concept of justice, *mishpat and tsedaqah* Isa. 28:17 and in Micah 6:8, "He has showed you, O man, what is good. And what does the Lord require of you? To act justly and to love mercy and to walk humbly with your God." Amos 5:21-24, "But let justice roll down like waters, and righteousness like an ever-flowing stream." Also Deut. 32:4; Psa. 89:14; Isa. 28:17; Rom. 3:26; Col.4:1;1 Jn.1:9; Rev. 15:3.
[213] Matt. 5:43; Lk. 10:36; Rom. 13:10; Acts 7:27.
[214] Mt. 19:21;Mk.12:42; Lk.4:18; Lk.14:21; Lk.18:22.
[215] Matt. 5, 6; Rom.12:9-21; Rom. 3:24; Eph. 2:8; Num.6:25; Pro. 3:34.
[216] Rom. 3:23, "For all have sinned and fall short of the glory of God."; 1 Jn. 1:18, "If we claim to be without sin, we deceive ourselves...."Our own

experience as well as world history affirm to us and constantly and poignantly remind us that sin is pervasive.

[217] Rom. 7:15-19, "...I have the desire to do what is good, but I cannot carry it out. For what I do is not the good I want to do; no, the evil I do not want to do— this I keep on doing...."

[218] W. Beach; H. R. Niebuhr, *Christian Ethics, sources of the Living Tradition* (New York: John Wiley & Sons, 1973), 24.

[219] I can well anticipate those who would challenge me on what I call the distinctive themes of the Christian Bible. The Hebrew bible, the Old Testament and the Koran also carry most or some of these themes. I would contend, however, that Jesus' kingdom ethics (loving one's enemies; going the second mile instead of "an eye for an eye"; submitting silently to God's will in the face of suffering and injustice; not mere religiosity but inner transformation: the deeper meaning of anger as killing, lustful thoughts as adultery; equivocation and insincerity in our speech and conduct as breaking an oath; God's gracious gifts and unmerited favors to us not because of what we deserve but solely on account of His mercy and goodness) is both revolutionary and without precedence. It supersedes in distinction and makes pale in comparison the theology and ethics of works righteousness of Hebraic and Islamic traditions.

As noted previously, the classical virtues in Plato's conception list only justice, temperance, courage and wisdom. Nowhere is found the theme of love, forgiveness so dominant in Christian thought. Furthermore, the Christian ethical stance of Biblical variety is incomprehensible to the secular mind whose ethics is based on rights, pleasure and good here and now, largely situation-based, relativistic (no absolute right or wrong) and devoid of a transcendent Source of morality. My argument for the distinctives of Christian ethics does not conflict with Lewis Smedes who believes "The commandment tell us to do what we already know we should do," which may give the impression that Christian ethical viewpoints are no different from any other variety in that everyone possesses the basic knowledge of morality as informed by "nature" or natural law or conscience. I shall address the compatibility between Smedes (*Mere Morality*, Grand Rapids:Eerdmans, 1995) and my concept later in the discussions.

[220] Beach and Niebuhr, *Christian Ethics*, op. cit., p.15. This human happiness and perfection they refer to usually have reference only to this world.

[221] Mouw, *The God Who Commands*, op. cit., 187. I interpret that these expressions of human restlessness are relevant to our many ethical issues held in tension in the Augustinian philosophical/ theological conceptual frame.

[222] Mouw, op. cit, p. 130. See also G. S. Harak, *Virtuous Passions* (Mahwah, NJ: Paulist Press, 1993). Also A. MacIntyre, *After Virtue: A Study in Moral Theory*, 2nd ed. (Notre Dame, Ind.: Univ. Notre Dame Press, 1984). and also S. Hauerwas, *Suffering Presence* (Notre Dame, Ind.: UNDP, 1986).

[223] Glen Stassen, *Just Peace-Making--Transforming Initiatives for Justice and Peace* (Louisville, Ky.: Westminster/John Knox Press, 1992), 53-113.

224 John B. Wong, *A Person-Based Triadic Model for Ethical Reasoning* (1997, unpublished).
225 Matthew 5:16, "Let your light (ethical light included) so shine before men, that they may see your good works (ethical tasks included) and glorify your Father in Heaven."
226 Christ's character is exemplified by His teachings which include the Ten commandments and all their implications that we have discussed with the principles of love and justice as their centrality, as well as His eschatological hope, the Resurrection—the final vindication of His life and mission and affirmation of His teachings.
227 pp. 228, 231 ff.
228 See my writings on "Biblical Relevance and Christian Reflection on the Issue of Abortion"; "Christianity and Homosexuality"; "Euthanasia and the Christian Perspective"; "Human Cloning Consonant with Christian worldview?"; "Stem-cell Research and Christian Reflection" (unpublished).
229 H. Thielicke. *The Ethics of Sex* (New York: Harper and Row, 1964).
230 Some comments need to be made on 1 Samuel 16:14-23. Verse 16 states, "Now the Spirit of the Lord had departed from Saul, and an evil spirit from the Lord tormented him...." God cannot be the source of evil. The word evil has been translated as injurious. I would interpret this evil spirit as a spirit of despondency, rejection, melancholy, severe depression, paranoia, intense emotional conflicts which typify the opposites of emotional and psychological wholeness. Because of Saul's free choice in deviating from God's plan for his life, God permitted such tormenting spirit, whether through the work of Satan or as a natural consequence of his decisions or because of his neurobiochemical imbalance. Whatever the cause of Saul's problem, David's music inspired by God and through which God continued to plead with Saul, at least temporarily helped restored Saul's mental equipoise.
231 Franz Schubert's version of *Ave Maria*, so the story goes, was rejected by the Pope because the music somehow had passed through the hands of a prostitute. Charles Gounod was then commissioned to write another version. Gounod based his composition on the first prelude of Johann Sebastian Bach and this new version is now the official Roman Catholic repertoire of *Ave Maria*.
Franz Schubert was the composer of the music of *Holy, Holy Holy* by John Neumann (See Adventist Hymnal #661). It was written a year before his death from typhoid fever in 1828. Of him on his death bed, Ludwig Beethoven said, "Truly in Schubert a divine spark there is!"
232 Wong, *The Resurrected Body...* In this book I posit the dual modes of God's expression, namely the dominant transphysical mode as well as the subsidiary, condescending, glorified-physical mode through the God-Man Jesus whenever and wherever The Father wishes to express Himself.
233 Donald Grout, *A History of Western Music.* Revised ed. (London, England, 1973), 7., as quoted by Wolfgang Stefani in *The Christian and Rock Music—A*

*Study on Biblical Principles of Music*, Samuele Bacchiocchi, ed.(Berrien Springs, MI: Biblical Perspectives,2000),348.

[234] Lin Yutang, *The Wisdom of Confucius* (New York, 1938), 251-272.

[235] Stefani, op. cit.,350

[236] Manfred Clynes, "On Music and Healing" in *Music in Medicine* (Ludenscheid, Germany, 1985), as quoted by Dr. Stefani, p. 351.

[237] Stefani, op. cit., 353.

[238] Ibid., p.353-354.

[239] Some of the ideas are from Aaron Copeland, the foremost American composer, as quoted by Samuele Bacchiocchi in *The Rock Rhythm and a Christian Response The Christian and Rock Music—A Study on Biblical Principles of Music*, Samuele Bacchiocchi, ed.(Berrien Springs, MI: Biblical Perspectives,2000), 130.

[240] Ibid., 131.

[241] Readers are urged to read Chapter 5, 7, 8,10,11, 12 of *The Christian and Rock Music—A Study on Biblical Principles of Music*, Samuele Bacchiocchi, ed.(Berrien Springs, MI: Biblical Perspectives,2000).

[242] *Time*, June 5, 2000, p.75.

[243] For further readings, see Thomas Derr's *Environmental Ethics and Christian Humanism* (Nashville: Abingdon Press, 1996). Also Larry Rasmussen's *Earth community Earth Ethics* (Maryknoll, NY: Orbis books, 1998).

[244] Rosemary Radford Ruether, *Gaia and God: An Ecofeminist Theology of Earth Healing* (San Francisco: Harper Collins, 1992).

[245] Peter Wenz, *Environmental Justice* (Albany: State University of New York Press, 1988).

[246] Pamela Smith, *What Are They Saying About Environmental Ethics?* (NY: Paulist Press, 1997) 56.

[247] Leonardo Boff, *Ecology and Liberation; A New Paradigm.* Translated J. Cumming (Maryknoll, NY: Orbis books, 1995).

[248] Sean McDonagh, *Passion for the Earth* ( Maryknoll, NY: Orbis Books, 1994).

[249] Donald MacKay, "Biblical Perspectives on Human Engineering," in *Modifying Man*: Implications and Ethics, editor, C. Ellison (Washington, DC: University Press of America, 1977), 68,69.

[250] Readers may want to refer to an extensive discussion of "soul" in my book John B. Wong, *The Resurrected Body--Y2K and Beyond* (Lanham, New York, Oxford: University Press of America, 2000), 95-126.

[251] William L. Reese, *Dictionary of Philosophy and Religion—Eastern and Western Thought* (London, New Jersey: Humanities Press, 1995), 573.

[252] Reese, p.504.

[253] Wong, *The Resurrected Body*, pp. 200-202.

[254] Malcolm Jeeves, "Brain, Mind and Behavior" in *Whatever Happened to the Soul? Scientific and Theological Portraits of Human Nature*, eds. W. S. Brown, et al (Minneapolis: Fortress, 1998), 87. Dr. Jeeves is president of the Royal

Society of Edinburgh, Scotland's National Academy of Science and Letters and Professor of Psychology at University of St. Andrews, Scotland.

[255] C. Trevarthen, general editor, *Essays in Honor of Roger W. Sperry* (Cambridge: Cambridge Univ. Press, 1990), 382-385., as quoted by M. Jeeves in "Brain, Mind and Behavior," op. cit, 88. Also consult R. W. Sperry, Psychology's Mentalist Paradigm and the Religion/Science Tension. *American Psychologist*, 607-613.

[256] Quoted by Jeeves in "Brain , Mind and Behavior," *Whatever Happened to the Soul? Scientific and Theological Portraits of Human Nature*, eds. W. S. Brown, et al (Minneapolis: Fortress Press, 1998), 90. Also consult

Donald M. MacKay, *The Open Mind and Other Essays: A Scientist in God's World* (Leicester: Inter-Varsity, 1991).

Donald MacKay, *Behind the Eye* (Oxford: Basil Blackwell, 1991).

[257] J.C. Polkinghorne, *One World* (London: SPCK, 1986), 75.

[258] Jeeves, op. cit., 89.

[259] *The Cambridge Dictionary of Philosophy*. General editor, Robert Audi (Cambridge: Cambridge University Press, 1996), 778.

[260] Ibid., 778.

[261] Simon Blackburn, Metaphysics, *The Blackwell Companion to Philosophy*. Ed. N. Bunnin and E.P.Tsui-James (Oxford: Blackwell Publishers, 1996), 84-86.

[262] J. C. Eccles, ed., *Brain and Conscious Experience* (Berlin: Springer-Verlag, 1966), 312. Quoted by Jeeves, op. cit., 88, (emphasis mine). Also consult

J.C. Eccles and K.R. Popper, *The Self and its Brain* (New York: Springer International, 1981).

[263] Brian McLaughlin, Philosophy of Mind, *The Cambridge Dictionary of Philosophy.*, 598.

[264] Ibid., 598.

[265] William Lycan, Philosophy of Mind in *The Blackwell Companion to Philosophy*. Editor N. Bunnin and E. P. Tsui-James (Oxford, Cambridge, Mass.: Blackwell Publishers, 1996) 167-191.

[266] Owen Flanagan, *Consciousness Reconsidered* (Cambridge, MA: MIT Press, 1992), 35-37.

[267] MacKay, Behind the Eye, (parenthesis mine).

[268] *The Cambridge Dictionary of Philosophy...* 602.

[269] One aspect of this uncertainty principle argues that instrumentation itself affects what is being measured: measuring the position of an object causes an uncontrollable change in its momentum. A corollary might infer that the closer one gets to an object, the more elusive it becomes. Reality is forever shrouded in mystery. What I want to say is that the future is rather dismal for any human attempts to equate electrical signals and biochemical data with complicated human thoughts, freedom, will, faith, hope, and spirituality.

KEY: f= and the following page; ff= and the following pages; n=Notes Section
**Example:** 191.2 refers to page 191 under note number 2

Abortion, 152
Acts [*4:12*], 3
Advent, second, 3
AIDS, 134
Allen, David, 100f
Ambrose, 74
Anderson, Ray S., 73, 77, 82, 86
Anthropic cosmological principle, 50, 201.75
Anthropology, Christian, 2
Athanasius, 74
Augustine, 74
Bach, Johann Sebastian, 160
Barth, Karl, 23,76
Beethoven, Ludwig von, 160
Bible, authority of, 5, 12, 19ff
Body, 69, 83, 89
Brain, 176ff
Brokenness, 4
Buddhism, 6,30
Calvin, John, 23,74
Christ, Divinity of, 5, 12, 22ff
Christian Wholism, definition, 1, 2; biblical locus, 2; 10, 24, 37
Clairvaux, Bernard, 160
*Cogito ergo sum* (I think, therefore I am), 39; see *Sum, ergo Deus est*
Commandment, first, 2
Confucianism, Confucius, 6,27ff,161
Consciousness, 181,185
Creation, 11,44; author's premise and conceptual model, 47ff to 51ff
Crick, Francis, Nobel laureate, 177
Cullmann, Oscar, 23
Dennett, Daniel, 181
Descartes, Rene, 180
Dianoias, 2
Dying whole 103
Eccles, Sir John, Nobel laureate, 180
Ecosystem, 1, 170ff
*Eirenen* (Gr. peace), 15
Emergence, 185
Endorphin, 9
Epiphenomenalism, 181
Erickson, Millard, 36

Erikson, Erik, 128
Ethics, 8, 142ff; virtue, 28; normative,143; definition,148; ethical decision-
    making schema, 149; sexual, 151ff
Evil, 49, 56ff, 65
Evolution, 44; theistic, 49; biological, 50, 199ff.69
Faith, 6, 39ff, 44
Felten, David, 134
Finance, 8, 165ff
Freedom, human, 60, 63, 65, 66
Freud, Sigmund, 6,127
Fromm, Erich, 128
Genesis [*1:26, 27; 2:8, 15*], 2,11, 69, 73, 82
Gestalt therapy, 129
God: love, omniscience, omnipotence, 61, 64; where was He on 9-11-01?, 67ff
*Hagios* (holy), 4
Handel, Frideric, 160
Haydn, Joseph, 160
Healing, 3
Health, 1, human nature, 91
Heisenberg uncertainty principle, 185
Henry, Carl F.H., 76f
Hermann, Robert, 104ff
Holy, 4
Homosexuality, 8 guidelines, 153ff
Humanism, 6, 34
Identity, human, 79ff; Christian core, 80; subjective, objective 80f
Immune response, 8
Intellect, 6, 39ff
Intelligence, definition, 44
*Ischus*, 2
Islam, 6, 31
James, William, 6, 123
Joy, 5,13
Judaism, 6, 31
Jung, Carl, 6, 124ff
Justification, 16ff
*Kardias*, 2
Kierkegaard, Soren, 75
Lin, Yutang, 161
Literature, 8
Loma Linda University, 105f
Love, 2, 59f, 65
Luther, Martin, 23, 74
MacKay, Donald, 173, 178ff, 184

Marxism, 6, 32
Matthew *5:48*, 3
Matthews, Dale, 99
McGrath,Alister, Oxford Univ., 12, 23ff, 36
Metaphor, 12
Mind-brain, 176ff
Mozart,Wolfgang, 160
Music, 8, 156ff
*Nephesh* , 86
Neuroscience, 7
New Ageism, 6, 34
Newton, John, 160
Nonreductionistic transphysicalism, 9, definition 182, 182ff
Origen, 74
Osler, William, 105
Paré, Ambroise, 98
Peace, 1, 5, peace of God 10
Pelagius, 75
Pellegrino, Edmund, 100, 107, 109
Perfect, perfection, 3,
Person, human, N.T. concept, 71ff, 89
Philippians [*4:4, 6, 7*], 10
Physical, 6
*Pneuma,* 88
Polanyi, Michael, 104
Polkinghorne, John, Cambridge University, 179 f
Postmodernism, 6, 35
Psychology, psychological, 6
*Psyches,* 2, 87
Psychoneuroendocrinoimmunology, 7, 132ff
*Quale,* 184
Ramsey, Paul, 76
Religious pluralism, 27ff to 44
Resurrected body, 26
Resurrection, 5. 26
Sabbath, Saturday, Sunday, 3, 191.2
Salvation history, 80
Schleiermacher, Fredrick, 75
Science, 44
Sexuality, human, 8, 138ff
*Shalom,* 5, 10, 13ff
*Soma,* 88
Soul, 9; definition, 78, 83; see *nephesh,* 86f, 89, 92
Sperry, Roger, Nobel laureate, 104

Spirit, 83; human spirit, 89
Stewardship, ecological, 8; see ecosystem
*Sum, ergo Deus est,* (I am, therefore God is), 39
Surrogacy, Mary's, 5
Taoism, 6, 29
*Telos,* 2
Theology, 9, 44; definition, 45
Transphysicalism, nonreductionistic, 9, 182ff
Watts, Isaac, 160
Wesley, John and Charles, 160
White, E. G., 76
Whole, wholeness, wholistic, 4, 13
Wholism, 4, 13; see Christian Wholism; spiritual wholism, 15
Wilcox, Bradley, 99ff
Winslow, Gerald, 188
Wong, John B., 1, 2, 39, 148-151, 182, 222.224
Wright, N. Tom, Oxford University, 44.63a, 197.63a

Dr. John B. Wong is a vascular surgeon with a deep interest in theology, ethics, and philosophy. He is an author, a university professor, and seminary lecturer. In addition to his MD, JD, ThD, he earned his Ph.D. in Theology and Ethics. Affiliated with many professional organizations, Professor Wong is a Fellow of the American College of Surgeons, International College of Surgeons, an active member of the American Academy of Religion and Society of Christian Ethics, and belongs to the Honorary Staff of Loma Linda University Medical Center. He is listed in the IBC's International Who's Who of Intellectuals, and 2000 Outstanding Scholars of the 20th Century, Cambridge, England. As Founder and President of the U.S.-China Christian Institute, Dr. Wong has involved himself in mission outreach and language instruction. He is married to psychologist Alice L. Wong, PhD. They have seven living children of whom three are adopted. JohnBWong@aol.com.

4891